Supreme Pressure

Victor Li

Supreme Pressure

The Rejection of John J. Parker and the Birth of the Modern Supreme Court Confirmation Process

palgrave
macmillan

Victor Li
Chicago, IL, USA

ISBN 978-3-032-07863-6   ISBN 978-3-032-07864-3 (eBook)
https://doi.org/10.1007/978-3-032-07864-3

Cover credit: Harris & Ewing/Library of Congress via Wikimedia Commons

This Palgrave Macmillan imprint is published by the registered company Springer Nature Switzerland AG
The registered company address is: Gewerbestrasse 11, 6330 Cham, Switzerland

For Kelly, Colin, BB, Dessie and Penny.

Acknowledgments

This book was a real labor of love for me. The idea came to me soon after I was done writing my first book, *Nixon in New York: How Wall Street Helped Richard Nixon Win the White House* (2018). As with the Nixon book, this project started out as me wanting to know more about something that interested me. Essentially, I had heard and read a bit about some high-profile Supreme Court rejections like Robert Bork and Abe Fortas. There wasn't much out there on John J. Parker and why his nomination failed. There were a few relevant law review articles, as well as *Duty and the Law: Judge John J. Parker and the Constitution* (1987) a book by Professor William Burris of Guilford College that focused more on his jurisprudence and ideology.

However, there was not a full-length book out there that covered his nomination and looked at the effects it had on the modern Supreme Court confirmation process. So I came to the same conclusion that I did when I wrote about Nixon: maybe I should write the book on Parker's Supreme Court rejection.

Despite having a clear objective, it took me a long time to get going. Part of it was life getting in the way—and I mean that in a good way (mostly). In the eight years between my two books, my wife, Kelly, and I became parents to a wonderful boy, Colin, and more recently to a loving puppy, Penny. However, we also lost our two sweet dogs, Bernie and Dessie. It was a real gut punch having to say goodbye to them and it continues to be a source of profound grief and pain for us. It was especially tough for me as a writer. BB had been next to me (or more often than not, in his bed near me) while I wrote most of my first book. Dessie did so for this one—at least for the first draft, which I completed right before she passed. As such, this one's for you, pretty girl.

And part of it was not being sure whether I wanted to get on the horse again. I imagine that whenever any writer starts thinking about writing a book, there's plenty of internal debate over whether it's worthwhile to commit to such an undertaking. That was definitely the case for me. Would anyone read this? Would anyone care about this subject? Is there a reason why it hadn't been written about at length?

Ultimately, I went for it and I have my wonderful wife to thank for that. She encouraged me and was always supportive—especially during low moments when I wasn't sure if I could pull this off. Thank you, my dear. I love you and I'm very lucky to have you as my wife and mother to Colin.

I'd also like to thank my parents for their continued faith in me. As I've mentioned before, my mom is probably the only person in the world who tries to read everything I've published going back to my movie reviews for my middle school paper (I stand behind my praise of *Teenage Mutant Ninja Turtles II: The Secret of the Ooze*—far, far behind). My Aunt Sandy has always been like a second mother to me and did such a great job taking care of my grandma for many years. We lost grandma in 2021—I miss you and wish you were still with us.

I'm very thankful to Jason Tomberlin and the folks at the University of North Carolina Wilson Special Collections Library. They were very professional and responsive and really helped me with my research needs. Additionally, Craig Wright and the people at the Herbert Hoover Presidential Library were very helpful and wonderful to deal with. Also, Katie Keegan and the people with the Kheel Center Labor & Management Microfilm Collections at Cornell University were exceedingly patient and quick to deal with my queries. Thanks to you all.

I'd also be remiss in not acknowledging Maddie Reichbart, who helped me with my research by going to the Library of Congress and copying documents for me. I've never hired a research assistant before, but Maddie made things very easy with her professionalism and thoroughness. And a big thank you to one of my good friends from college, Michelle Olson (Amherst '00), who recommended her to me. Finally, thanks to

Loretta Deaver and the people with the Library of Congress for their help with those files.

I've been extremely fortunate to work for the *ABA Journal*. Ever since I joined in 2013, they've made me feel welcome and helped me develop and enhance my skills while giving me opportunities that I might not have at other places. They were also really good about helping me promote my first book. The names have changed a lot over the years, but the level of support has not, and I'd like to thank my boss, John O'Brien, as well as my managing editor, Kevin Davis and my former colleague, Lee Rawles, who invited me onto her book podcast before my manuscript was even finished. It's great working with such a wonderful team of journalists (which is why we recently won our third consecutive Magazine of the Year award from the American Society of Business Publication Editors—I'd use the sports portmanteau of "three" and "repeat" but I don't want to get in trouble with Pat Riley).

Seeing my son start school has only reiterated how important good teachers are and how influential they can be. My interest in the Supreme Court started because of two great teachers I had in high school. Mr. Charles Hirsh was a great mentor to me and gave me lots of opportunities that he didn't have to but did because he believed and saw something in me. He had us research Supreme Court cases in 9th grade civics class, and that started my fascination with the Court (Clarence Thomas' confirmation hearings were around that same time, so that helped). Shortly after I started writing this book, I had a dream where my late mentor was helping me do research and organize my documents. A dyed-in-the-wool Democrat, he also complained about how I was writing about another Republican—something I could definitely see him saying to me in real life. I like to think he was helping me out one last time—and yes, Mr. Hirsh, I'll try and write about a Democrat next time.

I learned more about the courts, the Constitution and our judicial branch when I took A.P. U.S. History in 11th grade with Mr. Ed Metro. He encouraged my interest and helped me find books and movies that would allow me to learn more. Who knows if I would even be writing this if it hadn't been for them and the lessons they taught me. Thank you both.

A big thanks to the kind folks at Palgrave Macmillan for publishing this book. Finding a publisher can be a humbling, rejection-heavy endeavor, and this was certainly no different. As such, I'm very grateful that they said "yes" to me. Thanks to Palgrave's Christian Winting, Editor—U.S.

Politics & Political Theory, as well as Naveenprasath Malaikannu, Production Editor, Zeenathul Raeesa, Production Supervisor and Jill Balzano, Editorial Project Manager.

I'd also like to acknowledge James Ryan, a freelance editor I found on Reedsy who edited my manuscript. Thanks again for all of your help!

I'd like to thank the fine people who gave me editorial reviews/blurbs for my book: Professor Erwin Chemerinsky, Judy Perry Martinez, and Professor Thomas Edsall. Professor Edsall also gave me an editorial review for my first book and has been a wonderful mentor and teacher to me ever since I took his "Covering National Politics" class at Columbia University Graduate School of Journalism.

Finally, I know I already acknowledged them, but I just wanted to reiterate how grateful I am to have had grandma, Bernie and Dessie in my life and how much I miss them now that they're no longer with me. To quote a great philosopher: "In my life, I loved them all."

Prologue

Whereof what's past is prologue; what to come, in yours and my discharge.
—William Shakespeare, *The Tempest*, Act 2, scene 1

We all have skeletons in our closet. But when John J. Parker was nominated for a seat on the Supreme Court of the United States, the last thing he and his supporters believed was that the bag of bones his opponents were trying to drag into public view would amount to anything worth being concerned about. He was young, accomplished and respected. Most importantly, he had plenty of support, including most of the powerful figures in his state, many distinguished legal minds throughout the country, and the president of the United States who had won office in a landslide and whose party controlled the Senate that would be voting on his nomination. When he was nominated by President Herbert Hoover in 1930, his confirmation seemed like such a *fait accompli* that you'd forgive him for asking the chief justice for recommendations on what neighborhoods to live in and what kind of furniture he should get for his new chambers.

After all, it seemed as if the anti-Parker camp was grasping at straws, basing their opposition largely around two statements from his past. First was something he had said as the Republican nominee for governor of North Carolina in 1920. It was a race Parker was never going to win—a prototypical "dead man walking" campaign where a candidate's best-case scenario is to win a moral victory by keeping the margin of defeat as low as possible. Parker had done what many hopeless candidates do and focused on ideas and values while trying to expand his party's voter base for future elections. That had been the best he could hope for by running in a state where Democrats dominated and Republicans prayed they wouldn't lose in a landslide.

Nevertheless, Parker was going to do his best to win, and an important part of his strategy involved Black voters in North Carolina—or, more specifically, how he neither wanted nor welcomed their support. "The Negro as a class does not desire to enter politics," he said at the convention and in various forms throughout the campaign. "The Republican Party of North Carolina does not desire him to do so."

Civil rights groups were outraged and frightened at the prospect of seeing someone who uttered those words ascending to the highest court in the land and vowed to defeat the nomination with every tool and tactic at their disposal. After decades of Jim Crow and Supreme Court inaction, Black Americans were finally starting to notch some victories in the federal courts and were not about to cede their progress without a fight. Led by the National Association for the Advancement of Colored People (NAACP), civil rights groups mobilized against Parker and waged what they later called their most successful campaign since the Civil War.

They had company—thanks to something else Parker had previously said. In 1927, while comfortably ensconced on the bench as a U.S. Circuit Court of Appeals judge, Parker wrote an opinion that earned him the undying enmity of organized labor. In the case of *International Organization, United Mine Workers of America, et al v. Red Jacket Coal and Coke Company*, Parker cited existing Supreme Court precedent and ruled in favor of Red Jacket Coal and Coke Company, angering the United Mine Workers of America and many other labor groups that had been trying and fighting (in some cases literally) for years to unionize. Comparing the ruling to the infamous *Dred Scott* case, organized labor saw Parker as an enemy who was in the pocket of big businesses, and shuddered at the possibility of him joining the Supreme Court, which, at that time, was sharply divided between pro-business conservatives and pro-individual progressives.

Parker was nonplussed by the reaction from labor and their allies. As a lower court judge, it was his duty to follow the law as interpreted by the Supreme Court, and he believed that he had done his job in *Red Jacket*. Even though he may have been sympathetic to the aims and goals of labor—he had run on a pro-workers platform in 1920, after all—he maintained that his hands had been tied. Anyone could understand that, right?

Parker was also unimpressed by the furor over his comment about Black voters from 1920. He was a candidate running for office in the South—he wasn't about to ask the NAACP for an endorsement or anything. Plus, the way he saw it, he was actually trying to help Black North Carolinians and remove the issue of race from the campaign. Surely, no one was really going to hold that against him, right?

And, regardless of what those groups felt about him, Parker believed his impressive credentials and track record as a judge would take precedence. Sure, these civil rights and labor groups may have seen Parker as a menace who could not be allowed to bring his views to the Supreme Court; but Parker confidently believed that enough senators would understand that his statements were reasonable and consistent with the law and would not affect his ability to be a fair and impartial justice.

What Parker did not understand was that, while he may have demonstrated legal compliance, there were interest groups, as well as political and judicial figures, who believed there was more to being an effective judge or justice than simply following the law. They saw a country that had failed a large portion of its citizens and believed the courts had a duty to step up and help. In other words, Parker was being judged not just on his fealty to the rule of law but also on his willingness to use it to help people who needed it. He did not understand that until it was too late.

The Robert Bork nomination in 1987 is typically seen as the beginning of the modern-day Supreme Court confirmation process. The organized, well-coordinated opposition consisting of various civil rights, women's rights, civil liberties, and labor organizations, among other interest groups was so effective, and the pro-Bork forces were so shell-shocked and unprepared, that the confirmation fight left lasting lessons for everyone involved—to say nothing of future generations of politicians, judges, lawyers, lobbyists, and interest groups. In fact, "bork" has become a verb with its own definition in both the Oxford English and Merriam-Webster dictionaries describing, in essence, an organized political attack campaign against a person in order to defeat them. Nowadays, whenever any nominee receives a less than warm reception from the Senate, something that has become routine in today's hyper-partisan world, that nominee's allies will inevitably complain that he or she is being "borked" or that other side is unfairly "borking" an otherwise eminently qualified candidate who would have been easily confirmed in the halcyon days of old.

This book makes the case that maybe it should be "parkered" or "parkering" instead. In the case of John J. Parker, the nominee and his allies certainly felt like he was being unfairly targeted by an organized opposition that twisted and distorted his record in order to bring about a rejection that had nothing to do with qualifications or competence and everything to do with politics. The Parker nomination is not the first time outside interest groups mobilized against a Supreme Court nomination. However, it was the first time in American history where they were successful—and their victory provided the blueprint for future generations.

How these groups were able to mobilize and convince the Senate, which had rarely rejected Supreme Court nominees, to vote him down is more than just a story about a successful lobbying or pressure campaign. In many Supreme Court nomination fights, the battle often ends up being about more than the person whose name is being considered. In this case, the story is also about how the battle over Parker's nomination ended up becoming a proxy fight—one phase in a long-running war between Democrats and Republicans, progressives and conservatives, big business advocates and labor leaders, civil rights leaders and proponents of Jim Crow, Northerners and Southerners, and judicial activists and defenders of the status quo.

The effects of this war continue to be fought and felt today, as does Parker's legacy. While he was rejected for the Supreme Court, Parker ended up being a hugely consequential figure in American history. Thanks to his role in implementing *Brown v. Board of Education* in his judicial circuit, Parker's assertion that the decision only banned segregation in public schools and did not compel integration ended up providing the intellectual basis of the largest Southern resistance since the Civil War. Unlike that conflagration, this conflict has lasted decades and continues to be fought in various forms today. Arguably, Parker would never have had that kind of impact had he been successful in attaining his seat on the Supreme Court.

Perhaps it is surprising, then, that there is a dearth of material when it comes to Parker and his Supreme Court nomination. Oftentimes, he'll be mentioned in books about Herbert Hoover, the NAACP, Big Labor, and others, and there have been a few law journal articles written about him and his jurisprudence. William C. Burris, a professor of political science at Guilford College, wrote a short biography of Parker, but focused more on his jurisprudence and less on his confirmation battle. This book hopes to bridge that gap in scholarship and place Parker's doomed nomination in the right historical context, as well as demonstrate its significance in relation to Supreme Court nominations that came after it, particularly the controversial and contentious ones.

To quote a line from his confirmation battle, Parker was only an incident in a larger battle. To his supporters and opponents at the time, the actual issue was the Supreme Court. History has shown that even the Supreme Court was an incident. The actual issues were how Americans want their country to function, how the Constitution should be interpreted, and how the courts should, or should not, protect certain members of society.

John J. Parker, 1930 (Image by Harris & Ewing via Library of Congress/ Wikimedia Commons—https://commons.wikimedia.org/wiki/File:John_J_Parker_As_Judge_LOC.png)

John J. Parker, circa 1922 (Image from the N.C. Government and Heritage Library via Wikimedia Commons, https://commons.wikimedia.org/wiki/File:John_J_Parker_1922_NCPedia.png)

Cameron Morrison won a tightly contested 1920 gubernatorial primary and then handily defeated Parker in the general election. Like his two Democratic opponents, he became an ally and supporter of Parker's Supreme Court nomination (Image by State Archive of North Carolina via Wikimedia Commons—https://commons.wikimedia.org/wiki/File:T_81_8_Cameron_Morrison_(8407662085).jpg)

O. Max Gardner came up short to Morrison in the primary. Despite feeling like he had been robbed of the nomination, he campaigned for Morrison in the general election (Image by Harris & Ewing via Library of Congress/Wikimedia Commons—https://commons.wikimedia.org/wiki/File:GARDNER,_O.M._GOVERNOR_LCCN2016862610.tif)

Robert Newton Page defeated Morrison in 1902 and Parker in 1910. In the 1920 primary, however, he finished a distant third and retired to the private sector (Image via Wikimedia Commons—https://commons.wikimedia.org/wiki/File:RobertNewtonPageUSCongressman.jpg)

Senator Lee S. Overman of North Carolina emerged as one of Parker's strongest supporters in the Senate during his Supreme Court confirmation battle (Image by Harris & Ewing via Library of Congress/Wikimedia Commons—https://commons.wikimedia.org/wiki/File:OVERMAN,_LEE_SLATER._SENATOR_FROM_NORTH_CAROLINA,_1903-1933._BEFORE_MOVIE_CAMERA_LCCN2016866658.jpg)

One of the leaders of the Wilmington Massacre, Senator Furnifold M. Simmons of North Carolina strongly supported Parker. However, a tough primary limited his involvement in the confirmation fight. Ultimately, he lost renomination and later blamed his support of Parker for costing him his seat (Image by Harris & Ewing via Library of Congress/Wikimedia Commons—https://commons.wikimedia.org/wiki/File:SIMMONS,_F.M._SENATOR_LCCN2016857186_(cropped).jpg)

Senators William Borah (left) and George Norris (right) were two of the most influential members of an informal group of progressive, independent-minded senators that proved to be thorns in the side of the Republican majority. Dubbed "The Sons of the Wild Jackass" by one of their many detractors, Borah and Norris became implacably opposed to Parker's confirmation (Image by Harris & Ewing via Library of Congress/ Wikimedia Commons—https://commons.wikimedia.org/wiki/File:Sen._Borah_at_White_House_and_Sen._(George)_Norris_LCCN2016888706.tif)

The Taft Court in 1925. A conservative supermajority had drawn the ire of progressives who were sick and tired of the Court's long line of pro-business and freedom of contract rulings that went back decades. (L-R) (Seated): James McReynolds, Oliver Wendell Holmes, William Howard Taft (Chief Justice), Willis Van Devanter, Louis Brandeis. (Standing): Edward Terry Sanford, George Sutherland, Pierce Butler and Harlan F. Stone. Almost immediately after Sanford's death in 1930, Parker's friends and allies started pushing him for the now-vacant seat (Image by Harris & Ewing via Library of Congress/ Wikimedia Commons—https://commons.wikimedia.org/wiki/File:SUPREME_COURT,_U.S._TAFT_COURT_LCCN2016861491.jpg)

President Herbert Hoover with his wife, Lou. Hoover hoped to solidify electoral gains for the Republican Party in the South, and the Parker nomination was part of that strategy (Image by Harris & Ewing via Wikimedia Commons/Library of Congress—https://commons.wikimedia.org/wiki/File:Pres._and_Mrs._Hoover_at_Marine-Coast_Guard_football_game_LCCN2016889787.jpg)

Charles Evans Hughes was confirmed as Chief Justice right before Parker's nomination fight, but not without some difficulty and doubt (Image by Harris & Ewing via Library of Congress/Wikimedia Commons—https://commons.wikimedia.org/wiki/File:HUGHES,_CHARLES_E.,_HONORABLE_LCCN2016861989.jpg)

NAACP head Walter White helped spearhead the civil rights group's opposition to Parker, citing his 1920 comments about not wanting Blacks to vote for him or the Republican Party while calling Blacks who wished to participate in the political process "participation of the Negro in politics is a source of evil and danger to both races." (Image by National Portrait Gallery via Wikimedia Commons—https://commons.wikimedia.org/wiki/File:Walter_Francis_White_by_Clara_Sipprell.jpg)

AFL President William Green led organized labor's opposition to Parker due to the judge's opinion in the Red Jacket case. The UMWA had tried to unionize mine workers who were forbidden from joining a union thanks to a "yellow dog" contract. Parker upheld the injunction against the UMWA, citing Supreme Court precedent (Image by Harris & Ewing via Library of Congress/Wikimedia Commons—https://commons.wikimedia.org/wiki/File:GREEN,_WILLIAM_LCCN2016858934_Trim.jpg)

Owen J. Roberts was nominated by Hoover after Parker's defeat. Unlike Parker, Roberts was easily confirmed. The Justice would serve for 15 years and cast some important votes (Image via Harris & Ewing via Library of Congress/ Wikimedia Commons—https://commons.wikimedia.org/wiki/File:Owen_Josephus_Roberts_portrait.jpg)

Shortly after his rejection by the Senate, John J. Parker paid a visit to Hoover at the White House to thank him for his support (Image via New York World-Telegram and the Sun Newspaper Photograph Collection, Library of Congress—https://www.loc.gov/item/98502892/)

Alongside Francis Biddle (Left), Parker served as a judge at the Nuremberg Trials in 1945–1946. Parker was concerned the job would take him out of the running for a Supreme Court nomination – something which came true after President Truman nominated Harold Burton in October 1945 (Image by Harvard Law School Library via Wikimedia Commons—https://commons.wikimedia.org/wiki/File:Nurember_Trials_judges_Francis_Biddle_and_John_Parker_1945.jpeg)

Contents

About the Author

Victor Li is an award-winning multimedia journalist based in Chicago. He is the author of the book *Nixon in New York: How Wall Street Helped Richard Nixon Win the White House*. He is currently an Assistant Managing Editor with the *ABA Journal*, covering the business of law and legal technology and hosts the Legal Rebels Podcast under the auspices of Legal Talk Network.

Previously, he worked at ALM Media Properties in New York City for over three years, serving as a staff reporter for *Law Technology News* and *The American Lawyer*. His work has also been featured in *Corporate Counsel*, *The Am Law Daily*, *The New York Law Journal*, *The National Law Journal*, and *The Litigation Daily*, as well as *The Utica Observer Dispatch*, *The Huffington Post*, *The Columbia Journalist*, *Amherst Magazine*, *Soccerlens*, and *The Berkshire Eagle*.

He has an M.S. from the Columbia University Graduate School of Journalism, a J.D. from Tulane University Law School, and a B.A. in history from Amherst College. He lives in Chicago with his family.

Abbreviations

ABA	American Bar Association
ACLU	American Civil Liberties Union
AFL	American Federation of Labor
CCC	Committee of Colored Citizens
CIO	Congress of Industrial Organizations
DOJ	Department of Justice
FLP	Farmer-Labor Party
FTC	Federal Trade Commission
GOP	Grand Old Party (Republican)
ICC	Interstate Commerce Commission
IMT	International Military Tribunal
JD	Juris Doctor (or Doctor of Jurisprudence)
NAACP	National Association for the Advancement of Colored People
SEC	Securities and Exchange Commission
UMWA	United Mine Workers of America
UNC	University of North Carolina
WSA	War Shipping Administration

CHAPTER 1

Lily-White Republican: John J. Parker Makes a Big Political Decision

John Johnston Parker was born on November 20, 1885, in Monroe, NC, less than a decade after Reconstruction officially came to an end. The eldest of four children, Parker "came from good stock," as the saying went. On his father's side, he was a descendant of John Parker, a Revolutionary War veteran and Leonidas Parker, a former Confederate soldier who had died at the battle of Chancellorsville. On his mother's side, he was related to Samuel Johnston, the sixth Governor of North Carolina and one of the state's original two U.S. senators, as well as James Iredell, one of the original six justices of the U.S. Supreme Court and Abner Nash, governor of North Carolina from 1780 to 1781.[1]

Bloodlines and family ties had always been important in the South and, when it came to Parker, "[t]he finest blood in North Carolina flowed in his veins."[2]

That doesn't mean Parker grew up in wealth and privilege—in fact, it was quite the opposite. His father, John Daniel, did not have much in the way of a formal education and, instead, made a living as a "small merchant

[1] John J. Parker biography in the John Johnston Parker Papers #03464, Southern Historical Collection, The Wilson Library, University of North Carolina at Chapel Hill.

[2] William C. Burris, *Duty and the Law: Judge John J. Parker and the Constitution* (Bessemer, AL: Colonial Press, 1987), 12–13.

V. Li, *Supreme Pressure*,
https://doi.org/10.1007/978-3-032-07864-3_1

of very limited means."[3] During his life, he held several different jobs, including working at a cotton gin and owning a small meat market.

His mother, Frances Ann Johnston, on the other hand, was a music teacher and had received a good education. As a child, Parker seemed to take after his mother, inheriting most of her qualities and being inspired to achieve goals she helped set for him, including going to college and becoming a lawyer.[4]

Frances' influence also extended to Parker's religious upbringing. The daughter of an Episcopalian clergyman, Frances had gotten her husband to convert from Baptism and instilled in her son a strong religious identity and devotion that never left as he made his way through life. Parker would later serve as a Sunday school teacher and vestryman in his church, as well as take part in Episcopalian and Protestant conferences and conventions throughout the country. He even served as delegate to the 1937 General Convention of the Episcopal Church. "Religion, man's relationship to the Infinite, is the deepest force in his life. It enters into and colors his every activity and relationship, whether he be aware of it or not," Parker wrote in a letter to Reverend E.A. Penick of Charlotte. "Under its influence, he becomes a better husband and father, a better neighbor, a better citizen of the state."[5]

There was one major quality he had inherited from his father, however, and that was his boundless energy. He would lean heavily on this attribute during his childhood, which he later described as one of struggle. At the age of 13, he had to drop out of school to work at his father's meat market and help support the family. He was able to continue his schooling and balanced his education with working various jobs throughout Monroe. Parker applied that work ethic to his academics, excelling in school while demonstrating an aptitude for debate. One area he was not known to excel in was socially, as it was said he "never learned to play" and was derisively referred to by other children as "Johnny Bull"—either because of his work at his dad's meat market or because of his gift of gab.[6] When

[3] Burris, supra, 12–13.

[4] Parker biography, Parker Papers, supra.

[5] Parker Papers, supra, Letter from Parker to Penick, May 27, 1933.

[6] Burris, supra, 13–14.

he was nominated for the Supreme Court, a profile published in newspapers across the country described him as a "serious" man who was known as "John" and not "Jack," even among his friends and loved ones.[7]

When the time came, his family could not afford to send him to college, so instead he went to work selling suits for a clothing company to raise the money for his tuition at the University of North Carolina (UNC). He also studied Greek in his spare time in order to prepare himself for the school's classics requirements. "If we are to believe the comments of his fellow students, he arrived with a superior attitude, a certain lack of patience with the foibles of others, and something of a fixation about being in charge of everything around him," wrote William C. Burris, a professor of political science at Guilford College, in his biography of Parker.[8]

Despite that, Parker was well-liked and respected enough to be elected president of both his freshman and senior classes. He was on the debate team, served as president of the campus chapter of Phi Beta Kappa and won several college prizes for achievement in academics and leadership—including the Greek prize, something Parker was quite proud of given that he had learned the language during breaks from his job selling suits.

There were also times that he rejected his college's culture and challenged some of the norms that his fellow students had taken as a token of faith. He declined an invitation to the school's prestigious Order of the Golden Fleece honor society, criticizing the organization as undemocratic and elitist (he accepted membership a few years after his graduation, however). He also criticized the fraternity system as perpetuating unfair differences and distinctions among the student body and thought that the commonly accepted practice of hazing freshman (subjecting new students to initiation rituals) was stupid and reckless.[9] As Burris has pointed out, this behavior helps explain some of Parker's attitudes and actions in his later life, especially as a reform-minded candidate skeptical of political machines of all shapes and partisan identities.[10]

[7] Rodney Dutcher, "New Appointee to U.S. Supreme Court is Called a Middle of the Road Man," *The Reading Times*, April 3, 1930.

[8] Burris, supra, 14.

[9] Burris, supra, 16–17.

[10] Burris, supra, 16–17.

He graduated from UNC in 1907 with a Bachelor of Arts degree and, one year later, earned his Bachelor of Laws degree from UNC School of Law. His decision to go to law school made sense to the people who had known him well—brother, Samuel Iredell, later remarked that John had been a lawyer "even as a boy."[11] In law school, as was becoming customary throughout his academic life, Parker excelled in his studies, winning a prize for best thesis. One of his classmates later remarked that Parker came to UNC without so much as a trunk to his name, but left with a trunk full of medals and awards.[12] As his school days drew to an end, it was widely believed that "no position in North Carolina was beyond his reach if he chose to pursue it."[13]

Unfortunately for him, he chose the one profession that was beyond his reach—at least under the circumstances he chose for himself.

Republican

After earning his law degree, Parker worked for David Stern, a Greensboro, NC lawyer, for one year before going out on his own. He opened a law practice in Monroe and, in 1910, formed Stack and Parker with Amos M. Stack, who became a judge of the Superior Court of North Carolina in 1922.

Also in 1910, he married Maria Burgwin Maffitt, granddaughter of famous Confederate blockade runner John Newland Maffitt and member of the prominent Burgwin family in North Carolina. Like Parker, she also came from good stock, tracing her ancestors all the way back to the Mayflower and the Revolutionary War. According to a *Charlotte News* profile of her in 1930, she and Parker had grown up together and were, at least, distantly related, having both descended from Abner Nash. Described as a woman of "stately proportions" with "soft dark hair and brown eyes," who gave off an air of simplicity and repose, Maria Burgwin Parker would keep a low profile during her husband's subsequent rise to prominence, spending her time at her Episcopalian Church, participating with the local chapters of the Daughters of the American Revolution and

[11] Burris, supra, 13.

[12] "The History of John J. Parker," *VIP Mag*, www.vipmagsc.com/the-history-of-judge-john-j-parker/, accessed June 5, 2024.

[13] Burris, supra, 19.

Mayflower Descendants, and raising the couple's three children: Sara , John Jr., and Francis Iredell.[14]

While he soon established a successful and respected law practice, it was clear that his passion was politics, and he immediately started making moves to try and win elected office.

At first glance, Parker had the makings of a star in the political world. Standing six-foot tall, the blueish-grey-eyed Parker was young, appealing, genial, photogenic, charismatic, and articulate. He was also hard-working and intelligent and possessed a reputation for being a solid orator. In most instances, he would have been a highly sought-after candidate, with both parties beating down his door to secure his services.

In North Carolina, however, there was only one party that you wanted to have in your corner and, like most people in the state who were serious about winning elections, Parker had been a Democrat for most of his life. But when he decided to start pursuing elected office, he made the shocking decision to leave the dominant Democrats and join the Republican Party.[15]

The decision was confounding to people who knew Parker, since it was rare for ambitious, talented politicians to do anything other than register with the party that would allow them to put that all-important "D" next to their names. After all, by the time Parker had registered as a Republican to start his political and professional career, North Carolina was very much a one-party state, in line with most of the former Confederacy. It was a state where the Democratic primary was more competitive than the general election, and winning the nomination meant the only burning issue for the rest of the campaign would be where to hold the victory party. It was a state where Republican candidates often got the nomination by default and could have been spotted a 10-percentage point handicap and still lost handily.

It hadn't always been that way. In fact, Parker was old enough to remember a time when the GOP had actually managed to hold power in the state. From 1894 to 1898, long after Reconstruction had come to an end, Republicans had managed to pull off the seemingly impossible task of winning control of the state government, both U.S. Senate

[14] "Wife of Judge Parker is a Real 'Home-Maker,'" *The Charlotte News*, March 30, 1930.

[15] "Local and Personal," *The Monroe Journal*, April 21, 1916.

seats and various local races—all without the benefit of Union bayonets backing them up.

How did it happen? Like the rest of the former Confederacy, after Reconstruction officially came to an end in 1877, "redeemer" Democrats seized power and became the dominant political force in North Carolina. However, North Carolina differed from their Southern brethren in one sense: Republicans remained present in large numbers and represented a little less than half of eligible voters.[16] The GOP had a fairly strong base, with Unionist whites in the western and Piedmont counties and Black voters, who made up about one-third of the voting population.[17] The 1880, 1884, and 1888 gubernatorial races were all competitive, with the Democrats winning all three but by majorities ranging from less than 3 percentage points to slightly more than 7. Similarly, at the presidential level, Democratic nominees won the state in 1880, 1884, and 1888 by majorities ranging from approximately 3.5 percentage points to slightly over 6.

Another reason why the Republicans were able to stay competitive during this time was because of the state's newly enacted constitution. As with other defeated Confederate states, North Carolina had to draft a new constitution as a condition of readmission into the Union, and in 1868 a Republican-dominated convention drew one up that enshrined universal male suffrage with no property requirements. Outraged Democrats, who had been sidelined from the proceedings (Republicans had 107 of the 120 available seats at the convention), were reduced to complaining about it from afar or venting their anger to local newspapers. The *Wilmington Daily Journal* even used a series of insulting headlines, complete with racial slurs and stereotypes, to show how they felt about the proceedings. Other papers noted that white women and children were being kept indoors while the convention was happening in Raleigh so as to avoid the "motley horde."[18]

There were even some communities and localities where Black citizens were dominant and part of the majority. Wilmington was one such area,

[16] Daniel Farbman, "Redemption Localism," *University of North Carolina Law Review* 100 (2022), 1527, 1544.

[17] Alan Bromberg, "Pure Democracy and White Supremacy: The Redeemer Period in North Carolina, 1876–1894," University of Virginia Ph.D. dissertation, 1977.

[18] David Zucchino, *Wilmington's Lie: The Murderous Coup of 1898 and the Rise of White Supremacy* (New York: Atlantic Monthly Press, 2020), 39–40.

as the Cape Fear port had a lot of job opportunities for newly freed slaves. During the Reconstruction Era, Blacks made up approximately 55% of the population in Wilmington.

As a result, Democrats felt it necessary to maintain their power, lest the Blacks and Republicans gain power, and start to advocate for issues such as civil rights or ending segregation. So, they established a template that subsequent generations would follow to the letter, using race-baiting and the memories of Reconstruction to scare whites into voting Democratic. They also used groups like the Ku Klux Klan to terrorize Black citizens and enforce their vision of social and political order. In his PhD dissertation about the Redeemer Period in North Carolina, Alan Bruce Bromberg summed up the attitudes of Democratic officials during this initial post-Reconstruction era by pointing to the masthead of *The Caucasian*, a newspaper founded in 1884 in Clinton, NC, which read: "Pure Democracy and White Supremacy."[19]

However, as the nineteenth century drew to a close, the "panic" of 1893 had a tremendous impact on the state. Farmers and laborers were hit particularly hard, especially in the cotton industry, where the market collapsed as a result of the economic turmoil. They blamed the Democrats in power, accusing them of putting the interests of the wealthy and elite ahead of their own, and formed the Farmers' Alliance, an organization headed by Leonidas L. Polk, which eventually made up the base of the state's Populist Party.

The following year, sensing an opening, the state GOP agreed to enter into a political and electoral alliance with the Populist Party. It was an odd and certainly shaky union—the GOP still relied on Black voters and many poor white farmers were every bit as racist and committed to the rule of white supremacy as the Democrats. Black voters, for their part, were suspicious of their newfound allies in the so-called Fusion movement. However, they agreed to put their differences aside for the time being to team up against the Democrats, who they saw as the source of their difficulties.[20]

That decision paid dividends in 1894 when the so-called Fusionists won big at the polls, flipping both state houses, taking control of the

[19] Zucchino, supra, 39–40. See also: Digital NC, https://newspapers.digitalnc.org/lccn/sn91068244/1884-03-13/ed-1/seq-1/, accessed June 12, 2024.

[20] Zucchino, supra, 65.

state Supreme Court, and winning several other state and federal races, including both U.S. Senate seats. Democrats were stunned and dumbfounded. “Men who, a few years before, had been the most bitter in denunciation of the Republican Party and its Negro cohorts actually joined hands and defended the nomination of Negroes for office,” said Josephus Daniels, former Secretary of the Navy under President Woodrow Wilson and a newspaper magnate who managed the pro-Democrat *The News & Observer* in Raleigh, the largest paper by circulation in the state.[21] Two years later, Daniel Lindsay Russell, Jr., became the first Republican to win a gubernatorial race in the state since Reconstruction.

Once in power, Fusionists pursued policies designed to loosen the Democratic monopoly on power—particularly when it came to voting rights. In 1895, the Fusionist-dominated legislature passed a law that had the practical effect of making it easier for people of all races to vote by changing how election officials throughout the state were chosen and making it harder to challenge prospective voters. Two years later, the legislature curtailed the power of state party chairs even more. The legislature also passed laws restoring home rule, allowing Black-dominated counties to enact laws that not only made it easier for them to vote but to win.[22] During the period after Russell’s victory, there were an estimated 1,000 Black office holders in the state.[23]

Unsurprisingly, Democrats were not only upset about these developments but saw them as a direct threat to white supremacy. Daniels met with former U.S. Representative Furnifold M. Simmons and brainstormed ways to take back the government from the Fusionists and solve what they called “the Negro problem.”[24] Simmons, who was elected to the House in 1886, had been defeated for reelection in 1888 by a Black Republican and lost his bid for renomination in 1890 because of the Farmer’s Alliance. In the meantime, he served as state Democratic Party chair, resigning in 1894 to become collector of internal revenue for the Eastern

[21] Zucchino, supra, 67.

[22] Allen W. Trelease, “The Fusion Legislatures of 1895 and 1897: A Roll-Call Analysis of the North Carolina House of Representatives,” *The North Carolina Historical Review* 57, no. 3 (1980), 280–309, www.jstor.org/stable/23535481.

[23] William Alexander Mabry, “Negro Suffrage and Fusion Rule in North Carolina,” *The North Carolina Historical Review* 12, no. 2 (1935), 79–102, www.jstor.org/stable/23515171.

[24] Zucchino, supra, 65.

District of North Carolina. After the Fusion victories, Democrats begged him to come back in 1898 to help them re-establish their dominance, and he did so.

His plan, quite simply, was to scare North Carolina voters into putting the Democrats back into power. Once that happened, they could pass laws making it more difficult for Blacks to vote, enabling them to establish one-party rule in the state for generations. With Daniels there to help amplify his message, Simmons went about his campaign of race-baiting.

"[T]his is a white man's country and white men must control and govern it," an 1898 handbook prepared by Simmons and the Democratic Executive Committee of North Carolina read. "They must govern it not only because they are white men, but because they can do it better than the negro. The Negro has, whenever tried, demonstrated his unfitness and inability to rule. It is better for the Negro, as well as for the white man, that the white man should make and administer the laws."[25]

Other Democratic officials were less restrained. "North Carolina is a WHITE MAN'S State, and WHITE MEN will rule it [original emphasis], and they will crush the party of Negro domination beneath a majority so overwhelming that no other party will ever again dare to attempt to establish Negro rule here," wrote Simmons in an editorial entitled: "Chairman F.M. Simmons Issues a Patriotic and Able Address, Summing Up the Issues, and Appealing Eloquently to the White Voters To Redeem the State," published in *The News and Observer* on November 3, 1898.[26]

Daniels did his part, running photographs of Black elected officials and candidates to scare white voters and to sensationalize crimes committed by Blacks.[27] He amplified a story about a Fusionist sheriff who, in an effort to court Black voters, invited a Black politician to live with him and his daughter. The Black politician ended up getting her pregnant, and Daniels had a ready-made scandal to play to the fears of white residents

[25] "The Democratic Handbook. 1898. Prepared by the State Democratic Executive Committee of North Carolina: Electronic Edition." *Documenting the American South*, https://docsouth.unc.edu/nc/dem1898/dem1898.html, accessed March 31, 2025.

[26] "Chairman F.M. Simmons Issues a Patriotic and Able Address, Summing Up the Issues, and Appealing Eloquently to the White Voters To Redeem the State," *Raleigh News and Observer*, November 3, 1898, *Civil War Era NC*, https://cwnc.omeka.chass.ncsu.edu/items/show/552, accessed February 24, 2022.

[27] Mabry, supra, 95.

frightened of the prospect of miscegenation and race-mixing.[28] Any story about rapes committed by Black men against white women was sure to draw breathless, front-page coverage from *The News and Observer*, even though Daniels later admitted that the actual number of rapes committed by Black men against white women was "few in number."[29] To hammer home the point, Daniels, who likened the Black man to an incubus, a winged demon who raped women while they were sleeping, hired a top editorial cartoonist to use his artistic skills to draw extreme, frightening caricatures of Blacks, often portraying them as evil, savage rapists and murderers.[30]

Some went even further, calling for outright acts of violence and terrorism. "Before we allow the Negroes to control this state as they do now, we will kill enough of them that there will not be enough left to bury them," said U.S. Representative and future North Carolina Governor William Walton ("W.W.") Kitchin.[31] Meanwhile, large numbers of white supremacists, known as "Red Shirts" after their attire of choice, patrolled the streets, using tactics ranging from intimidation to outright violence to keep anyone who might vote against the Democrats from the polls.

Leaving nothing to chance, Democrat officials stuffed and tampered with ballot boxes—in one precinct, the Democratic candidate's vote total was higher than the number of registered voters. Red Shirts and others went around intimidating Blacks from voting; one majority Black district ended up giving the Fusion candidate an astonishingly low 39 votes compared to over 250 for the Democrat. The fear factor went both ways—Democrats rounded up white voters by spreading rumors of Black residents plotting to unleash violence or, even worse, attempt a military coup.[32]

Of course, the threat of violence was there, but from the likes of the Red Shirts and other disaffected whites. Russell felt worried enough about his safety that he made sure he was escorted to his polling place in Wilmington by two Democratic officials. When he left Wilmington to travel

[28] Zucchino, supra, 77–78.

[29] Zucchino, supra, 79–80.

[30] Zucchino, supra, 76.

[31] Billy Ball, "North Carolina's Wilmington Massacre and Trump's Insurrection Really Aren't So Different," *Cardinal & Pine*, November 10, 2021, accessed February 24, 2022.

[32] Zucchino, supra, 168–169.

back to Raleigh, a small group of Red Shirts led by a young man named Cameron Morrison boarded his train and informed him that a lynch mob was waiting for him at an upcoming stop. Morrison advised a terrified Russell to hide in the baggage car until the threat passed, whereupon he was escorted back to the governor's mansion safely.[33]

Ultimately, the Democrats' campaign of fear and intimidation worked even better than they could have anticipated. Panicked, Republicans and Populists split, with the former trying desperately to make the election about good governance and reform while the latter tried to co-opt white supremacy for their own means. With their disciplined campaign strategy and their opposition in disarray, Democrats swept the 1898 elections, taking back both state legislative houses. Fewer than half of registered Black voters ended up casting ballots and the white supremacy campaign peeled off thousands of Populist voters. The two leaders of the successful effort took victory laps, with *The News and Observer* proclaiming that "white supremacy receives a vote of confidence" while Simmons would be declared "the little giant of New Bern" who single handedly destroyed Black rule.[34]

Having learned their lesson, one of the first things they did once they got back in power was to make sure they would stay there. The now Democratic-controlled legislature drafted a constitutional amendment enacting all sorts of restrictions on voting designed to disenfranchise Blacks, including the infamous poll tax, literacy test, and Grandfather clause that existed in other Southern states at the time.[35] The amendment was approved by voters in 1900, with Democrats using many of the same tactics that had worked two years before.[36]

[33] Zucchino, supra, 172–173.

[34] Zucchino, supra, 174–175.

[35] The Grandfather clause was a legal mechanism used in some Southern states after Reconstruction to disenfranchise Black voters while allowing many white citizens to continue voting. These laws stated that a person could only vote if their grandfather had been eligible to vote before a certain date—usually before the Civil War or the passage of the Fifteenth Amendment (1870), which granted Black men the right to vote. Since most Black people's grandfathers had been enslaved and therefore unable to vote, they were effectively barred from voting. Meanwhile, many poor and uneducated white voters were exempt from literacy tests or poll taxes that would have otherwise prevented them from voting.

[36] Helen G. Edmonds, *The Negro and Fusion Politics in North Carolina, 1894–1901* (Chapel Hill, NC: Univ of North Carolina Press, 2003).

For some, waiting two years, or even a couple of months, for the next legislative session to begin was simply intolerable. In Wilmington, for instance, the day after the elections, a group of nine prominent white men (known by the nickname "The Secret Nine") called a meeting at the courthouse to discuss "business in the furtherance of white supremacy."[37] During the meeting, Alfred M. Waddell, a former U.S. representative, read *The White Declaration of Independence* to the crowd. "Believing that the Constitution of the United States contemplated a government to be carried on by an enlightened people; believing that its framers did not anticipate the enfranchisement of an ignorant population of African origin; and believing that the men of the State of North Carolina who joined in forming the Union did not contemplate for their descendants a subjection to an inferior race," the *Declaration* stated, "We, the undersigned citizens of the city of Wilmington and county of New Hanover, do hereby declare that we will no longer be ruled, and will never again be ruled, by men of African origin."[38]

Waddell went on, claiming that since white residents owned 95% of the property in Wilmington and paid taxes on it, they should be ruled by their fellow white residents. Arguing that Blacks, and their white enablers, had demonstrated that they were incapable of ruling fairly, Waddell demanded that Wilmington's mayor and chief of police resign so that a new government could be installed. That new government, Waddell promised, would deal with Blacks fairly—albeit only after whites got a "large part of the employment heretofore given to Negroes." Waddell also pointed to an August 1898 editorial in the Black-owned *Wilmington Daily Record* by editor Alexander Manly in which he took issue with the racist trope of Black men raping white women, and argued that it was more common for white men to rape Black women. Responding to an incendiary editorial from Rebecca Latimer Felton in Georgia, a former slave owner and advocate of lynching Black men accused of rape who would make history as the first woman to serve in the U.S. Senate, Manly went a step further and accused white men of not taking care of their women enough so

[37] "Announcement in the Wilmington Messenger on November 9, 1898," *Wikipedia*, https://en.wikipedia.org/wiki/Wilmington_massacre#/media/File:Attention_White_Men.jpg, accessed June 14, 2024.

[38] "The White Declaration of Independence," reprinted from *The News and Observer*, November 10, 1898, https://people.uncw.edu/schmidt/Misc/1898/1898WhiteDec.html, accessed June 13, 2024.

that, as a result, some of them might have even wanted to be with a Black man.[39]

Predictably, Waddell and his allies were outraged and reacted like they had been slapped across the face with a hundred leather gloves. One might wonder why they were still so angry about it in November when the editorial had been published in August. Turns out, Simmons had advised his allies in Wilmington to wait until closer to election day to display their anger.[40]

Waddell and his allies did so, using the text of the *Declaration* to call the editorial "vile and slanderous," and to demand Manly's immediate resignation and exile from Wilmington and the closure of the *Wilmington Daily Record*. In any other city or community, Manly would have been lynched, and even that would have been too good for him, Waddell declared. Getting rid of him and his paper was the best way to protect residents from such horrific lies in the future and, if their demands weren't met, Waddell warned, Manly would be "expelled by force."[41]

Waddell and his followers issued an ultimatum to the Committee of Colored Citizens (CCC), a group of 30 or so prominent Black residents of Wilmington, to comply or risk violence. "Stern and determined, the white[s] looked the masters they proposed to be – anxious and expectant, the Negro realized his day of dominancy had passed," the *Semi-Weekly Messenger* wrote in an account subtitled: "radicalism overthrown and Wilmington redeemed."[42] Whether they meant "master" to refer to the historical context of slavery or meant it in a more general sense, the implication was clear—Waddell was not interested in negotiating.[43]

After the frightened CCC claimed they did not speak for and were not responsible for Manly, Waddell ended the meeting and dismissively gave them until 7:30 the following morning to respond, or else his mob

[39] Zucchino, supra, 87–88.

[40] Zucchino, supra, 90.

[41] "The White Declaration of Independence," supra.

[42] "Recent Occurrences: Wilmington's Second Declaration of Independence. Historical Review. The Sons of Cape Fear Again Establish a Glorious Record – the Example of Illustrious Sires Followed. Radicalism overthrown and Wilmington Redeemed – Cool, Calm and Deliberate Action of White Men in Resenting an Insult to Their Women. Thrilling Narrative of the Burning of the Negro Newspaper Office – The Bloody 10th of November," *The Semi-Weekly Messenger*, November 22, 1898.

[43] Wilmington's Second Declaration of Independence, supra.

would torch the *Wilmington Daily Record's* offices. The CCC drafted a letter again disclaiming responsibility for Manly, but offering to work with Waddell and his group to carry out his demands. The CCC representative went to deliver the letter to Waddell at his home, but got intimidated after seeing a bunch of Red Shirts outside; he got scared and put the letter in a public mailbox, instead.

So, Waddell received no response to his self-imposed deadline and unleashed his mob, which destroyed several Black-owned businesses, assaulted and killed numerous Black residents and inhabitants and, as promised, torched the offices of *The Daily Record*.[44] The mob then forced Wilmington's mayor and aldermen and police chief to resign at gunpoint, and installed Waddell as mayor. One of the first things the new mayor did was to banish several prominent Black residents from the city. Waddell also allowed some of the white Republicans to leave, too, but not before the deposed chief of police was nearly lynched. "Negro rule is at an end in North Carolina forever," *The News and Observer* declared triumphantly.[45] "The events of the past week in Wilmington and elsewhere place that fact beyond all question."

There's never been a definitive death count for the Wilmington Insurrection. Historians have estimated the death toll to be close to 300, with thousands more Blacks forced to flee Wilmington.[46] However, some contemporaneous sources downplayed the insurrection and kept the numbers artificially low (*The New York Times*, for instance, had the death toll at 19).[47] Meanwhile, Waddell wrote a widely read account that was published in several outlets, including *Collier's Weekly* and *The News and Observer*, that largely whitewashed the event and maintained that everything had been done by the book.

[44] Scott Neuman, "A North Carolina city begins to reckon with the massacre in its white supremacist past," *NPR*, November 10, 2021.

[45] "Order Now Reigns: Wilmington's New City Government Has Done its Work Well," *The News and Observer*, November 13, 1898.

[46] Timothy B. Tyson, "The Ghosts of 1898," *The News & Observer*, November 17, 2006, archived PDF from the original https://web.archive.org/web/20200821164033/http:/media2.newsobserver.com/content/media/2010/5/3/ghostsof1898.pdf, August 21, 2020.

[47] "Nineteen Negroes Shot to Death," *The New York Times*, November 11, 1898, *Civil War Era NC*, https://cwnc.omeka.chass.ncsu.edu/items/show/673, accessed March 2, 2022.

> As to the government we have established, it is a perfectly legal one. The law, passed by the Republican Legislature itself, has been complied with. There was no intimidation used in the establishment of the present city government. The old government had become satisfied of their inefficiency and utterly helpless imbecility, and believed if they did not resign they would be run out of town. Therefore they came forward, after consulting with men of our city, and they said each one of them wanted to resign was anxious to do so. They wanted to get rid of the responsibility. If our people would organize, they would be glad to resign and let us take the responsibility.[48]

Waddell portrayed his mob as acting mostly peacefully and maintained that, while they may have trashed the *Record's* office, they were as surprised as anyone that a fire broke out and even tried to put it out. He also noted the lengths he had gone to let the Black and Republican officials leave town safely and, now that they were gone and the crisis had abated, everything was great in Wilmington. In fact, he claimed that Blacks in Wilmington were as happy as the whites that order had been restored to the city, and that some Black residents had even gone up to him and expressed happiness that he had taken charge. He even went as far as to say that things were so peaceful now that he could patrol the city with six women in tow, which was a pretty bold claim considering how a big part of his justification for leading the coup had been to protect the women and children.[49]

In any event, what followed was the restoration of one party rule in the Tar Heel state.[50] Democrats won back the governor's mansion in 1900 and held it for the next 73 years. Simmons was elected to the Senate in 1901, and his party would hold both North Carolina seats until 1972, when Republican (and former Democrat) Jesse Helms was elected. After George White, a Black Republican who was first elected in 1896, decided

[48] "The Story of The Wilmington, North Carolina, Race Riots." *The News and Observer*, November 27, 1898, *Civil War Era NC*, https://cwnc.omeka.chass.ncsu.edu/items/show/771, accessed February 28, 2022.

[49] The Story of The Wilmington, North Carolina, Race Riots." *The News and Observer*, supra.

[50] The nickname's origin is somewhat debated, but it most commonly relates to the state's early industry in tar, pitch, and turpentine—products derived from the state's extensive pine forests. During the Civil War, North Carolina soldiers were said to have "tar on their heels," implying they stuck firmly in battle and refused to retreat. Over time, "Tar Heel" became a proud symbol of resilience and determination for North Carolinians.

not to run for reelection in 1900, another 92 years would pass before North Carolina sent another Black person to Congress.

"That Young Fellow from Monroe Almost Beat Me"

According to Burris, Parker's friends and associates got upset with him after he joined the GOP in 1908, believing he had taken whatever promise and potential he had in electoral politics and flushed it down the toilet.[51] After all, it had been nearly a decade since the Democrats had begun re-asserting their dominance in the state and driving Republicans and Fusionists from power—either by the ballot or the bullet. Republicans had very little electoral success in the years since, and Parker risked irrelevancy and obscurity by joining a minority party that could conceivably point to a 10-point loss as a "strong showing."

Democrats later accused Parker of making the move in order to curry favor with national Republicans, who may have been weak in the South but were the majority party at the federal level. For context, when Parker ran for governor in 1920, there had only been two Democratic presidents since the end of Reconstruction. Therefore, during the years when Republicans ran Washington, they would distribute money, federal positions, judicial appointments, and other patronage to party members throughout the country—including the South. To Democrats, Parker wasn't a serious candidate for state office—instead, he was just trying to make a name for himself so that he could cut to the front of the GOP "pie counter," waiting for his piece.[52]

They also accused Parker of being upset over a personal snub that took place shortly after his graduation from college. In 1910, Parker admitted in a speech that he had approached the state Democratic committee to see if he could be a speaker and advocate for them throughout the state. "His services were not needed, it seems, and in a short time, Mr. Parker was making Republican speeches," *The Greensboro Telegram* reported.[53]

Others, however, believed Parker's decision had more to do with the policies of the national Republican Party rather than its state chapter.

[51] Burris, supra, 34–35.

[52] Burris, supra, 34–35.

[53] *The Greensboro Telegram*, September 24, 1910.

Parker greatly admired Theodore Roosevelt and proudly cast his presidential vote in 1908 for William Howard Taft, Roosevelt's hand-picked successor. After Roosevelt and Taft fell out in the run-up to the 1912 presidential election, Parker remained publicly neutral, although others have claimed that he favored the former president over the then current one.

Another reason why the national GOP appealed to him was due to his strong belief in free markets with minimal economic regulations, and his extreme concerns over the rise of socialism. During his 1920 campaign, he would go as far as to say that defeating socialism "is the supreme patriotism of today."[54]

And, of course, he liked the national GOP because they weren't the national Democratic Party, which was then dominated by anti-big business populist William Jennings Bryan.[55] In one of his first big speeches after joining the Republican Party, Parker argued that Democrats had been on the wrong side of every major issue since the days of Thomas Jefferson and warned that they would destroy American businesses.[56] When he ran for governor 12 years later, he expounded on those themes, saying during a campaign speech: "One of the things in my life of which I am most proud is that fact that in 1908, when the Democratic party nominated Mr. Bryan and adopted a platform in which I could not believe, God Almighty gave me the courage to do my duty as I saw it. And I stand ready to part company with the Republican party if it ever repudiates the principles in which I believe."[57]

There were, no doubt, practical concerns as well. Since most of the state's rising stars and political heavyweights were in the Democratic Party, there were fewer people in Parker's way if he wished to rise to the top of the GOP in a short amount of time. Indeed, shortly after he joined, he was immediately entrusted with running the campaign for John Motley Morehead II for U.S. Representative for North Carolina's 5th District. Not only did Morehead win, but Parker made a name for

[54] "Parker Nominated," *The Charlotte News*, May 4, 1920.

[55] Burris, supra, 35.

[56] "Republicans Did Not Name Ticket," *The Daily Record*, August 17, 1908.

[57] "Parker Scores Revaluation in Speech at Hill," *The Charlotte Observer*, April 18, 1920.

himself traveling the state and making speeches, developing a reputation as a good orator and campaigner.

In 1910, however, Morehead decided not to run for reelection—instead he became chairman of the state's Republican executive committee and set about trying to reform the party, moving it away from its Fusionist past (complete with constant charges of catering to "Radicals and Negroes") and putting it more in line with the national party and its pro-big business policies. Believing, perhaps naively, that with Blacks closed off from voting in North Carolina for the foreseeable future, the racial issue had been neutralized, Morehead and other "lily-whites" within the state GOP wanted their party to be exclusively white and compete with Democrats for those voters. Therefore, with the full support of President Taft, who had become the first GOP candidate for president ever to campaign in North Carolina in 1908,[58] Morehead and his group of progressives tried to remake the GOP in the image of its national counterpart.[59]

So, when Parker ran his first race, a 1910 contest for U.S. Congress for North Carolina's 7th District, he focused on national issues, such as lowering tariffs and busting trusts. He also hit his opponent, incumbent Representative Robert Newton Page, on pocketbook issues, noting that the congressman had only secured $115,000 in federal appropriations in his eight years in Congress while Morehead had once brought home $300,000 in one shot. And while Parker may have disliked Bryan, he wasn't below using him as a weapon—in this case, he made a political issue out of Page not voting for Bryan for president in 1896.[60]

Parker also spoke of the need for a vibrant, two-party system in North Carolina—and the South, as a whole. He understood the South was seen as backwards, poor and unsophisticated by the rest of the country and believed a strong two-party system could help his state, as well as others in the former Confederacy, become more modernized and prosperous. He frequently spoke about the need for a strong Republican Party and how

[58] "Come quick, Pa—it's a Republican candidate!" *NC Miscellany*, October 17, 2015, https://blogs.lib.unc.edu/ncm/2015/10/17/come-quick-pa-its-a-republican-candidate/, accessed April 28, 2024.

[59] Joseph F. Steelman, "The Trials of a Republican State Chairman: John Motley Morehead and North Carolina Politics, 1910–1912," *The North Carolina Historical Review* 43, no. 1 (January 1966), 31–42.

[60] "Parker and Page Meet," *The Davie Record*, October 12, 1910.

breaking the Democratic stranglehold on electoral politics in the South would be better for the region in the long run.[61]

As the 1910 elections unfolded, however, it became clear that Morehead's hope that the race question would be settled was wishful thinking. Ironically enough, those dashed hopes were personified in the form of a white supremacist who had emerged as the symbol of Black rule and effective boogeyman for Democrats and their base of white voters.

Marion Butler had been a leading figure in the populist movement and one of the main architects of Fusion. After graduating from UNC in 1885, Butler had hoped to study law, but his father's untimely death meant that he was now in charge of his family's farm. That ended up being his gateway into politics; he was elected president of his local Farmers' Alliance at the young age of 25, before becoming president of the national Farmers' Alliance in 1893. He also acquired *The Caucasian*, becoming the paper's main editor and turning it into a mouthpiece for the Farmers' Alliance. Starting out as a Democrat, Butler was elected to the North Carolina Senate in 1890, but split with his party in 1892 over Grover Cleveland's pro-business and anti-free silver policies.[62] The state Democratic Party, under Simmons' leadership, essentially warned unhappy party officials that they had to support the entire ticket, including Cleveland. If anyone dared to split their ticket or back everyone but the former president, the party decreed, they would not be allowed to take part in county and congressional district conventions.[63]

As a result, Butler and his followers bolted and joined the fledgling Progressive Party. Understanding that they needed help to compete with Democrats, and seeing the potential in a strategic alliance with the Republicans, who were still a strong minority party in the state at that time, Butler met with Black and white members of the state GOP and agreed to cooperate with them against the Democrats. The 1894 Fusion victory also had implications for Butler, as he was elected to the U.S. Senate by the Populist and GOP-dominated state legislature. Two years later, as

[61] Burris, supra, 39–40.

[62] The Free Silver movement was a political campaign that advocated for the free coinage of silver as a means to expand the money supply and promote economic growth. This policy was particularly popular among farmers and working-class Americans who believed it would help address economic hardship.

[63] James L. Hunt, "The Making of a Populist: Marion Butler, 1863–1895, Part II," *The North Carolina Historical Review* 62, no. 2 (1985), 187–188.

national chairman of the Populist Party, Butler made a deal for his party to endorse Bryan for president, a move that catapulted Butler into the national spotlight. Despite that, Populists and Republicans continued to cooperate up until the fateful elections of 1898.

With Democrats back in power, they picked Simmons to succeed Butler after his term in the Senate was up. Butler then practiced law in Washington, D.C. but remained a high-profile political figure in his home state, where he joined the North Carolina Republican Party. Whenever his name came up, either because he showed up at a state GOP convention or because he worked with Morehead to try and rebuild the party, it gave rise to the old "Radicals and Negroes" line of attack that Democrats had utilized so effectively in the past. "The man who votes the Republican ticket, whether he does so knowingly or not, votes to hasten the reopening of the question of Negroes voting in North Carolina," the Raleigh-based *News and Observer* warned in August 1910.[64]

It was an ironic charge, considering Butler's background as an ardent white supremacist. He had even tried to position the Populist Party as the true "white man's party," writing in an 1894 editorial about how Democrats were "changing their tune" on Black voters by courting their support at the ballot box[65] and how the Democrats, not Republicans had become the "Negro Party."[66] And, in arguments Parker would later adopt, Butler claimed that injecting race into politics distracted voters and politicians from focusing on more important issues. "As long as the toiling masses remain divided because of appeals to race prejudice and party love, so long will they be at the mercy of organized capital," *The Caucasian* said in a March 1893 editorial.

Democrats had another reason for hating Butler. During Reconstruction, the state legislature had issued large numbers of bonds to pay for various projects, most notably building the Western Carolina Railroad. However, some corrupt officials stole money from the project and the railroad was not completed, rendering the bonds worthless. When Democrats regained control after Reconstruction, they settled with bondholders, buying the bonds back for about 25% of their face value. One major bondholder, a company based in New York, wanted the full amount

[64] *The News and Observer*, August 20, 1910.

[65] "It Is Now 'Our Colored Brethren,'" *The Caucasian*, August 16, 1894.

[66] "The Negro Party," *The Caucasian*, August 30, 1894.

back, but their options were limited. Under the Eleventh Amendment, citizens of one state cannot sue another state in federal court, ruling out a lawsuit to recover their money. So in 1901, during the dying days of Russell's administration, the bondholders reached out to the outgoing governor for help.

Russell, seeing a chance to save himself from financial ruin as well as to stick it to his Democratic enemies, devised a scheme whereby the New York bondholder would donate some of their bonds to another state and then that state could sue North Carolina for full repayment, with Russell getting some of this money for his troubles. "Now, whenever these repudiating State[s] see that they can be sued by other States, my opinion is that they will come to a compromise with the holders of these Bonds, who would say, we have donated to that State or to this State which has sued you," Russell wrote to friend and lawyer Alfred Russell (no relation).[67]

South Dakota was chosen, and the ensuing case ultimately went to the Supreme Court. In 1904, a 5–4 majority ruled in favor of South Dakota, holding that the state was entitled to the full value of their security.[68] The case had its predicted effect of bringing North Carolina to the bargaining table with the New York bondholders to see about making a compromise as to the outstanding bonds. Russell ultimately did get some money out of his deal, but he remained in the red for the rest of his life—which came to an end in 1908 after years of declining health.

The bond controversy long outlived him and became a noose around Butler's neck—one that Democrats were only too happy to tighten when facing Republican opponents in the ensuing years. Russell had contacted Butler, asking to see if he knew of any states that might be interested in receiving a charitable donation. Butler, who claimed he didn't know about Russell's plot to use the bonds, nevertheless became tagged as an accomplice with Russell's scheme, which not only saw the North Carolina governor side with another state against the one that elected him, but also harkened back to Reconstruction and the hated "Radicals and Negroes" legislature.

Indeed, throughout the 1910 campaign, Page did not hesitate to play that card and called Parker a "pawn" of Butler's and others who wished to

[67] Robert Durden, "Governor Daniel L. Russell Explains His 'South Dakota Bond' Scheme," *The North Carolina Historical Review* 38, no. 4 (1961), 532.

[68] *South Dakota v. North Carolina*, 192 U.S. 286 (1904).

"turn the state government over to the Negroes."[69] During a September 1910 debate between Parker and Page, the incumbent put his challenger on the defensive, charging that Butler had returned to the state for the sole purpose of collecting on repudiated Reconstruction bonds, and asking whether Parker supported paying him. According to *The News and Observer* and *The Charlotte Observer*, Parker dodged the question and did not answer it directly.[70]

Parker made things worse by defending his association with Butler and Morehead and trying to turn Page's invocation of Butler against him, telling the audience that Butler did more for the state than Page ever had. *The Dispatch* reported that the line went over poorly with the audience, and a palpable chill filled the room as more people interpreted Parker's line as a defense of the boogeyman Butler rather than an attack against Page.[71]

As expected, Parker was defeated by Page, but ran a respectable campaign and only lost by a little over 3,300 votes out of over 25,000 cast, resulting in a 56.62–43.38% margin. The result was pretty consistent with how Page did in 1908, in which he defeated Republican and former state Attorney General Zeb Vance Walser by 3,325 votes, and better than his 1906 showing, where he beat G.D.B. Reynolds by 2,772 votes.[72] Nevertheless, Page later singled out Parker as the one who came closest to knocking him off. "That young fellow from Monroe almost beat me," Page said.[73]

Landslide

That strong showing made Parker a hot commodity with the state GOP and an obvious choice for higher office. However, that didn't make his prospects for winning a general election any brighter or less daunting. Six years later, Parker won the GOP nomination for state attorney general and ran against Democrat James S. Manning, a former justice on the North

69 Burris, supra, 42.

70 "Political Pawns of Marion Butler," *The News and Observer*, September 23, 1910.

71 "The Page Parker Debate," *The Dispatch*, October 5, 1910.

72 "A Pocket Manual of North Carolina," 1911, www.carolana.com/NC/NC_Manuals/NC_Manual_1911.pdf.

73 Burris, supra, 43.

Carolina Supreme Court. Manning had been appointed to that position by Governor W.W. Kitchin and, after the expiry of both of their terms, they formed a law firm together in Raleigh. Manning finished first in the June 3 primary with 43,332 votes out of 93,117 cast, or 46.5%. Former U.S. army captain (and Confederate army veteran) Edmund Jones came in a distant second with 18,902 votes.[74] Ordinarily, he would have been entitled to a runoff, but with Manning so close to an outright majority, he chose not to ask for one and conceded defeat ten days later.[75]

"For a great many years, it has been conceded by the legal profession of the State, and others who have watched his career, that Judge Manning is one of the most profound and learned and active lawyers now practicing at the bar in North Carolina," the Bar of Durham County said in a resolution.[76]

As in the 1910 contest, Parker came into the race as a huge underdog. However, he had made a name for himself as a result of his prior run for office and in the years since. Newspapers often praised Parker as a talented orator, excellent campaigner, and forceful advocate—even Democratic outlets like *The Greensboro Daily News* referred to Parker as having a "splendid reputation."[77]

He had also developed a reputation as a good attorney, with his hometown newspaper, *The Monroe Journal*, dubbing him "one of the ablest young lawyers in the State."[78] In the middle of the campaign, Parker took a detour to the courthouse, defending a Black mail carrier on federal charges of setting a mail car on fire. According to the *Charlotte News*' write-up of the case, the defendant was "ably defended" by Parker, his partner, A.M. Stack and co-counsel, with the paper being sure to point out that the defendant was, essentially, "the only witness for himself, aside from character witnesses he put up."[79]

[74] A Pocket Manual of North Carolina," 1917, https://www.carolana.com/NC/NC_Manuals/NC_Manual_1917.pdf.

[75] "Jones Will Not Ask for Second Primary," *The News and Record*, June 13, 1916.

[76] "James S. Manning: A Candidate for Democratic Nomination for Attorney General," *The State Journal*, May 26, 1916.

[77] "J.J. Parker Will Speak In This City Tonight," *The Greensboro Daily News*, November 1, 1916.

[78] "Mr J.J. Parker has been designated ...," *The Monroe Journal*, April 21, 1916.

[79] "Massey Negro Cleared of Charge of Burning Mail Coach on Seaboard," *The Charlotte News*, April 7, 1916.

Parker focused on a few main issues during his campaign. Like his 1910 campaign, he seemed more interested in issues of national importance, often talking about the need to protect American interests at home and abroad—especially with a major war then raging in Europe and in parts of Asia and Africa. He called for the institution of protective tariffs to protect American businesses against the disruption brought by the war, and blamed the Wilson administration and Democrats in Congress for lowering tariffs during their years in power.[80] "I don't believe there is a Democrat who in his heart of hearts is not ashamed of his party's record," he said during an October speech in Raleigh.[81]

Parker also railed against the Adamson Act, a federal law that established the eight-hour workday and overtime pay for interstate railroad workers, calling it "the darkest blot on the history of this country in the past decade," and questioning its constitutionality. "The President was simply afraid to meet a crisis," said Parker, noting that the Act was passed to avoid a nationwide railroad strike, "and if such policies are to be followed in the future, the integrity of this government is seriously threatened."[82]

By necessity, Parker also talked about state issues, complaining that taxes were too high and promising to investigate the Cape Fear and Yadkin railway to see if they were operating in violation of antitrust law. He criticized the state's education system, calling it unworthy of the state and inferior even to "heathen Japan."[83]

He also hammered home the need to have a competitive Republican Party in North Carolina—an issue he had talked about in 1910 and one that he would return to in the future. Simply put, having one party in power for so long was bound to make things inefficient and stagnant, and he used the tax issue as an illustration. Parker pointed out that, during the Democrats' 16 consecutive years in power, the tax rate had gone up even while other states were cutting taxes. He blamed Democrats for paying too much for schools, doubling the size of the government, and ignoring the plight of farmers or laborers. The only thing they accomplished, in

[80] "Mr. Parker Wishes to Investigate Railway," *The Greensboro Daily News*, November 2, 1916.

[81] "Parker Spoke in Raleigh," *The Wilmington Dispatch*, October 16, 1916.

[82] Ibid.

[83] "Parker Speaks to Republicans," *The News and Record*, October 15, 1916.

Parker's mind, was to keep North Carolinians in a state of perpetual fear that the Fusionist regime and their Black base might make a comeback if they didn't vote Democrat.[84]

And he was right in the sense that Democrats could play the old "Radicals and Negroes" card and have it pay dividends. In the 1916 electoral cycle, Butler appeared at the GOP state convention; he immediately gave Democrats a ready-made, tried-and-true line of attack. "The Republicans want the Negro to have an unrestricted ballot, so that he may use the Negro again and make his vote of personal value in Republican assaults upon Democracy," *The News and Observer* warned, adding that Butler was "again in control of the Republican party of the State" and calling him "an unworthy son of the State" whom "men of character do not hesitate to denounce."[85]

As with 1910, Parker couldn't help himself and felt compelled to defend his party. In an October speech in Raleigh, Parker defended the Fusionist government, arguing that the 1897 legislature had produced some excellent results and had accomplished more than its Democratic successors had. He also invoked the ghost of Daniel L. Russell, calling Democrats hypocrites for complaining about the Republican's extravagance in office when the then current governor, Locke Craig, made almost twice as much in salary and allowances. According to the *Wilmington Dispatch*, unlike what happened in 1910, when Parker tried to defend Butler, the audience—even the Democrats in attendance—seemed amused by the reference to Russell.[86]

In the end, Parker lost to Manning in a blowout (60.93–39.07%), taking just 120,211 votes to Manning's 187,312.[87] Manning actually ran ahead of President Wilson, who easily carried North Carolina with 168,383 votes, while Parker's total tracked fairly closely with what Charles Evans Hughes, the GOP nominee for president, got in the state (120,890 votes). In other words, Parker had the misfortune of running against a candidate who was seemingly more popular with the North Carolina voters than the guy at the head of the ticket. Despite *The Wilmington*

84 "Mr. Parker Wishes to Investigate Railway," supra.

85 *The News and Observer*, April 29, 1916.

86 "Parker Spoke in Raleigh," *The Wilmington Dispatch*, October 16, 1916.

87 Peter G. Fish, "A 'Freshman' Takes Charge: Judge John J. Parker of the United States Court of Appeals, 1925–1930," *Journal of Southern Legal History* 10 (2002), 59–113.

Dispatch praising Parker for making great speeches and acquitting himself well during the campaign,[88] there was really no way to put any positive spin on this race—Parker got shellacked and, typically, a loss like this would spell the end of one's political career.

Instead, it made him the unquestioned leader of the North Carolina GOP and front-runner for the gubernatorial nomination in 1920—a race that would have profound short- and long-term implications for his career and life.

[88] "John Parker Made Good," *The Wilmington Dispatch*, November 10, 1916.

CHAPTER 2

1920 and Beyond: A Fateful Gubernatorial Election

The 1920 North Carolina gubernatorial race featured three well-known, heavyweight candidates who were all more than capable of winning that November. None of them were John J. Parker.

Maybe if Parker had run as a Democrat, he might have stood a chance. Instead, he was in the unenviable position of waiting to see which Democrat he would have the privilege of losing to that November. If he were fortunate, maybe the Democrats would beat each other up so badly that whoever ended up winning the nomination would be so weakened that Parker would only lose by single digits. Surely that would go a long way towards strengthening the party and positioning it well for the future, while maybe even helping a few Republicans pull off down-ballot upsets in the process.

The early front-runner in the Democratic field was Lieutenant Governor Oliver Max Gardner (he went by the name O. Max Gardner in his professional and political life). The youngest of 12 children, Gardner was born on March 22, 1882, in Shelby, North Carolina. Both of his parents died during his childhood, so Gardner was raised by his older sisters until he went to college. An outstanding football player, Gardner captained the team at North Carolina College of Agriculture and Mechanic Arts (now North Carolina State University). After graduating in 1903 with a degree in chemistry, he enrolled at UNC for law school and ended up captaining their football team too. He remains the

V. Li, *Supreme Pressure*,
https://doi.org/10.1007/978-3-032-07864-3_2

only person to ever to accomplish that feat at both UNC and the school known today as NC State.[1]

Upon earning his law degree, Gardner moved back to Shelby in 1907 where he, like Parker, balanced his practice with a budding career in politics. He also co-owned a local cloth mill. The same year he moved back to Shelby, Gardner married Fay Webb, whose father was local superior court judge James L. Webb and whose uncle was Congressman E. Yates Webb. Gardner's brother-in-law through his sister, Bess, was Clyde R. Hoey, a Shelby newspaper owner and lawyer, who would later serve as governor and U.S. senator. This so-called Shelby Dynasty would eventually control politics in the state for much of the 1930s and 1940s, with Gardner wielding a tremendous amount of power and influence as a governor and then kingmaker within North Carolina.[2]

A staunch Prohibitionist, Gardner was elected to serve two terms in the state Senate before successfully running for lieutenant governor in 1916 at the age of 34. As Douglas Carl Abrams pointed out in his retrospective of the 1920 race, at the time, Gardner was trying to defy history since no one had ever managed to get elected governor from the lieutenant governor's job.[3] Nevertheless, Gardner had earned plaudits from the press for how he had presided over the state Senate and became a leading candidate for governor in 1920. He had also picked up endorsements from former governors W.W. Kitchin and Robert B. Glenn and Kitchin's brother Claude, who was U.S. House majority leader.[4]

As far as Democrats went, Gardner was considered to be part of the progressive wing of the party. On the other end of the ideological spectrum was Cameron Morrison, the man who had advised Russell to hide

[1] Richard Walker, "Early UNC-State rivalry featured the first Shelby High football star and a man who went on to far greater fame," *Carolinas Sports Hub*, https://carolinassportshub.com/early-unc-state-rivalry-featured-the-first-shelby-high-football-star-and-a-man-who-went-on-to-far-greater-fame/, accessed June 5, 2024. Given how NCAA eligibility rules have changed since then, as well as the fierce the rivalry that has developed between the two schools, he will probably remain the only person to ever captain both NC State's and UNC's football teams.

[2] Paul McCraw, "The Shelby Dynasty," *NCPedia*, https://dev.ncpedia.org/shelby-dynasty, accessed: January 16, 2025.

[3] Douglas Carl Abrams, "A Progressive–Conservative Duel: The 1920 Democratic Gubernatorial Primaries in North Carolina," *The North Carolina Historical Review* 55, no. 4 (1978), 421–443.

[4] Ibid.

in the baggage car of his train to avoid a lynch mob during the 1898 elections. Born on October 5, 1869, in Richmond County, North Carolina, Morrison was a lawyer by trade who, like Parker, had moved to Charlotte to formally practice.

He also had another thing in common with Parker. Morrison was a party-switcher, although in his case he did a reverse-Parker, having originally joined the Republican Party. Morrison's father was a former Confederate veteran who, after the Civil War, had taken the rare step of throwing in with the GOP instead of the Democrats. But then, in 1891, the younger Morrison could no longer stomach the Fusionist regime, so he joined the Democrats and soon became a leader of the Richmond County Red Shirts, making a name for himself by challenging the voter registrations of over 200 Blacks in the state, and giving speeches throughout the county extolling the virtues of the white race.[5] A participant in the Wilmington Insurrection, Morrison later claimed that he never hurt any Black person, only intimidated and scared them.[6] Nevertheless, his impact was clear. After Wilmington, Simmons toasted Morrison and praised him for his "splendid leadership" while adding that "when the history of the movement for white supremacy came to be written no man would be given greater credit for the victory than Cameron Morrison."[7]

Morrison was unable to parlay his notoriety into a long, distinguished career in politics—at least, not at first. After an unsuccessful bid in 1896, Morrison won a seat in the North Carolina Senate four years later, but only served for one term. In 1902, he ran for U.S. House of Representatives in the 7th District, but lost in the Democratic primary to Robert N. Page—the man who would defeat Parker in 1910. Morrison then took a 20-year break from politics, during which time he practiced law and served in a variety of capacities for the state Democratic Party. When Morrison decided to make his comeback, he immediately got the endorsement of Simmons and his powerful political machine, which made him a

[5] "Historical Background of Governor Cameron Morrison," *Charlotte Mecklenburg Library*, https://www.cmlibrary.org/blog/historical-background-governor-cameron-morrison#_ftn14, accessed June 5, 2024.

[6] "Governor Cameron Morrison," *State Archives of North Carolina*, https://archives.ncdcr.gov/morrison-cameron/open, accessed June 5, 2024.

[7] Historical Background of Governor Cameron Morrison, supra.

formidable candidate despite his long layoff and lack of previous electoral success.[8]

According to Abrams, Morrison nearly lost that endorsement before 1920 even started. In November 1919, Morrison's wife died suddenly, and a grieving Morrison stopped campaigning. Concerned that they were losing ground, Simmons and his allies considered pulling their support for Morrison and making a deal with Gardner.[9] Whether they were truly considering dumping him or they just wanted to give him a kick in the pants to motivate him, it had the effect of getting Morrison out of his perpetual state or mourning. Now, he vowed to stay in the race regardless of whether Simmons supported him or not—an attitude that suited his political patron just fine.[10]

The other leading candidate in the field was Parker's 1910 opponent, and Morrison's 1902 conqueror, Robert N. Page. The eldest of the three main contenders, Page was born in Wake County on October 26, 1859. His father owned timber yards in the county before moving the family to Moore County and continuing the family business there. His family became quite prominent in the coming years, being dubbed the "House of Page" as Page and each of his brothers made big reputations for themselves. His oldest brother, Walter Hines Page, became Ambassador to Great Britain under Wilson, while his three younger brothers became well-known businessmen and/or politicians.

After completing his studies, Page went to work for his family's lumber company while starting his career in politics. He was mayor of Aberdeen from 1890 to 1898 and served two years in the state house before being elected U.S. Representative for the 7th District in 1902. Page served seven terms in the House and was a member of the powerful Appropriations Committee. Fervently against entering World War I, Page opposed the Wilson Administration's neutrality policies as being insufficiently neutral, causing him to become unpopular in his heavily Democratic district. Therefore, he decided against running for reelection in 1916 and chose to retire.

Four years later, he decided to make a comeback and entered the gubernatorial race. In addition to arguing for the usual good roads and

[8] Abrams, supra, 421–443.

[9] Abrams, supra, 421–443.

[10] Abrams, supra, 428–429.

better schools, Page also called for funding the government by making it more efficient rather than relying on undue taxation. He also advocated for improved public health policies and protection for agricultural goods. Most radically of all, he proposed the concept of "industrial democracy," in which employers would share some of their profits with their workers as a means of ending ongoing labor unrest and giving both sides an incentive to succeed. "[P]rejudice must be eradicated; antagonism must give place to mutual consideration; capital must cease to be an orgy in the eyes of labor, and capital must cease to view labor as a commodity," Page said in a statement to *The Messenger and Intelligencer*.[11] Predictably, Morrison called it socialism and said it was the "most fallacious, dangerous and undemocratic utterance ever made by a Democratic aspirant for high office in North Carolina."[12]

Page's campaign of ideas stood in contrast to those of his main opponents. Morrison and Gardner ran more personality-based campaigns, with the former giving fiery speeches attacking his main rivals and tying himself to the legacy of the former governor, Charles Aycock, a virulent white supremacist and prominent proponent of the Wilmington Insurrection, and the latter portraying himself as the principled candidate of change standing up to the powerful Simmons machine. Morrison responded to the machine charge by proudly trumpeting his association with Simmons while calling out his opponents for having similar power bases ("Shelby Dynasty" and "House of Page").[13] Meanwhile, Gardner justified his lack of campaign promises by pointing out that, since the governor had no power of veto and could not direct the state legislature to pass certain bills, it was "unjust to the general public to enter into pledges" that might affect his ability to govern when the time came.[14]

Page, however, was never able to get much traction in the race. For one thing, his base of support overlapped with Gardner.[15] Also, despite his time in Congress, Page wasn't as well known in the state outside of his home district, putting him at a disadvantage to Gardner, who had been

[11] "Vote for Page for Governor," *The Messenger and Intelligencer*, May 29, 1920.

[12] Abrams, supra, 432.

[13] Abrams, supra, 431.

[14] "Max Gardner for Governor: Equipped for Office," *The Reidsville Review*, June 4, 1920.

[15] Abrams, supra, 424–425, 432–434.

elected statewide, and Morrison, who had Simmons backing him. Page was also considered a poor campaigner and speaker, which didn't help matters.

In the end, the issue that may have helped decide the race was women's suffrage. At the federal level, the Nineteenth Amendment guaranteeing women the right to vote had been approved by both houses of Congress but had not yet been ratified by North Carolina and was one state short of reaching the requisite three-fourths majority for it to go into effect for the entire country. Democrats in North Carolina were split over whether the state should ratify the amendment. On the anti-suffrage side, there were some who were against the idea of women voting in general, while others worried that extending the franchise to women would open the door to Black women voting. Others in the party, however, saw women's suffrage as inevitable—as such, it made sense that they should try and appeal to this new base of voters and not be identified with the forces that had tried to keep them from the ballot box.[16]

The issue had, similarly, split the Democratic primary field. Gardner had been a strong supporter of women's suffrage since 1916 while Morrison was an outspoken opponent. On the campaign trail, Morrison used what he referred to as the "Susan B. Anthony Amendment" as a convenient boogeyman, equating it to socialism and calling it a threat to the status quo. Page, for his part, had tried to stay quiet about the issue—perhaps reflecting his personal opposition towards the issue.[17]

According to the newspaper accounts of the race, Morrison's fortunes took a turn for the better after the Democrats' state convention in April, where, in a proxy fight between Gardner's budding dynasty and Morrison's Simmons-led machine, Gardner and his allies defeated Morrison's attempt to place an anti-suffrage plank into the party's platform and replaced it with a pro-suffrage plank. That victory may have been a Pyrrhic one, as Morrison started gaining ground and newspaper accounts at the time credited his anti-suffrage position. Gardner even started to retreat slightly from his pro-suffrage stance, not mentioning the issue in his speeches as much and even emphasizing his pre-1916 opposition to it.[18]

[16] Abrams, supra, 434–438.

[17] Abrams, supra, 434–438.

[18] Abrams, supra, 434–438.

The Democratic primary, which was held June 5, did not settle matters. Morrison and Gardner were neck-and-neck in the final vote—so much so that the result would not be known for another 11 days, during which time there were allegations of fraud and vote-stealing. Gardner led the initial vote but, as more ballots trickled in, Morrison ended up winning the primary by 87 votes. Page finished in third place, albeit with a surprisingly high 23.5% of the vote, winning 11 counties.

A runoff beckoned, but Morrison benefited by being able to look like the front-runner going into the race.[19] Also helping Morrison was that, despite his stark policy differences with Page, he ended up winning eight of the 11 counties that had gone to Page in the primary. The July runoff was not close—Morrison won easily by a margin of 53.5% to 46.5%. Gardner would later grouse that the nomination had been stolen from him.[20] Nevertheless, he understood he was a young man and would have more chances—but only if he was a good soldier and stayed loyal to his party. As a result, he made nice with Morrison and campaigned for him in the general election. In the end, Morrison's victory was widely credited to his stance on suffrage—although his endorsement by the Simmons machine and by many of the largest newspapers in North Carolina—an important factor in the pre-television, pre-radio era—also played a part.[21]

"A Source of Evil and Danger to Both Races"

At least Parker did not have to go through a bruising primary. Instead, thanks to his previous campaigns and the lack of viable statewide candidates in his party, Parker won the GOP nomination in a walkover. While waiting to see who his opponent would be, Parker was able to focus on ideas and issues. When it came to the Nineteenth Amendment, both the state GOP and Parker had been outspoken advocates for women's suffrage and supported ratification. "Two years ago, the Republican Party declared in favor of women's suffrage," he said during an April speech at

[19] "Today's Returns Appear to Have Eliminated Page," *The Charlotte News*, June 7, 1920.

[20] Rob Christensen, *The Paradox of Tar Heel Politics* (Chapel Hill, NC: University of North Carolina Press, 2008), 50.

[21] Abrams, supra, 438.

his alma mater, UNC.[22] "I should be ashamed for it to be said that the men of other states gave to our wives and mothers and daughters the privilege which we are unwilling to give them ourselves." By the time the general election campaign kicked into high gear, however, the issue had become moot. In August, Tennessee had become the thirty-sixth state to ratify the amendment, putting it into effect for the entire country.

Nevertheless, there were a lot of other things Parker was able to focus on, including upgrading infrastructure as a means of helping residents while attracting businesses to the state, improving public education, and protecting laborers. "Labor must be protected from the evils of the factory system. The protection of women and children, the limitation of hours of labor, insurance for the benefit of the employee against industrial casualties are too important to leave to private judgment. We must enact adequate labor legislation," Parker said during his acceptance speech at the 1920 state GOP convention.[23] Ironically enough, ten years later, with his nomination to the Supreme Court hanging in the balance, Parker would be accused of being anti-labor or, rather, not sufficiently sympathetic towards the plight of the working class. This part of his speech would, seemingly, be forgotten about as pro-labor senators looked for an excuse to reject his nomination.

"Laboring men have a right to organize. They have a right to strike. They have a right collectively to enter into agreements with their employers. These rights are fundamental and should not be abridged by the state," he said during a campaign speech at Wake Forest.[24]

As with his 1916 campaign, Parker also tackled taxes—he condemned the state's Revaluation Act of 1919, which provided for reassessment of property values for taxation purposes. Arguing that the act only came about because the state needed more revenue but was constitutionally prohibited from raising income tax rates, Parker excoriated it for putting an undue burden on farmers and farmland owners, who he claimed were being taxed at five or six times their former value.[25] Parker promised to

[22] "Parker Scores Revaluation in Speech at Hill," *The Charlotte Observer*, April 18, 1920.

[23] Burris, supra, 50.

[24] "Independent Voter is Hope of the Country," *The Monroe Journal*, May 14, 1920.

[25] "Candidate John Parker Pleads for Tax Reform," *The Monroe Journal*, June 25, 1920.

have the act repealed and replaced with a more equitable system, criticizing the current plan for allowing corporations and railroads to pay less than their fair share of taxes while putting more of the burden on individuals, especially farmers.[26]

In that regard, he advocated that North Carolina governors be granted the power to veto, putting it in line with most of the other states in the country. Such a move would make the governor a more active participant in the law-making process and make it so they couldn't shirk responsibility for bills passed under their watch. He argued for another expansion of gubernatorial powers, agreeing with Page that government needed to be more efficient. However, he went further, arguing in favor of the short ballot, a measure that would allow the governor to function as a president of sorts by giving them the power to appoint executive officers such as secretaries of state and auditors so that their interests would be aligned and they could work together more easily.[27]

He also returned to one of his favorite topics: the need for a strong two-party system in the South. In a late October speech, Parker argued that one-party rule had stunted Southern innovation and industrialization and relegated the region to second-class status when it came to national politics. Without a viable opposition party, Parker argued, Democratic incumbents could simply hold onto power without actually accomplishing anything in office, helping their constituents or improving the state. "We must break the 'Solid South' as a means to political freedom and to the intellectual and industrial upbuilding of the South," he said.[28] In another speech, he cautioned against showing blind loyalty towards a political party as if it were a sports team.[29]

Much of his criticism about how being a one-party state handicapped North Carolina was directed towards the Democratic Party bosses like Simmons, who relied on reactionary policies and race-baiting to maintain their power and win elections. Parker had contempt for the tactic of

[26] "Mr. John J. Parker in an Address Here," *The Oxford Public Ledger*, October 15, 1920.

[27] "State Tax System 50 Years Out of Date Declares Parker," *The Asheville Times*, May 18, 1920.

[28] "Mr. Parker Says South Is In Need of Political Freedom," *The News and Record*, October 31, 1920.

[29] "John J. Parker Heard by People of Duplin," *The Greensboro Daily News*, October 22, 1920.

utilizing demagoguery and fear to hold onto power—not only because it was a losing issue for his side but because it meant that platforms, promises, and records, or lack thereof, didn't matter. The only thing that did was who would do more to stop Black voters from taking over.

In his critique of bossism, Parker made sure not to spare his own party from the rod. "Nothing better ever happened to the Republican Party than its defeat in 1912. That defeat killed the machine, and the men in the Republican Party who stand for something have come to the front," Parker said in the 1920 race while vowing not to be the governor of a "faction or a party but of the whole people."[30]

Parker's words were also meant to disassociate himself from his perceived political bosses, Butler and Morehead. He very much wanted to be seen as his own man, with his own set of ideas, who was untainted by the past, particularly the Fusionist government that still inspired so much hatred and fear from so many voters in the state. "The Republican Party of today is not the party of Reconstruction," he said during the 1920 campaign.[31] "It is not the party of 1896."

In the hopes of underscoring that the GOP of 1920 was not the GOP of 1896 or 1865, Parker tried his best to neutralize the racial issue. During his acceptance speech at the North Carolina Republican Convention, Parker took a page from the lily-whites' playbook and also drew on his own training as a trial lawyer by drawing the sting.

> The Negro as a class does not desire to enter politics. The Republican Party of North Carolina does not desire him to do so. We recognize the fact that he has not yet reached that state in his development where he can share the burdens and responsibilities of government. This being true, the attempt by certain petty Democratic politicians to inject the race issue into every campaign is more reprehensible … In the first place, there can be no such thing as social equality or intercourse between the races. In the second place, the participation by the Negro in politics is a source of evil and danger to both races and is not desired by wise men of either race. These things are settled.[32]

[30] Burris, supra, 54–55.

[31] Burris, supra, 55.

[32] John J. Parker GOP Convention Speech, John J. Parker Papers.

Parker repeated these claims on the campaign trail. During an April speech at his alma mater, he again emphasized that Blacks in North Carolina were better off not participating in politics and that everyone, particularly state Republicans, accepted it. Parker added that Blacks were entitled to a "square deal," but did not talk about what such a deal would entail or include.[33] He went even further in a late October speech, declaring that the Republican Party in North Carolina was a "white man's party," and that the state was in no more danger of being taken over by Blacks as it was by the Japanese.[34]

Meanwhile, in an October 30 speech in Greensboro, Parker made clear he believed in white supremacy and quoted from a poem written by John Charles McNeil that wondered, among other things, what would politicians talk about if it weren't for Blacks. "What would we do without you, Mr. N-----?" Parker said, quoting from the poem which ultimately promised Black Americans that, despite being a problem, "the heart of all this mighty nation is set to work out your salvation, but don't you fear expatriation."[35] In another late October speech, Parker accused Morrison of having no ideas and plans to help the people of the state and was only interested in running a "n----- campaign."[36]

Parker quickly learned that, while he may have hoped to settle or quiet the racial issue, his opponents were perfectly happy to keep exploiting it. In his speeches, Morrison did his best to tie Parker to Butler and Morehead and the Fusionist past they represented. In his acceptance speech for the Democratic nomination, he referred to Parker as Butler's nominee

[33] "Parker Fires Broad Side at Democrats, Condemns Article Ten," *The Daily Tar Heel*, April 24, 1920.

[34] "Mr. Parker Says The South Is In Need of Political Freedom," *The News and Record*, October 31, 1920.

[35] "Parker Speaks to Greensboro Crowd," *Winston-Salem Journal*, October 31, 1920. John Charles McNeil, *Lyrics from Cotton Land* (Charlotte: The Stone & Barringer Company, 1907) (site: https://ia800209.us.archive.org/27/items/lyricsfromcotton00mcne/lyricsfromcotton00mcne.pdf) (accessed July 18, 2025). It was fairly common for politicians in this era to use the n-word during public appearances, speeches, and campaign ads.

[36] "Parker Declares He Will Be Next Governor," *The News and Record*, October 30, 1920.

and expressed pride in how he, along with Simmons and others, helped drive Butler and his Black allies from power.[37]

Perhaps unwittingly, and definitely unwisely, Parker then played into his opponent's hands by criticizing Morrison for his affiliation with the Red Shirts, calling him a "lawless citizen" whose actions made him "unfit to be Governor." For Morrison, however, the charge might as well have been a gift from Heaven; he not only leaned into it like any savvy politician from that era would have, but he also doubled down. "It is true that I wore a Red Shirt then," he told a cheering crowd in Brevard.[38] "I wore it to help roll back the black clouds of Negroism and throw protection around the white womanhood of North Carolina. I wore that Red Shirt and I am proud of it as you Johnny Rebs of having worn the grey." *The News and Observer* noted that Morrison received an extended ovation from the women in attendance, although it was not for the "white womanhood" line but for a later portion of his speech in which he talked about how the Democratic Party had "made the church and the school the center of moral and political influence in the State."[39] In fact, Morrison seemed to be paying almost no price of his longtime opposition to women's suffrage. *The Greensboro Daily News* reported Parker, identified twice in the piece as a "rash and romantic young man," had been making significant inroads with women voters in Raleigh. However, with suffrage no longer an issue, women were flocking to the Democrats for a variety of reasons, including cultural and economic interests.[40]

In North Carolina, candidates for governor do not have running mates, but Parker might as well have had two given how often Morrison uttered his opponent's name alongside Butler's and Morehead's. Morrison even did it on issues that were not, ostensibly, about race. On education, for instance, he accused Parker and his party of denouncing the state's school system "as inferior to that of the Fiji Islands," while wondering if the people of North Carolina were "willing to risk John J. Parker, Marion Butler and John M. Morehead and a lot

[37] "Parker Nominated by Marion Butler, So Claims Cam Morrison, Who Opens Fire on the Young Monroe Republican Nominee," *The Monroe Journal*, August 24, 1920.

[38] "Morrison Closes Speaking Tour in Mountain Towns," *The News and Observer*, October 12, 1920.

[39] Ibid.

[40] "Gov. Bickett To Hear The Final Appeal for Ed. Alexander Today," *The Greensboro Daily News*, October 12, 1920.

of Republican politicians to overthrow our great system of schools."[41] On taxes and revaluation, Morrison stated that he supported a proposed constitutional amendment to reform the income tax system, and criticized the press for painting him and his fellow Democrats as the party of revaluation. He then performed a bit of political jiu-jitsu by pointing out that Republicans in the legislature had backed the measure and that it had passed with bipartisan support—he criticized Parker for not acknowledging that. Accusing the GOP and Parker of hypocrisy on the issue, Morrison then brought it back to his favorite boogeyman, saying: "They are now making a campaign more audacious and more shameless than the damnable Butler ever made."[42]

And if Morrison ever missed an opportunity to invoke Butler and the specter of a return to the Fusionist days of the past, then his allies in the press were sure to fill the void. *The News and Observer* warned that Parker was using his "good round voice and pleasant manner" to try and get North Carolinians to "forget about the past and give the Republican Party a chance" even while his lieutenants were using every underhand tactic available to try and register Black voters[43] The paper also lamented that such an honorable and able young man like Parker would throw away his political fortunes in order to be a pawn of the likes of Butler and Morehead.[44]

That Fusionist past—to say nothing of the Reconstruction era—was still too recent for many voters. For all intents and purposes, Morrison won this race the moment he was declared the winner over Gardner in the runoff—arguably, he secured it the moment he was declared the winner by 87 votes in the primary. Morrison certainly thought so—he refused to even debate Parker or make joint appearances with him.

And he was right to do so. Morrison easily won the election, taking 57.2% of the vote to Parker's 42.7%. However, unlike his 1916 race, Parker could take some bragging rights from his otherwise heavy defeat.

[41] "Morrison Gives Republicans of State Hard Hit," *Winston-Salem Journal*, October 29, 1920.

[42] "Morrison Flays Parker; Defends Taxation System," *The News and Observer*, September 10, 1920.

[43] "Democracy Will Poll Its Usual Heavy Majority," *The News and Observer*, October 31, 1920.

[44] "Butler Wanted to Get Whole Cheese," *The News and Observer*, March 5,1920.

He polled 230,175 votes, which was more than any gubernatorial candidate had ever earned other than Morrison, who got 308,151. Parker's total was 37% more than what the outgoing governor, Thomas Walter Bickett, got in his 1916 race, and almost 50% more than Daniel Lindsay Russell received in 1896.

Parker could also take solace in the fact that, while he may not have won the governor's mansion, some of his ideals ended up being victorious. Despite campaigning as a conservative, Morrison amassed a fairly progressive record during his tenure in office. Parker had advocated improved roads and the building of a statewide highway system while Morrison had expressed general support for such endeavors but warned they would cost money.[45] Once in office, Morrison plunged ahead and improved the state's roadways, adopting Parker's argument that doing so would help residents and attract businesses into the state. He pushed through two multimillion-dollar bond projects to build over 5,000 miles of highway to the point that he would eventually be remembered as the "Good Roads Governor."[46] Morrison also increased funding for public schools—albeit while successfully pressuring the state board of education to ban the teaching of evolution.[47]

And, as with his prior campaigns, Parker managed to accumulate a lot of personal goodwill and prestige. *The Monroe Journal* chalked up his failure to win as "due more to his party affiliation rather than to his lack of personality or ability"[48] while *The Western North Carolina Times* praised him for running a great campaign and credited his tireless campaigning and excellent speech making for the increase in GOP votes up and down the ballot.[49] For instance, in the Senate race that year, Republican A.E. Holton got more than twice as many votes as Morehead got in his 1918 Senate race against Simmons. In the congressional

[45] "Improved Road Through Every County Seat in N.C.," *The Asheville Citizen-Times*, August 12, 1920.

[46] Douglas Carl Abrams, "Cameron Morrison (1869–1953)," *North Carolina History Project*, https://northcarolinahistory.org/encyclopedia/cameron-morrison-1869-1953/, accessed May 17, 2024.

[47] Ibid.

[48] "Mr. John J. Parker to Locate in Charlotte," *The Monroe Journal*, July 7, 1922.

[49] "J.J. Parkers Great Campaign," *The Western North Carolina Times*, December 10, 1920.

races, Republican nominees all saw their vote totals increase considerably compared to 1918—albeit all in losing efforts.[50]

Nevertheless, the fact remained that Parker had now lost three major campaigns in ten years and looked no closer to winning elected office than when he started out. "[T]here is nothing so disappointing and heart-breaking as politics," Parker noted.[51] And, as he found out ten years later, sometimes politics can have long-term consequences and repercussions in ways you never thought would be possible.

"I am a Lawyer and Not a Politician, Anyway"

With his political career, seemingly, on ice, John J. Parker did what a lot of people in his position do. He focused on his law practice.

In 1922, Parker moved to Charlotte to expand his law practice and joined Stewart, McRae and Bobbitt as its new senior partner. According to *The Charlotte Observer*, the firm, which was renamed Parker, Stewart, McRae, and Bobbitt, was the oldest in the city and had a reputation as one of the best in the state.[52] In a newspaper interview, Parker explained that he wanted to come to Charlotte because it was *the* city of North Carolina, and because the train system would allow him to easily serve clients in other parts of the state.[53]

And it was clear that Parker had plenty to offer the firm. Newspaper accounts of his move to Charlotte, even from Democratic publications, were respectful and full of praise for Parker, calling him an excellent and capable attorney. "His coming to Charlotte is expected to add much to the importance of Charlotte as a legal center and to greatly strengthen the well-known firm with which he has associated himself," *The Charlotte Observer* wrote.[54]

He stressed that he was not doing this for political reasons and made clear that he was out of the game—at least for the next few years. "I am

[50] "A Pocket Manual of North Carolina," 1921, www.carolana.com/NC/NC_Manuals/NC_Manual_1921.pdf.

[51] Letter from John J. Parker to Morris Ames Soper, May 20, 1930, in Parker Papers.

[52] "Parker Forms A Partnership," *The Charlotte Observer*, August 12, 1922.

[53] "Mr. John J. Parker to Locate in Charlotte," *The Monroe Journal*, July 7, 1922.

[54] "Parker Forms A Partnership," supra.

a lawyer and not a politician, anyway," Parker said.[55] "I feel that I owe it to my clients to stick to my law practice."

He may have also felt that he owed it to himself and his family to stay out of politics for a while and make some money in the private sector. While figures are not available, Parker had expended much of his own money to help fund his campaigns and, in his correspondence with GOP officials, he noted that he did not think he could make another sacrifice like that—especially so soon after his last one.[56]

The state GOP, though, had other ideas. Republicans implored him to stay involved, offering him various positions, including chairing the state GOP, replacing Morehead on the National Republican Committee or even running for office in 1924, either in another race for governor or challenging for a Senate seat. "In urging you to indicate your willingness to make the race again, I do not do so without having first sounded out our influential friends in various parts of the state," Republican state chairman William G. Bramham wrote to Parker in 1923. "I have yet to find anyone who does not heartily approve of the suggestion I have made to you."[57]

There was one option for Parker that, thanks to the Republican domination of the federal government, was within his grasp. Indeed, it was the reason why some Democrats believed Parker had joined the Republican Party in the first place—so he could cut to the front of the pie counter and get a federal job, in this case a judgeship. News articles published a month after his gubernatorial defeat even speculated that this could be Parker's next move—assuming he wasn't going to run for office again.[58]

Instead, Parker threw himself into his law practice, taking on a number of big cases during this time. In January 1922, months before his move to Charlotte was officially announced, he defended a murder suspect in a high-profile case, delivering an impassioned summation that earned him front-page coverage in the local papers.[59] His client had been

[55] "John J. Parker Out of Politics," *The Greensboro Daily Record*, May 29, 1922.

[56] John J. Parker papers, Letter from William G. Bramham to JJP, February 28, 1923.

[57] John J. Parker papers, Letter from William G. Bramham to JJP, February 15, 1923.

[58] "If At First You Don't Win, Try, Try Again," *The Winston-Salem Journal*, December 24, 1920.

[59] "State Outlines Alleged Motive in Murder Case," *The Charlotte Observer*, January 26, 1922.

charged with first-degree murder, but ended up being convicted on second-degree.[60]

He also represented nearly 250 state banks against the Federal Reserve Bank of Richmond in the "par clearance" case. At issue was a state law that permitted North Carolina banks to charge exchange rates against Federal Reserve banks. The law was enacted in 1921 by the North Carolina legislature and captioned with the title: "An act to promote the solvency of state banks." In that regard, the banks argued that they needed to charge the rates in order to stay in business, and that they would save upwards of $500,000 to $1 million a year by doing so. The Federal Reserve Bank of Richmond, however, countered that the law violated their due process and equal protection rights, and ran afoul of the Constitution's requirement that states only accept gold and silver coins as tender in payment of debts. The Union County Superior Court issued an injunction against the Federal Reserve Bank of Richmond, but the North Carolina Supreme Court reversed. Parker and his clients then appealed to the Supreme Court.[61]

When oral arguments took place on April 30 and May 1, 1923, Parker found himself going against two giants in the legal and political fields. A similar rule in Georgia was also being challenged, and the Federal Reserve Bank of Atlanta had hired John W. Davis, famed Supreme Court litigator and solicitor general, who founded a prestigious law firm known today as Davis, Polk & Wardwell. He was also a political heavyweight—one year after arguing this case, he would be nominated by the Democratic Party for president, running against incumbent Calvin Coolidge. Representing the Federal Reserve Bank of Richmond was Henry W. Anderson, who founded a prestigious law firm known today as Hunton & Williams. A prominent Virginia lily-white Republican and gubernatorial nominee, Anderson had been a vice presidential candidate in 1920, finishing fourth at the GOP convention that year.

Nevertheless, Parker emerged victorious, convincing a majority of the court to rule in favor of his clients. Written by Justice Brandeis, the opinion made clear that the North Carolina law "does not obstruct the performance of any duty imposed upon the Federal Reserve Board and

[60] "Second Degree Murder is Jury's Verdict; Thomas Given 18 Years in Penitentiary," *The Concord Times*, January 30, 1922.

[61] *Farmers & Merchants Bank v. Federal Res. Bank*, 262 U.S. 649 (1923).

the federal reserve banks. Nor does it interfere with the exercise of any power conferred upon either."[62] Parker, for his part, told his clients that the opinion was strong and made clear that any state bank in the country could now do what they did.[63]

That same year, Parker was appointed Special Assistant to the Attorney General to prosecute World War I fraud cases. Parker handled two cases on behalf of Attorney General Harry Daugherty, a controversial figure in the administration of President Warren G. Harding, who had himself been accused of corruption. In fact, three years later, Daugherty would be indicted for allegedly receiving funds in the sale of assets seized from American Metal Company (he was tried twice with a mistrial the first time and an acquittal the second time).

In a case that went to trial in January 1924, Parker, along with a team of additional Special Assistants to the Attorney General, prosecuted several defendants in *U.S. v. United States Harness Company* in West Virginia, accusing them of conspiring to defraud the country out of more than $15 million in materials during the war. Specifically, the prosecution alleged that seven former War Department officials ordered a grossly excessive amount of material to make harnesses out of. Then, four of those officials left and started the United States Harness Company. With the help of the three remaining War Department defendants, these four then allegedly misrepresented the quality of the harnesses to the government so that they could sell them at a large profit to private companies.[64]

After a week-plus long trial, the defendants were acquitted—but that only tells part of the story. According to press reports, U.S. District Judge D. Lawrence Groner declared that the government had failed to produce evidence of a conspiracy to defraud the United States and dismissed charges against two of the defendants while instructing the jury to return verdicts of not guilty for the remaining five. "I have concluded that, if a jury should find a verdict of guilty, I would have to set it aside," Groner

62 *Farmers & Merchants Bank v. Federal Res. Bank*, 262 U.S. 649 (1923).

63 "Parker Tells Clients Par Clearance is Won," *The Greensboro Daily News*, July 21, 1923.

64 "Trial of Harness Cases Is Started," *The Baltimore Sun*, January 15, 1924.

said in court.[65] "Not even the affirmative evidence in the case indicated that the defendants were guilty of any misconduct."

A few months later, Parker and his team tried six defendants in Washington D.C. federal district court for conspiring to defraud the government out of more than $1 million in lumber sales. The defendants argued that the contract between them and the government was a no-strings-attached sale agreement, which allowed them to resell the lumber for a profit.[66] The lead defendant was John Phillips, a former Georgia GOP state committee chair and a wealthy lumber dealer. Additionally, one of Phillips' co-defendants, former War Department official Ernest C. Morse, had been one of the defendants acquitted in the Harness case.

Unlike the Harness case, the Lumber case took several months to try. Nevertheless, the result was the same. The defendants were acquitted, and the presiding judge didn't think much of the case before him. During the trial, U.S. District Judge Jennings Bailey even dismissed the charges against two defendants, one of whom was Morse.[67]

Despite losing two high-profile cases, Parker's reputation did not really suffer. In both cases, defense attorneys pointed the finger of blame at Representative William J. Graham (R-IL), chairman of the House committee that investigated war contracts, accusing him of playing politics. The failures also ramped up the pressure on Daugherty, who had resigned under pressure in March 1924, but was still the subject of two special investigations. The first one was handled by special counsel Atlee Pomerene, a former Democratic U.S. senator from Ohio, and prominent Philadelphia lawyer Owen J. Roberts, who was best known for his involvement in the Teapot Dome scandal during the Harding Administration and whose fate would become entangled with Parker's. The second was a wide-ranging probe led by Senator Burton K. Wheeler (D-MT) that would have long-term implications for both the senator and Daugherty's successor as attorney general, Harlan Fiske Stone. "Every single charge in the indictment was shown to be false by official documents taken by representatives of your department from the files of the War Department more than two years ago and in the hands of your assistants ever since,"

65 "All Defendants in the U.S. Harness Case Acquitted," *The Baltimore Sun*, January 25, 1924.

66 "4 Freed of Lumber War Fraud Charges," *The St. Louis Dispatch*, July 19, 1924.

67 "Ex-War Sales Head Cleared By Judge," *The Evening Star*, July 1, 1924.

Morse's defense attorney Frank J. Hogan said, in remarks addressed to Daugherty.[68]

Despite the poor results, Parker got plaudits for his courtroom performance in the Lumber case. Charles A. Douglas, one of the defense attorneys, would later recount that Parker was "fair, able, and thorough in the conduct of the prosecution" and "did nothing that merited just criticism by the defense." "I never knew a case so thoroughly and wonderfully prepared in every part of its detail, and I have at no time ever encountered a more dangerous and formidable trial lawyer than he," he said.[69]

He also found a strong supporter in Stone. "[T]he impression I gained was that the cases were well conducted by him and that the failure to secure conviction was due to the perversity of juries in this class of case," he said about Parker.[70]

So, as 1924 drew to a close, Parker had developed a reputation as a sharp legal mind, a compelling orator and a charismatic campaigner. However, thanks in large part to his party affiliation, he had also a well-deserved reputation as a loser at the ballot box and was no closer to his dream of securing elected office in North Carolina than he had been at the start of his adult life.

But in life, when one door closes another one often opens—and that was certainly the case for Parker. In 1925, he would be presented with a golden opportunity—one that put him on a path that very nearly took him to one of the most prestigious and powerful jobs in the land. First, he had to talk himself into it.

[68] "Daugherty Flayed on Harness Case," *The Baltimore Sun*, January 26, 1924.

[69] "Confirmation of Hon. John J. Parker to be an Associate Justice of the Supreme Court of the United States," United States Government Printing Office, 1930.

[70] Herbert Hoover Papers, Memo from Harlan F. Stone, 1929.

CHAPTER 3

On the Bench: Landing a Coveted Federal Judgeship

Even though it was clear to many Republicans in the state that their best chance to exert power was through federal positions, Parker had always seemed reluctant to go that route.

For one thing, he wasn't sure being a judge was for him. "It is a most honorable position, and as you point out in your letter, it might lead to advancement in the judiciary, but I must confess the more I think about the judgeship, the further I am from desiring it," Parker wrote in a February 1925 letter to Herbert Seawell, a friend and fellow prominent Republican lawyer in the state who had served as U.S. attorney under Taft.[1] "I am afraid that I am temperamentally unfit for a judgeship. I feel quite certain that I would not be a good trial judge."

Maybe Parker was being honest. Or maybe he was trying to assure his friend that he didn't have designs on a job that Seawell definitely wanted. Seawell had been nominated for a U.S. District Court seat by Roosevelt in January 1909, but the Senate did not confirm him, and the nomination was withdrawn.[2] When Henry G. Connor, U.S. District Judge for the Eastern District of North Carolina, died in November 1924, Seawell

[1] Parker Papers, Parker Letter to Herbert Seawell, February 19, 1925.

[2] "Unsuccessful Nominations and Recess Appointments," *Federal Judicial Center*, www.fjc.gov/history/judges/unsuccessful-nominations-and-recess-appointments, accessed: January 2, 2025.

V. Li, *Supreme Pressure*,
https://doi.org/10.1007/978-3-032-07864-3_3

actively pursued the job with Parker, serving as one of his chief lieutenants and advocates with the GOP decision-makers in Washington.

In fact, the day after Connor's death, Parker sent letters addressed to President Coolidge and Attorney General Stone asking them to consider Seawell for the now vacant seat. Decorum might have dictated a bit of a waiting period. However, Parker, no doubt, knew that there would be a lot of jockeying among Republican lawyers in the state for the plum position.

And, indeed, there was. Several prominent lawyers and friends asked Parker for his help in securing the judgeship. Some aspirants claimed that there had been secret deals or arrangements for certain people to step aside that now were not willing to do so. Others lamented that they had sacrificed for others in the past and now wanted their fair reward. Nevertheless, Parker always reiterated his commitment to Seawell, but also promised not to actively campaign against anybody and to support whoever ended up with the nomination. "I know that it was a crushing humiliation to Mr. Seawell and to his family that his name should be withdrawn," Parker wrote in a letter to another candidate for the position, Isaac Meekins, general counsel for Enemy Insurance Companies and Parker's successor as GOP nominee for governor of North Carolina. Parker also called Seawell's unsuccessful nomination a blow to the growth of the state Republican Party and recounted how Page had used the issue against Parker during their 1910 contest as evidence of the GOP's weakness.[3]

The contest eventually took on the look and feel of a bare-knuckled political contest, complete with mudslinging and hurt feelings. "I very much regret that the Judgeship has again reached the level of cesspool politics," lamented William Bramham, chair of the North Carolina GOP, to Parker.[4] "The candidates are spreading poison in old time fashion against each other." Ultimately Meekins got the nod and was nominated by Coolidge in January 1925 for the seat. Parker sent Meekins a letter congratulating him and wishing him well.[5]

At around the same time, there was speculation that the federal government might create a new federal district court in North Carolina. Once

[3] Parker Papers, Parker Letter to Isaac M. Meekins, December 1, 1924.

[4] Parker Papers, Letter from William Bramham to Parker, December 29, 1924.

[5] Parker Papers, Letter from Parker to Meekins, January 10, 1925.

again, Parker's name came up for that, but he disclaimed interest, reiterating his commitment to Seawell. "I am disposed not to say anything about the judgeship until the district is created, but you understand, of course, that all I have said about your qualifications and availability for the judgeship stands," he wrote to Seawell.[6] "I am not and will not be a candidate for the appointment."

Another possible reason for Parker's recalcitrance was his prior attacks on bossism and machine politics in North Carolina. In that vein, it would have been somewhat hypocritical for him to then rely on that machine to get a federal job—especially a life-tenured position like a judgeship. But as a successful career in politics seemed less likely, Parker started to soften a bit when it came to the judiciary. For one thing, he recognized that the courts could serve as an important bulwark against the Democratic machine in the state. "All of the judges of the state are elected by the Democratic party, which commands a majority of the voters," he noted.[7] "I think the fair administration of justice is best preserved by the appointment of Republican lawyers to the federal bench."

And, he may very well have been sincere when he said he felt like he wasn't cut out to be a trial judge. An appellate judge, however, was a different story. Federal appellate judges don't conduct trials—they review them for constitutional or procedural problems, taking the cases they choose and applying the law as they see fit and as instructed to by higher courts—in this case, the Supreme Court. Speaking of which, being a federal appellate judge doesn't guarantee a promotion to the Supreme Court, but it can put you on a lot of shortlists—especially if the political situation lines up in your favor. Republicans had won 11 out of 15 presidential elections since the end of the Civil War and were coming off two straight landslide victories. The only Democratic nominees to win the White House during that time were Grover Cleveland, who prevailed in two close elections (and lost a third), and Woodrow Wilson, who benefited from a GOP split in 1912 and nearly lost in 1916. With that recent history in mind, it looked like Republicans would surely hold onto the White House for the foreseeable future. Who knows what could happen for Parker in the future?

[6] Parker Papers, Letter from Parker to Seawell, January 17, 1925.

[7] Burris, supra, 66.

When Charles A. Woods, a judge on the U.S. Court of Appeals for the Fourth Circuit, died in June 1925, Parker made it clear that he was interested in the job. "I believe I can render a public service on the Circuit Bench, and have made up my mind that if the opportunity to serve in this way comes to me, I should accept the opportunity," he wrote in a letter to Marion Early, co-counsel in the Harness case.[8]

However, he did not want to seem too eager for the seat, calling contests for judicial seats "unseemly."[9] Instead, his friends and supporters did the work for him. "Mr. Parker will not enter the contest, but has agreed, upon urgent solicitation, that if the place is tendered him, he will accept it," Parker's law partner Plummer Stewart wrote in a letter to a South Carolina lawyer asking for his support.[10]

Far from being a passive participant, Parker actively supervised the effort to get him onto the bench. He noted that geographic balance was always important when it came to political appointments and the Fourth Circuit, which consisted of Maryland, West Virginia, Virginia, North Carolina and South Carolina, only had judges from Maryland and Virginia at that point (the third seat had been held by South Carolina's Woods). North Carolina hadn't been represented on the bench in several years and, with the national GOP taking more of an interest in the state for presidential elections, Parker argued that it made sense that a Tar Heel would get the seat.[11]

Unlike the contest that developed within the state for the District Court seat that ultimately went to Meekins, there wasn't much jockeying or positioning among prominent lawyers in the state. Instead, Parker emerged as the consensus choice, with most of the North Carolina bar backing him. There was one exception: a prominent Greensboro lawyer named William Bynum was endorsed by his city's bar for the position. Bynum had served as an assistant attorney general during the McKinley Administration and had run, unsuccessfully, for chief justice of the North Carolina Supreme Court in 1918. However, Bynum didn't seem interested in the position, writing to Seawell that, while he appreciated the

[8] Parker Papers, Parker Letter to Marion C. Early, June 27, 1925.

[9] Parker Papers, Parker Letter to Rush Holland, June 26, 1925.

[10] Parker Papers, Letter from Plummer Stewart to R.S. Stewart, June 26, 1925.

[11] Parker Papers, Letter from Parker to Rush Holland, June 26, 1925. Also: Letter from Parker to Charles Kerr, June 26, 1925 and Letter from Parker to W.S. Ward, June 27, 1925.

support, he would be happy to see Parker get it.[12] Additionally, Bynum was already in his mid-60s and seen as someone whose best days were behind him (indeed, he passed away less than a year later).

Parker did not consider Bynum a strong candidate; nevertheless he worried that Bynum could split his support within the North Carolina legal community and doom his chances of securing the nomination. "I feel the only chance of my being appointed is to have the unanimous support of the Bench and Bar of the State," he wrote to his brother, Silas.[13] "Consequently, Judge Bynum's candidacy cannot help him, and may hurt me."

There was another factor to consider. While Parker's internal logic for why his state deserved the seat may have made sense to him, it didn't necessarily work for others. West Virginia had no qualms about trying for a second judge on the panel and Senator Guy Goff (R-WV) pushed for Judge George Warwick McClintic, who had been appointed to the U.S. District Court for the Southern District of West Virginia by President Harding in 1921. Bramham believed that Goff was going to insist on the nomination and that he wouldn't need to twist the arm of the assistant attorney general in charge of nominations, who was also a native West Virginian. Additionally, he pointed out that Coolidge had carried West Virginia in the most recent presidential election, despite it being Democratic nominee John W. Davis' home state, so maybe the now vacant judgeship would be the state's reward.[14]

Nevertheless, Parker encouraged his allies to continue putting pressure on the White House—even going in person to make their case if necessary. When Parker heard that one of his prospective colleagues on the circuit court, Judge Edmund Waddill, Jr., had asked about him and some other candidates, Parker wrote to several of his friends trying to find out what was said and what that meant for him. He even took a more active role in promoting himself and solicited support from prominent Democrats in the state, including Senator Simmons and his colleague, Lee Overman, and Governor Angus McLean. Luckily for Parker, the Democrats in charge of the state did not hold any grudges towards him and, understanding that the job was always going to go to a Republican,

[12] Parker Papers, Letter from William Bynum to Herbert Seawell, June 29, 1925.

[13] Parker Papers, Letter from Parker to Silas I. Parker, July 7, 1925.

[14] Parker Papers, Letter from Bramham to Parker, August 5, 1925.

wanted to see one of their own on the federal bench. Even Morrison, his 1920 opponent, wrote to Simmons and recommended Parker for the job. "I have no doubt, my dear sir, as to your character, ability and equipment to discharge the duties of this high office," Simmons wrote to Parker, promising him that, if he had an opportunity to express his views to the attorney general or president, he would recommend him without reservation.[15]

Parker need not have worried. According to news reports printed in September 1925, McClintic took himself out of the running because he sensed he might have a rocky confirmation with the Senate as a result of some recent, controversial rulings on Prohibition and labor cases.[16] The following month, Parker was given a recess appointment to the Circuit Court and was subsequently confirmed by the Senate in December.

Despite getting what he wanted, Parker clearly did not enjoy the process. "This is the first time I have ever been up for a federal appointment, and 'if the Court know herself, and she think she do,' this will be the last time," he said to Bramham.[17] "Having allowed myself to get in the position of being considered for the place, I naturally want to be appointed, but whether I am appointed or not, I don't think I will ever allow myself to get in such a position again."

"He Is a First-Class Judge"

Parker joined a court that was known to be fairly sleepy and not too demanding. Part of the reason was age. Parker's predecessor, Wood, had been 72 when he passed, and his new colleagues were 64-year-old John Carter Rose and 70-year-old Waddill. During the early days of Parker's tenure, both Rose and Waddill were stricken with health problems, causing them to be absent for extended periods. Therefore, Parker immediately distinguished himself as the workhorse of the court, taking on nearly half of the written opinions.[18] Within five years, he was running the place, first on an unofficial basis after Waddill got ill. After Waddill's death,

[15] Parker Papers, Letter from Furnifold Simmons to Parker, August 21, 1925.

[16] "Federal Judgeship Offer Is Declined by McClintic," *The Virginia-Pilot*, September 11, 1925.

[17] Parker Papers, Letter from Parker to Bramham, August 6, 1925.

[18] Fish, "A 'Freshman' Takes Charge," supra, 59–113.

Parker simply assumed the senior judge role, assigning opinions, running the courthouse, and representing the court at judicial conferences despite statutory ambiguity as to how the senior judgeship is determined.[19]

He didn't just churn out content, either. Parker's opinions were usually praised by his colleagues and fellow judges for being well crafted, reasoned and written. "He is a first-class judge," Waddill told Chief Justice Taft after Parker's first year on the court.[20]

The start of Parker's career on the bench coincided with a time of growing public dissatisfaction with federal courts, particularly the Supreme Court. In November 1930, months after his failed Supreme Court nomination, the *ABA Journal* published a piece from Parker in which he noted that "[o]ne of the favorite pastimes of this unsettled age is criticizing the law and denouncing lawyers" thanks to "an unconscious jealousy of the men who play so large a part in the control of the state, from impatience with the rules which preserve the present institutions of society against those who would destroy them, or from lack of understanding of the nature and history of our jurisprudence and of what has been accomplished by the profession in shaping it to meet the needs of the times."[21]

Parker's strong words were likely influenced by his Senate rejection, however, he was correct in his assessment that large swaths of people in the country had long believed the courts had failed them by not doing enough to help them economically, politically or socially. One of the most persistent criticisms against the courts came in the area of economic rights. For nearly three decades, the High Court had used its power of judicial review to strike down federal and state laws that interfered with the freedom of contract. In essence, governmental regulations designed to protect employees, like limiting the work week, restricting child labor or allowing them to unionize more easily were usually found to be unconstitutional. Named after *Lochner v. New York*, a 1905 Supreme Court case that struck down a state law limiting the number of hours bakers

[19] Ibid., 86. Chief Justice Charles Evans Hughes and others believed the senior judge had to be specifically appointed, similar to the chief justice of the Supreme Court. Parker argued the job automatically went to whoever had the most seniority in the circuit. Subsequent statutes and amendments largely codified Parker's interpretation.

[20] Ibid., 75–76.

[21] John J. Parker, "Social Progress and the Law," *ABA Journal*, Vol. 16, No. 11 (November 1930), 701–707.

could work, the *Lochner* era stood for the proposition that individuals and businesses were free to agree to whatever terms they wished without governmental oversight[22]—essentially taking the doctrine of *laissez faire* economics to its logical extreme.

Of course, just because parties were free to enter into contracts with one another didn't mean they were on equal footing or negotiating from similar positions of power. In fact, most of the time, individual employees felt compelled to sign whatever terms were offered to them for fear of getting fired or never hired in the first place. Therefore, judicial protection of the right to contract seemed like less of a constitutional ideal and more of a way to protect businesses and business owners from governmental regulations that would cut into their profits.

Some progressives, including several who would loom large over Parker's life in the near future, tried to do something about it. In 1911, Senator Robert Owen Jr. (D-OK) proposed giving both houses of Congress the power to remove a federal judge from office by a majority vote. "The Federal courts have invaded the Constitution and invaded the rights of the States and invaded the legislative function of Congress and of the States, and have become an instrument through which the special interests have been enabled to block all progressive legislation of recent years," he said in a floor speech.[23] That didn't go anywhere—the Constitution is clear that the only way to get rid of Article III judges is through impeachment, despite Owen's assertions that recalling judges was a milder remedy that covered all situations short of the impeachment standard of high crimes and misdemeanors.

But Owen and his allies continued battling the court. In 1918, after the Supreme Court had declared unconstitutional a bill that he had co-sponsored banning child labor, Owen proposed passing the bill again, only this time with a provision stating that the Supreme Court could not strike it down.[24] That didn't go anywhere, either. Nor did an attempt by

[22] *Lochner v. New York*, 198 U.S. 45 (1905).

[23] "Election and Recall of Federal Judges: Abstract of Speech," Statements and Speeches of Robert Owen, *Federal Reserve Bank St Louis*, https://fraser.stlouisfed.org/title/statements-speeches-robert-l-owen-5328/election-recall-federal-judges-535691, accessed: June 20, 2024.

[24] "Senate Progressives vs. the Federal Courts," *U.S. Senate*, https://www.senate.gov/artandhistory/senate-stories/senate-progressives-vs-the-federal-courts.htm, accessed June 20, 2024.

progressive Senator William Borah (R-ID) to require a supermajority of seven justices to invalidate an act of Congress. Calling 5–4 decisions on constitutional questions "a matter of deep regret" that "justify a want of respect for the decisions of that great tribunal" and "breed an atmosphere of distrust in the solidity and worth of our Federal judicial system," Borah thought it was ridiculous that one justice could single handedly decide if a bill passed by Congress and signed by the president could stand or not.[25]

After a federal law imposing taxes on employers who use child labor was invalidated by the court in 1922, influential Senator Robert La Follette (R-WI), who would run for president in 1924 as the nominee of the Progressive Party, argued for a constitutional amendment allowing Congress to override a Supreme Court decision. "Today, the actual ruler of the American people is the Supreme Court of the United States," La Follette said in a speech to the Annual Convention of the American Federation of Labor in 1922.[26] "In fact, five of these nine men actually supreme rulers, for by a bare majority the court has repeatedly overridden the will of the people as declared by their representatives in Congress, and has construed the Constitution to mean whatever suited their peculiar economic and political views." La Follette argued that the power the Supreme Court claimed to have to invalidate acts of Congress as unconstitutional was not only absent from the Constitution, but had been considered and rejected by the Founding Fathers. Instead, he claimed the Supreme Court has usurped power and become a "Frankenstein which must be destroyed or else it will destroy us."

The stakes were especially high by the time Parker made it to the circuit court. With Chief Justice Taft, Justice Edward T. Sanford, and four other justices that would eventually be known as the Four Horsemen (Willis Van Devanter, George Sutherland, James McReynolds and Pierce Butler), conservatives had a supermajority and frequently upheld the right of contract while striking down governmental regulations. Taft may not have been the most conservative justice on the court, especially when compared to the Four Horsemen. But given his stature as a former president, as well as his belief in the need for a strong, independent judiciary

[25] William Borah, "Five to Four Decisions As Menace to Respect for Supreme Court," *The New York Times*, February 18, 1923.

[26] Report of the Proceedings of the 42nd Annual Convention of the American Federation of Labor, https://archive.org/details/sim_american-federation-of-labor-proceedings_1922, accessed June 23, 2024, 232–233.

with the chief justice as its head—a foreign concept back then when the job was seen as little more than being first among equals on the Supreme Court—he became a lightning rod for criticism by Congressional progressives, some of whom he had been odds with during his time as president and during his ill-fated reelection campaign in 1912.

In keeping with his view of himself as the head of the judiciary, Taft had some pretty big plans that required Congressional approval. Thanks to Prohibition and World War I-related litigation, including war fraud cases like the ones Parker prosecuted, judicial caseloads had exploded, and some circuits were facing huge backlogs. Taft argued that he should have the authority to temporarily reassign judges from one circuit to another in order to help alleviate any congested dockets or judge shortages. In 1922, he and Attorney General Daugherty drafted a bill that would create a group of at-large federal judges Taft could deploy at his discretion (dubbed the chief's "flying squadron"), as well as call for a regular conference in which senior federal circuit judges would give the chief justice information about their dockets and needs, allowing the chief justice to make informed personnel decisions.

While it may have sounded eminently practical, some senators were concerned about what they considered a power grab by the chief justice. Progressives looked at the bill as Taft wanting to stack the courts with additional Tafts who would give even more protection to businesses and corporations at the expense of regular people. George Norris (R-NE), a progressive senator, went even further and proposed a fairly radical solution—getting rid of federal judges and letting state courts deal with everything. Arguing that life tenure made federal judges indifferent to the suffering of regular people, Norris added that having two types of courts doubled expenses for taxpayers, making them poorer. With big corporations starting to take over, they could then run roughshod over regular people. "Justice is too expensive," Norris said on the Senate floor on April 6, 1922, "so expensive, in fact, that the poor man cannot afford to buy it."[27]

They got help from an unlikely area: conservative Southern Democrats who were worried about federal overreach and the idea of "carpetbagging judges" coming into their states and imposing their values. Overman compared Taft's bill to the infamous "midnight judges bill" of 1801 in

[27] George Norris, Speech on Additional Judges Bill, *Congressional Record*, April 6, 1922.

which outgoing President John Adams attempted to pack the courts with Federalists after he and his party lost control of the White House and Congress in the 1800 elections. "If a judge is needed in any district, let a Senator from that State introduce a bill, have it referred to the committee, and let it be reported back to the Senate, and passed," Overman said on the Senate floor on April 6, 1922, calling it a "pork barrel judges bill" that would just add a bunch of Republicans to the federal judiciary.

Overman and others also raised alarm over Taft's idea of a conference, seeing the entire concept as an attempt by the chief justice to throw his weight around and exert undue influence on lower court judges. "Chief Justice Taft says in his testimony that they want to have supervision over them and watch them," Overman said. "Watch a circuit judge? Watch a district judge? Why, they ought to be independent of Congress, independent of the Chief Justice, independent of everybody." Senator John Shields (D-TN) tried to amend the bill by requiring the chief justice to get consent from a judge before he could be reassigned, but was voted down.

A watered-down version of the bill passed by the Senate on April 7, 1922, by a 44–21 tally,[28] with progressive Republicans like Borah, Norris, and La Follette voting in opposition, and went into effect later in the year. Taft got his conference, which is known today as the Judicial Conference of the United States and continues to meet regularly. The bill did create new judgeships, but assigned them to specific circuits. The chief justice did get some power to reassign judges but not the "flying squadron" he wanted.

Despite getting quite a bit of what he had asked for, Taft was upset about the opposition to his bill—especially from the progressives, or as he dubbed them the "yahoos of the west."[29] So when he went back to Congress a few years later, he decided to bury them in legalese.

He also brought backup. Concerned about the High Court's backlog of cases, which in some instances went back five years, Taft asked Justices Van Devanter, McReynolds and Sutherland to draw up a bill that would give the justices more discretion over the cases they heard and then lobbied tirelessly for its passage. The Judiciary Act of 1925 (colloquially

[28] Roll Call Vote To Pass H.R. 9103, *Voteview*, https://voteview.com/rollcall/RS0670317, accessed: June 24, 2024.

[29] "Senate Progressives vs. The Federal Courts," supra.

known as "The Judges' Bill"), essentially set up the system we still have today, in which the Supreme Court votes on which cases to hear, typically only granting certiorari in a small number of cases that they deem to be important enough to merit their intervention. There would still be some cases they would be required to hear, but otherwise, their docket would be mostly set at their discretion. The plan would also have the effect of strengthening the circuit courts, since they would now have the final word in most cases.

To get the bill passed, Taft took a lower profile, lest he draw the ire of his progressive critics. Perhaps learning from his clashes with them, Taft attempted to frame the bill as a means of helping poorer, less-privileged litigants by eliminating long delays and streamlining the appellate process, making litigation more efficient and less time and resource consuming.[30] Of course, what was left unsaid was that, by strengthening the courts, Congress was, essentially, preserving or even expanding the status quo.

Nevertheless, progressives put up little fight. The bill passed by a voice vote in the House and by a 76–1 margin in the Senate (Alabama Democrat J.Thomas Heflin was the only one who opposed it), with Borah and several others voting for it while Norris and La Follette did not vote.[31]

Like Taft, Parker was also deeply committed to increasing efficiency in the justice system. As a judge, he sought to cut down on or eliminate needless steps or procedures that had no bearing on the final result. According to Duke University Professor Peter Fish's "A 'Freshman' Takes Charge: Judge John J. Parker of the United States Court of Appeals, 1925–1930," Parker favored "liberal rules of practice" and was not as concerned about legal technicalities or forms as he was about scrutinizing the facts of a particular case and getting to the right result based on an application of the law to those specific facts.[32]

For instance, Parker was not shy about invoking "harmless error" if the right result came about in spite of deficiencies during the pendency of a case. For instance, in *Belvin et al v. United States*, a case Parker and his colleagues handed down in 1926, one of the issues on appeal was

[30] Jeremy Buchman, "Judicial Lobbying and the Politics of Judicial Structure: An Examination of the Judiciary Act of 1925," *The Justice System Journal* 24, no. 1, Court Administration (2003), 13.

[31] Roll Call Vote To Pass H.R. 8206, *Voteview*, https://voteview.com/rollcall/RS0680199, accessed: June 24, 2024.

[32] Fish, supra, 80–81.

that the indictment in a Prohibition conspiracy case did not specify that intoxicating liquids in question were meant for beverage consumption. Parker was not moved by this argument and held that it was "well settled that an indictment for conspiracy to commit an offense need not describe the offense which is the object of the conspiracy with the same certainty as would be required in an indictment for that offense" and that, as long as the indictment "contained a sufficient description of the object of the conspiracy to fairly and reasonably inform the defendants of the character of the offense charged, it was sufficient."[33] Similarly, in a 1929 opinion, Parker found that an indictment alleging defendants possessed a car they knew to be stolen was sufficient even though it did not directly state that the car was actually stolen.[34]

Parker's approach was similar in civil cases. In one case handed down in 1928, Parker upheld a lower court decision in which the plaintiffs in an insurance case had erroneously sought a legal remedy instead of an equitable remedy, in this case, reformation of the policy and enforcement against the defendants. Typically, courts would dismiss cases for pursuing the wrong remedy and, according to Fish, defense counsel did not bother to introduce any evidence because they had been so confident that the case was going to be tossed. Parker, though, found that, despite the error, the trial court had reached the correct result and saw no point in making everyone go through the process once again just to arrive at the same destination. "In such case justice has been done, and courts exist to do justice, not to furnish a forum for intellectual skill or prowess," Parker said in his opinion.[35]

He went even further in the *ABA Journal* article mentioned earlier that was published months after his unsuccessful Supreme Court nomination. Arguing that indictment by grand jury should be eliminated in all but the most serious cases, Parker claimed that prosecutions initiated by information were more than sufficient so long as they fairly apprised the accused of the charges they faced and protected them against double jeopardy. Similarly, he argued that civil pleadings that accurately laid out the facts underlying a cause of action or defense were more than sufficient. Most radically, Parker suggested getting rid of the requirement for

33 *Belvin v. United States*, 12 F.2d 548 (4th Cir. 1926).

34 *Wendell v. United States*, 34 F.2d 92 (4th Cir. 1929).

35 *Great American Ins. Co. v. Johnson*, 25 F.2d 847 (4th Cir. 1928).

unanimous jury verdicts. "Nothing need be feared from allowing a verdict by a three-fourths majority of the jury, when the judge has the power to set aside the verdict and grant a new trial when satisfied that it is wrong," he said, adding that unanimous verdicts can lead to corruption and delay and serve "no good purpose."[36] He added: "I do think that one of the crying needs of the times is reform in procedural law, and that one of the great services which the profession can render to the cause of social progress is to simplify the procedure of the courts, to abolish technicalities and the cumbersome machinery which tends only to delay, and to provide a system which will go simply and directly to the only matter in which the court should be interested, the matter of doing justice between the parties."[37]

Parker took that approach with his fellow judges on the Fourth Circuit, looking for ways to be more efficient in dispensing justice. In one instance, he looked to cut down on "frivolous petitions for rehearing" that "take up considerable time and involve considerable delay in the disposition of cases."[38] Relatedly, Parker argued that judges should refrain from writing too much *obiter dicta*, parts of written opinions that are not essential to the decision and do not have precedential value. For one thing, he argued that if a judge wrote too much about what a party could have done or how the law might have applied if certain facts had been different, it might invite more frivolous petitions for rehearing. For a fact-centric judge like Parker, it was far more important for the court to announce "our conclusion based on the facts of this case, without suggesting what we might do if the facts were not as they are."[39] That approach to economy of writing and sticking to the facts of a particular case without opining on what might or should be would have dramatic unintended consequences for him when he was nominated for the Supreme Court.

Ideologically, his jurisprudence as a circuit court judge has been described by other commentators as complex and hard to categorize. Peter Fish made clear that Parker was not an economic *laissez faire* jurist in the mold of The Four Horsemen and had no problems upholding the

[36] John J. Parker, "Social Progress and the Law" supra, 704.

[37] Ibid.

[38] Fish, supra, 82–83.

[39] Ibid., 83.

use of state police power if he thought it would promote economic development in the South.[40] Fish cited a 1929 opinion in which Parker upheld municipal ordinances requiring railroads to replace wooden bridges with concrete or other fireproof ones citing safety and efficiency. The railroads had objected, claiming that the ordinances violated their freedom of contract. In writing for a unanimous three-judge panel, Parker turned aside the railways' arguments, writing: "No facts are alleged upon which the conclusion can legitimately be based that the extension of the fire limits was not justified by the growth and development of the town, or that the replacing of wooden by concrete bridges was not required for the safety of the public, or that the building of concrete bridges would entail any undue hardship or unreasonable expense upon complainant."[41] He added that many towns have "grown greatly" over the last 25 years thanks to these types of fire limits.

When it came to national economic regulation, however, his jurisprudence was more complex and fact-determinative. In some cases, he took a narrow view of interstate commerce and was not overly deferential to Congress and its ability to regulate it. In *Atlantic Coast Line Railroad and Seaboard Air Line Railway Co. v. Standard Oil Company of New Jersey*, for instance, Parker held in 1926 that oil transported by rail into the state from outside North Carolina that was then stored in Wilmington became intrastate commerce once the company shipped the oil to other places within the state's borders.[42] The rail companies had maintained that the oil was still interstate commerce, which would allow them to charge higher rates, because it originated from outside North Carolina. However, Parker ruled that the oil's out-of-state journey came to an end in Wilmington, when it was stored in the tank and mixed with the rest of Standard Oil's reserve there. Therefore, the oil then became intrastate commerce once it was shipped to other locations within the state. In a related case involving the same parties that originated in Florida, the Sixth Circuit came to the opposite conclusion, finding that interstate

[40] Peter G. Fish, "Judge Parker and the Public Service State," *Duke Law Magazine* 37–44 (1985).

[41] *Carolina & NW Ry. Co. v. Town of Lincolnton*, 33 F.2d 719 (4th Cir. 1929).

[42] *Atlantic Coast Line R. v. Standard Oil C., N.J*, 12 F.2d 541 (4th Cir. 1926).

rates should have applied. The Supreme Court in 1927 reversed the Sixth Circuit, with Taft's opinion closely mirroring Parker's reasoning.[43]

In another commerce case, Parker ruled that the Interstate Commerce Commission exceeded its authority when it enjoined Southern coal producers from reducing their tonnage rates on shipments to the Great Lakes region in order to better compete with Northern producers, who had just reduced their rates. According to the opinion, the ICC had refused the Southern rate reduction for a variety of reasons, including the longer haul from Southern fields to ports in the Great Lakes and differences in industrial conditions. Parker, however, found that the ICC had exceeded its authority, holding that the commission was charged with maintaining an adequate system of transportation, not dictating national economic policy. "Congress certainly did not intend by this language to create in the Commission an economic dictatorship over the various sections of the country, with power to kill or make alive," Parker wrote in his opinion, warning that, if the commission had the power to choose winners when it came to tonnage rates, it could do the same for anything—fruit growing, cotton manufacturing, furniture building, to name just three.[44]

That's not to say Parker always took a restrictive view of federal commerce power. In fact, Fish argued that Parker generally sided with the federal government in commerce cases and took a broad interpretation of the commerce clause—especially when it came to promoting economic development and modernization in the South, something he believed the region desperately needed.[45] In *Chandler v. Pennsylvania Railroad Company*, Parker wrote in his 1926 opinion that the imposition of interstate rates on a shipment of potatoes from Norfolk to Cuba was proper. Parker rejected the plaintiffs' argument that the railroads had to file an explicit export rate with the ICC and that because they did not, the lower intrastate rate should apply. Parker held in his opinion that since the shipments were obviously not intrastate, then the higher interstate rates should apply.[46]

[43] *Atlantic Coast Line R. Co. v. Standard Oil*, 275 U.S. 257 (1927).

[44] *Anchor Coal Co. v. United States*, 25 F.2d 462 (S.D.W. Va. 1928).

[45] Fish, "Judge Parker and the Public Service State," supra, at 42–43.

[46] *Chandler v. Pennsylvania Railroad Co.*, 11 F.2d 39 (4th Cir. 1926).

And, in the same case alluded to earlier in which his penchant for judicial efficiency had severe, unintended consequences for him, Parker took a broad view of Congressional commerce power to justify his decision. As will be covered later, it made him a target of organized labor and helped set the stage for his ultimately unsuccessful Supreme Court nomination.

"He Is, I may Almost Say, Idolized by His Friends in North Carolina"

As a judge, Parker made sure not to appear overtly political or partisan. He had resigned his GOP National Committee membership immediately upon receiving his commission and stayed out of politics for the duration of his time on the bench. That's not to say he completely cut himself off from the political world. He maintained open lines of communication with members of Congress, as well as the executive branch, passing along names of people to be considered for jobs and making his views clear on issues relevant to his circuit or state. For instance, he sent letters to members of Congress to lobby on behalf of the long-rumored creation of a new judicial district in North Carolina. Much like how others went to bat for him when he was nominated for his judgeship, Parker also helped out other nominees for federal judgeships, helping them weather the confirmation process and using his political connections to advocate on their behalf.

Sometimes his correspondence was of a personal nature. In June 1925, he exchanged letters with Secretary of Commerce Herbert Hoover. Both had an interest in reorganizing their respective branches to be more efficient and Parker praised Hoover for a recent speech to that effect. "Allow me to congratulate you not only on the address, but also on the great work that you are doing in your Department," Parker said.[47]

Whether Parker was truly impressed and sincerely wanted to acknowledge Hoover, or he sensed that there were benefits to cultivating a relationship with a popular, well-respected cabinet official who was widely seen as a potential future presidential contender, isn't known.

Either way, after Hoover became president in 1929, Parker ended up on his radar for a role in his administration. Assistant Attorney General Mabel Walker Willebrandt, a strong Hoover ally who had served as

[47] Parker Papers, Letter from Parker to Herbert Hoover, June 8 1925.

a controversial surrogate for him during the campaign, recommended Parker for attorney general, citing Stone's high opinion of him from the war fraud cases and his strong performance as a circuit court judge. "He is, I may almost say, idolized by his friends in North Carolina and regarded as the most representative member of their Bar," she said to Hoover in a February 1929 memo.[48] "He represents the new South."

The reference to the new South surely appealed to Hoover, who had managed to break the Solid South in the 1928 presidential election. The Hoover campaign invested heavily in Southern states and coordinated with local lily-whites in the hopes of peeling off white voters suspicious of the Democratic nominee, New York Governor Al Smith, the first Catholic to win a major party's nod for president. To be fair, Smith's religion wasn't the only reason he was unpopular with many Southerners—Smith was also a "wet" who was skeptical of Prohibition. Southern Democrats were dismayed that their party had seemingly transformed into an "organization in which the whiskey-soaked and the corrupt Gotham politician would feel quite at home" and one that would "destroy the fruits of decades of progress towards national sobriety."[49] Whether it was Smith's Catholicism or stance on Prohibition, or the fact that Hoover represented continuity with the Harding and Coolidge Administrations, which were popularly perceived as being responsible for the nation's prosperity, Hoover ended up winning in a landslide and even carried several states that hadn't voted for a Republican since Reconstruction, including North Carolina.

During his administration, Hoover tried to consolidate his and his party's gains in the South, aligning with the lily-whites and removing Black Republicans from positions of power within the party. Hoover's GOP even kept Oscar De Priest of Illinois, the first Northern Black Republican Congressman, at an arm's length and made sure federal patronage went to whites first.[50] The thinking went that, if the GOP could make significant in-roads into the South, it would help everyone,

[48] Herbert Hoover Papers, Memo from Mabel Walker Willebrandt to Hoover, February 8, 1929.

[49] Martin Fausold, *The Presidency of Herbert Hoover* (Lawrence, KS: University Press of Kansas, 1985), 30.

[50] James Chapin, "Analysis: The end of the Southern strategy, part 2," *United Press International*, www.upi.com/Archives/2001/02/22/Analysis-The-end-of-the-Southern-strategy-part-2/7841982818000/.

including Black Southerners, by allowing the region to modernize and improve its economic and educational systems.[51] In other words, it was exactly what Parker had advocated during his various campaigns for office about the need for two strong parties in the South.

The attorney general job ended up going to William D. Mitchell, who was still serving as Coolidge's solicitor general at the time of the appointment. According to press reports, Parker was then considered for Mitchell's old position, and had even met with administration officials to talk things over. However, the *Greensboro Daily News*, while referring to Parker as "exceptional," sounded skeptical that a circuit court judge would really give up a life-tenured job for what was a prestigious position but a clear step down for someone in his position.[52]

Instead, the president selected Charles Evans Hughes, Jr., son of the former justice and 1916 GOP nominee for president of the United States. The younger Hughes was an accomplished lawyer in his own right, having served as a secretary to future Supreme Court Justice Benjamin Cardozo and made a name for himself on Wall Street as a corporate lawyer with the firm his father founded. Famed judge Learned Hand later said that Charles Evans Hughes Sr. was the greatest lawyer he ever saw—except for his son, who was even better.[53]

Unfortunately for the younger Hughes, his tenure as solicitor general was destined to be a short one. When Chief Justice Taft resigned in February 1930 due to declining health, he had requested the senior Hughes as his replacement, and Hoover decided to grant that political last wish. Therefore, Hughes Jr. had to step down to avoid the appearance of a conflict of interest. As the next chapter will show, the Hughes' chief justice nomination ended up having tremendous implications for Parker.

Those implications started to come into focus the following month, when Justice Edward Sanford suddenly died. Much like with his circuit court nomination, Parker's friends and allies immediately started boosting his case for the Supreme Court. "I hope you will decide to stand for

[51] G.F. Garcia, "Black Disaffection From the Republican Party During the Presidency of Herbert Hoover, 1928–1932", *The Annals of Iowa* 45, no. 6 (1980), 462–477.

[52] "Judge John J. Parker is Mentioned for Post of Solicitor General," *The Greensboro Daily News*, April 16, 1929.

[53] "A Storied Law Firm With a Strong History," *Hughes Hubbard & Reed*, www.hughesshubbard.com/culture/firm-history.

appointment to the Supreme Court of the United States," Greensboro lawyer C. Clifford Frazier wrote to him in a letter dated March 8, 1930, the same day that Sanford died.[54] "North Carolina certainly deserves some fitting recognition from President Hoover."

As was the case when Parker was named to the circuit court, North Carolinians evidently felt that it was their turn at the feeding trough when it came to the High Court vacancy. Noting that the last Tar Heel to serve on the Supreme Court was Alfred Moore, an obscure eighteenth-century jurist who held the ignominious distinction of having only written one opinion during his four years on the court, Seawell argued that the state was long overdue for another shot and encouraged the lawyers and judges in the state to get behind Parker.[55]

It wasn't just his geography that made him a viable candidate for the job. Parker's judicial opinions were considered first rate, and he was widely respected among his fellow judges. "Judge Parker possesses, in a remarkable degree, those characteristics so important in a judge – the power of correct analysis and a clear grasp of principle – and in the preparation of his judicial opinions, there is always evidence of his painstaking care and of a thirst for complete information in the collection of the materials," Judge D. Lawrence Groner wrote to President Hoover on March 11, 1930.[56] McClintic was no less effusive in his praise of Parker, emphasizing his intelligence, work ethic and physical and mental vigor. "John Parker would add the force of continuity, for a great many years, to the Supreme Court," he wrote to Hoover on March 15, 1930.[57]

Meanwhile, Charles Jonas, U.S. representative and member of the Republican National Committee representing North Carolina, sketched out a plan of attack for Parker and his allies, talking about how the judge should follow his playbook from when he got the circuit court judgeship and let his friends and allies lobby on his behalf while he stayed above the fray. Cautioning that they didn't want to seem too eager to replace a departed justice, especially one who hadn't even been buried yet, Jonas recommended that they start by building up support within the bar and

[54] Parker Papers, Letter from C. Clifford Frazier to Parker, March 8, 1930.

[55] Parker Papers, Letter from Herbert Seawell to Kenneth G. Royall, March 10, 1930.

[56] Parker Papers, Letter from D. Lawrence Groner to President Hoover, March 11, 1930.

[57] Parker Papers, Letter from George McClintic to President Hoover, March 15, 1930.

bench in the state before the party itself would get openly involved. "Of course, you will want to have nothing to do with it openly, but you can direct your friends," Jonas wrote to Parker.[58]

Not that they really needed to do much to put Parker at the top of the shortlist. *The Washington Post* ran a story on March 10, 1930 identifying Parker as the presumptive front-runner for the spot—ahead of other luminaries like Owen J. Roberts, Learned Hand, Borah, former President Coolidge and John W. Davis. While wondering if Parker was too young for the job (he was 44 at the time he was nominated to the Supreme Court), the *Post* speculated that the president would want to nominate a Southerner to replace Sanford, who had hailed from Tennessee. Parker, the *Post* maintained, was the logical choice and "the most eligible candidate from the South."[59]

He wasn't the only candidate, of course. North Carolina's two Democratic senators had one of their own in mind: Chief Justice of the North Carolina Supreme Court Judge Walter P. Stacy. While Senators Simmons and Overman both hoped Hoover would make a bipartisan gesture and give Stacy the nod, they were also realistic and understood that the job was likely to go to a Republican. Therefore, they both made it known that Parker would be an acceptable alternative.[60] "He is as good a man as there is in the South," Simmons said.[61]

With that in mind, Willebrandt drafted a memo encouraging Parker's nomination for the vacancy, arguing that, not only was he eminently qualified, but also that it made sense politically. She argued that Hoover could appease Simmons, who was upset about one of his candidates being passed over for the ICC, and allow the administration to elevate Groner to Parker's old seat, a move she called "very desirable politically."[62]

She wasn't the only one pushing for Parker. In the days following Sanford's death, Hoover received many recommendations for the young North Carolinian, including one such note dated March 19 from

[58] Parker Papers, Letter from Charles Jonas to Parker, March 9, 1930.

[59] "Speculation is Rife on Court Selection: Justice Parker is Considered as Logical Choice to Succeed Sanford," *The Washington Post*, March 10, 1930.

[60] Parker Papers, Letter from Senator Overman to J.G. Merrimon, March 15, 1930 and Letter from Senator Simmons to J.G. Merrimon, March 14, 1930.

[61] "Judge John J. Parker, North Carolina, Named for U.S. Supreme Court," *The News and Advance*, March 22, 1930.

[62] Hoover Papers, Memo from Willebrandt to President Hoover, March 20, 1930.

Overman. The senator also included a number of pro-Parker telegrams in his endorsement and sent them along to the White House.[63]

For his part, Hoover seemed willing to let others take the lead on the nomination process. According to *Making the Supreme Court: The Politics of Appointments, 1930–2020* by Charles M. Cameron and Jonathan P. Kastellec, Hoover was not very interested in the Court—perhaps because he was dealing with the Great Depression for most of his term in office. According to their data, he displayed the lowest amount of interest compared to the other presidents they studied. He did not have a process for identifying and vetting candidates, instead consulting with a few trusted advisors, getting a name or two and then picking one of them.[64]

The Parker nomination was one such quick decision. There is little in Hoover's presidential papers relating to why Parker was considered and why he ultimately got the nod, which he did on March 21, 1930, when Hoover officially announced the nomination. In a news conference that same day, Hoover made clear that fitness was the most important issue, but noted that each circuit had a representative on the court over the last 20 years—except Parker's Fourth Circuit, which hadn't sent anyone to the court in nearly 70 years. When quizzed by reporters, Hoover came with his homework, pointing out the last time was 1860, when Justice Peter Daniel retired.[65]

At first, the move was widely acclaimed—far more than Hoover's previous nomination of Hughes had been—and the assumption was that Parker would sail through the Senate confirmation process, perhaps without a single dissenting vote.[66] Justice Stone even sent Parker a note dated March 22, 1930, welcoming him to the court and promising that he would find an "interesting career there."[67]

[63] Hoover Papers, supra.

[64] Cameron, Charles M., Kastellec, Jonathan P., *Making the Supreme Court: The Politics of Appointments, 1930–2020* (New York: Oxford University Press, 2023).

[65] *Public Papers of the Presidents of the United States: Herbert Hoover. January 1 to December 31, 1930* (Washington, D.C.: United States Government Printing Office, 1976), 98.

[66] "Carolina Jurist for Supreme Court," *The New York Times*, March 21, 1930. "North Carolina Judge Named By Hoover To Supreme Court; Succeeds Late Judge Sanford," *The Greensboro Daily News*, March 22, 1930.

[67] Parker Papers, supra, Letter from Harlan Fiske Stone to Parker, March 22, 1930.

His fellow Tar Heels were exceedingly pleased with the nomination, which many of them assumed was a slam dunk. "It should be gratifying to realize that North Carolina as a whole rejoices with you," U.S. District Judge Johnson Hayes of the Middle District of North Carolina, and a man mentioned as a possible replacement for Parker on the circuit court, wrote in a letter to the nominee.[68] "No appointment has ever brought such universal satisfaction." Similarly, Simmons wrote to Parker congratulating him and expressing pride at the prospect of finally getting another Tar Heel on the court.[69] Bailey Groome, Parker's friend and president of the North Carolina Commercial Secretaries Association, even prophesied that his college buddy's rise was only just beginning. "[W]ithin six more years, you will be the nominee of the Republican party for President of the United States," he vowed.[70]

Parker, for his part, took the news in stride and went about his day as if nothing had happened. According to press reports, on the day he was nominated, he still showed up for work as usual and went about his daily tasks despite the fact that he was now one of the most well-known individuals in the country. His only statement on his nomination was a four word missive that, the Associated Press observed, reflected the overall simplicity of his speech, demeanor and manner. "I feel very humble," he said.[71]

While some newspapers did stress that his appointment was hardly a done deal, even that level of caution seemed more theoretical than anything specific. Especially since progressive wildcards like Norris and Borah seemed positively disposed to the nominee. "I know very little about Judge Parker," Senator Norris of Nebraska, the chairman of the Senate Judiciary Committee, told the *Lincoln Nebraska State Journal*.[72] "But what I do know is favorable."

[68] Parker Papers, supra, Letter from Johnson Hayes to Parker, March 22, 1930.

[69] Parker Papers, supra, Letter from Furnifold Simmons to Parker, March 22, 1930.

[70] Parker Papers, supra, Letter from Bailey Groome to Parker, March 22, 1930.

[71] "Plain John J. Parker Bears Gracefully the Honor of New Appointment to the Supreme Court," *The Salisbury Post*, March 23, 1930.

[72] "Southern Judge to Fill Supreme Court Vacancy," *The Lincoln Nebraska State Journal*, March 22, 1930.

CHAPTER 4

Precedents: How Prior Confirmation Battles Set the Stage for Parker

When John J. Parker was nominated to the Supreme Court in 1930, he had good reason to be confident of his chances for confirmation. The Senate rarely turns down a Supreme Court nominee—as of the end of 2025, there have been 121 nominees that were confirmed by the Senate and ended up serving on the court compared to only 12 that were rejected by a formal vote. There have also been a handful of nominees who were not confirmed due to Senate inaction, as well as some who withdrew under pressure once it became clear they could not prevail.[1] There have even been some nominees who turned the job down, but that hasn't happened since the 1880s.[2]

[1] Some of the nominees who were not considered by the Senate ended up being confirmed later on, including Roger Taney, who was nominated for an associate justiceship in 1835 but then landed the Chief Justiceship the following year and Stanley Matthews. The most recent example of a nominee who failed due to Senate inaction was Merrick Garland, who was nominated by President Barack Obama in 2016 to replace Justice Antonin Scalia.

[2] This was more common in the early days of the republic, as being a Supreme Court justice wasn't always a glamorous job. John Jay, for instance, resigned the chief justiceship in 1795 to become governor of New York. When President John Adams nominated him to his old seat in 1800, he turned it down, citing the court's "lack of energy, weight and dignity which are essential to its affording due support to the national government." John Marshall ended up with the seat and did a lot to give the court the energy, weight and dignity Jay thought it lacked. As of this writing, the last person to be formally

V. Li, *Supreme Pressure*,
https://doi.org/10.1007/978-3-032-07864-3_4

Otherwise, the Senate seemed committed to upholding the "consent" part of its constitutional power to advise and consent to judicial nominations. At the time Parker was nominated, the Senate hadn't rejected anyone since 1894 and, in many cases, they had barely even put up a fight. Most Supreme Court nominees between 1894 and 1930 were confirmed quickly and easily—some were even approved the same day they were nominated.[3]

Prior to the Parker fight, the few times that the Senate formally rejected a High Court nominee were usually the result of political considerations. For instance, Alexander Wolcott was rejected in 1811, in large part, because he was seen as a political crony of then President James Madison who possessed a less-than-first-rate legal mind. One Washington, D.C. reporter called the nomination "abominable,"[4] and even Wolcott's allies seemed unable to say much to help his cause. One even paid him a backhanded compliment, opining that with hard work and determination, he might, one day, reach the level of his colleagues on the court.[5] The Senate rejected him by a lopsided 24–9 tally despite Madison's Democratic-Republicans holding a large majority. Upon his defeat, *The Virginia Patriot* would gloat that Wolcott was more qualified to appear before a judge than to be one.[6]

Several times, individual senators or influential politicians were able to get a nominee rejected on an up-and-down vote. John Canfield Spencer's 1844 nomination ran into trouble; thanks to an ongoing feud between

nominated to the Supreme Court only to turn it down was Roscoe Conkling. The former Senator and Representative who had been a leading candidate for President in 1876 was nominated by President Chester Alan Arthur in 1882 and confirmed by the Senate, only to refuse the job.

[3] Edward D. White was confirmed on the same day as nomination as both an associate justice (1894) and chief justice (1910). Former President William Howard Taft and ex-U.S. Senator George Sutherland (R-Utah), two Warren Harding nominees, were also extended similar courtesies.

[4] Mark Lawrence, "Supreme Court Nominees Rejected By The Senate," *The Washington Post*, September 15, 1987, www.washingtonpost.com/archive/politics/1987/09/15/supreme-court-nominees-rejected-by-the-senate/28abe505–180f-423d-a774-adfb861ef2e0/.

[5] Paul Simon, *Advice & Consent: Clarence Thomas, Robert Bork and the Intriguing History of the Supreme Court's Nomination Battles* (Washington, D.C.: National Press Books, 1992), 173.

[6] Quoted in J. Myron Jacobson and Ron M. Mersky, *The Rejected: Sketches of the 26 Men Nominated for the Supreme Court but Not Confirmed by the Senate* (Milpitas, CA: Toucan Valley Publications, 1993), 16.

President John Tyler, a nominal member of the Whig Party, and Henry Clay, the intellectual and political leader of the party. Clay, who was running to succeed Tyler as president, wielded tremendous influence over Senate Whigs, to the point where they probably would have rejected Jesus Christ if he had been nominated by Tyler. Therefore, Spencer, a mere mortal, never stood a chance and his nomination went down in defeat by a 26–21 vote.[7]

The following year, Senator Simon Cameron of Pennsylvania led the fight against his intrastate rival, George W. Woodward, when the latter was appointed by President James K. Polk (who had narrowly defeated Clay in the 1844 election). Woodward was controversial and incendiary—especially when it came to espousing his anti-immigrant views.[8] He also had poor relationships with some powerful politicians in Pennsylvania, and had already crossed swords with Cameron. The two had previously contested a vacant Senate seat and a "bitter" Woodward would claim he had been cheated.[9] Cameron didn't forget, and took advantage of unwritten rules and customs whereby senators, out of courtesy to one of their own, would often refuse to support a nomination if one or both senators from that nominee's home state objected. With Secretary of State James Buchanan, another influential Pennsylvanian, making noise about being interested in the seat, Cameron lined up enough senators to deny Woodward,[10] who was defeated by a vote of 20–29. Buchanan ultimately decided not to go for the seat and Polk nominated another Pennsylvanian, Robert Cooper Grier, who was confirmed in 1846.

In 1869, Cameron and others helped take down another nominee. President Ulysses S. Grant had picked his attorney general, Ebenezer Hoar, to fill a newly created seat on the court. Despite having a sizable Republican majority in the Senate that had voted to confirm him as attorney general earlier that year, Hoar found himself on hostile ground when his nomination to the court was considered. Senate Republicans had grown to dislike him for a variety of reasons, one of which was

[7] Tyler made subsequent attempts to fill the seat, but the Senate tabled the nominations. Ultimately, he nominated Samuel Nelson for the seat, and he was confirmed.

[8] Simon, supra, 184–185.

[9] Daniel Curran, "Polk, Politics, and Patronage: The Rejection of George W. Woodward's Nomination to the Supreme Court," *The Pennsylvania Magazine of History and Biography* 121 (1997), 163.

[10] Ibid.

Hoar's refusal to follow individual senators' recommendations for lower court nominations. At one point, a senator even introduced a resolution demanding to know why Hoar had disregarded their choices.[11] Angry senators got their revenge by rejecting Hoar by a 33–24 vote. "What could you expect for a man who has snubbed seventy Senators?" Cameron said afterward.[12]

Another senator who took advantage of the body's rules and customs was David Hill, a powerful Democrat from New York. Hill had lost the 1892 Democratic nomination for president to his intrastate rival, former President Grover Cleveland, and after Cleveland won the election that year, Hill seemed intent on making him pay. After Justice Samuel Blatchford died in 1893, vacating the seat that had, traditionally, gone to a New Yorker, Cleveland nominated prominent New York lawyer, and avowed political enemy of Hill, William Hornblower to the seat.

Predictably, Hill refused to support the nomination and utilized Senate customs and traditions to his advantage.[13] Hill objected and, much like how Cameron had used senatorial courtesy to block his instate rival Woodward, enough Senators deferred to their colleague that Hornblower's nomination went down by a vote of 30–24. Cleveland then tried another New Yorker, former New York County District Attorney and New York City Bar Association President Wheeler Hazard Peckham. Once again, Hill invoked senatorial courtesy, and Peckham was rejected by an even larger margin of 41–32.

Cleveland then decided to beat the Senate at their own game. Another feature of senatorial courtesy was that they would almost always vote to confirm one of their own. With that in mind, Cleveland tapped Senator Edward Douglass White (D-LA) to the seat, and he was easily approved. White would later be promoted to chief justice by President Taft in 1910,

[11] Lawrence, supra, 74–75.

[12] Simon, supra, 202.

[13] Historians often assign Hill, to say nothing of the Senate's arcane rules and "boys club" atmosphere, the lion's share of credit or blame for torpedoing these two nominations. However, see Jacobstein and Mersky, supra. They argue that there were larger political issues at play, including a growing schism between Democrats and Republicans regarding protective tariffs and between free silver politicians from the West and South and gold supporters, which had the effect of galvanizing opposition to Cleveland in the Senate with his nominees serving as convenient targets.

becoming the first associate justice to serve as chief justice since John Rutledge.

Precedents

There were a few confirmation battles that ended up having major implications for Parker when his name was submitted to the Senate in 1930.

In 1795, John Rutledge saw his nomination for chief justice go up in smoke thanks to his public comments. One of the preeminent legal scholars in America and a Founding Father who had signed the Declaration of Independence, the South Carolinian Rutledge had been one of the dominant figures at the Constitutional Convention. He chaired the Committee of Detail, a group consisting of the finest legal minds at the convention that was charged with drafting much of the Constitution's actual text. According to author Richard Barry, who penned *Mr. Rutledge of South Carolina*, the job had to go to someone so skilled that he could deftly reduce to writing the various agreements and compromises made by the members of the convention while drafting the various clauses and sections in an artful way so as not to inflame or exacerbate any underlying tensions or limit or foreclose any changes or reforms in the future.[14]

Rutledge was the consensus choice, which spoke to just how respected and admired he was as a legal mind. Through his work on the committee, Rutledge was largely responsible for drafting the judiciary clause of the Constitution and purposefully leaving it vague and open-ended rather than enumerating its powers like in Article I for the legislature.[15]

When it came time for President George Washington to staff the Supreme Court, he had his pick of the best legal minds in the nascent United States. He nearly picked Rutledge to serve as the nation's first chief justice,[16] before appointing him as one of the five original associate justices. Rutledge resigned after two years without ever hearing a case,

[14] Richard Barry, *Mr. Rutledge of South Carolina* (New York: Duell, Sloan & Pearce, 1942), 337–338.

[15] Ibid., 345–350. Barry argued that it was because he and others knew that if they were explicit about how the final authority lay with the courts and its unelected judges, then it never would have been ratified.

[16] "John Rutledge," *Oyez*, https://www.oyez.org/justices/john_rutledge.

but when original Chief Justice John Jay stepped down in 1795 after being elected governor of New York, the South Carolinian jumped at the chance to return to the court.

Rutledge's confirmation seemed like a done deal. Indeed, he had accepted a recess appointment and was already hearing cases as chief justice.[17] Surely, the Federalist-dominated Senate would rubber stamp anyone the popular and venerated Washington nominated. The fact that it was a legal giant like Rutledge who had, more or less, created the federal judiciary, made it all the more unlikely that the Senate would pick this moment to rebel.

Thanks to Rutledge's predecessor as chief, that's exactly what happened. Jay had negotiated a treaty with Great Britain that had resolved some of the outstanding issues stemming from the American Revolution, including trade terms, repayment of debts, and other matters. The treaty had been very poorly received back home. Angry New Yorkers threw stones at Secretary of the Treasury Alexander Hamilton, arguably the most influential man in D.C. after Washington, while residents in Rutledge's South Carolina registered their discontent by burning Jay in effigy. Many prominent politicians spoke out against it, particularly Thomas Jefferson and James Madison, the leaders of the Democratic-Republicans. Jefferson even wrote to Rutledge's brother, Edward, calling the treaty an "infamous act, which is really nothing more than a treaty of alliance between England and the Anglomen of this country against the legislature and people of the United States."[18]

However, most Federalists either backed the treaty or loyally toed the party line to support two of its luminaries in Washington and Jay. One exception was Rutledge. Calling it less of a treaty and more of a "humble acknowledge[ment] of our dependence on his majesty" and a "humble surrender of our rights and privileges," Rutledge showed off his legal

[17] The Rutledge court heard two major cases: *United States v. Peters*, 3 U.S. 121 (1795), which ruled that U.S. federal courts lacked jurisdiction over criminal law matters committed on international waters and *Talbot v. Janson*, 3 U.S. 133 (1795), which held American citizens did not give up all of their rights simply by becoming a citizen of another country.

[18] "From Thomas Jefferson to Edward Rutledge, 30 November 1795," *Founders Online*, National Archives, https://founders.archives.gov/documents/Jefferson/01-28-02-0419. [Original source: *The Papers of Thomas Jefferson*, vol. 28, *1 January 1794 – 29 February 1796*, ed. John Catanzariti. Princeton: Princeton University Press, 2000, pp. 541–542.]

mind by arguing that there were certain terms and phrases in the pact that were vague, potentially giving England latitude to act in bad faith without any recourse.[19]

Had he stuck to making legal arguments, he might have survived the coming storm. Unfortunately for Rutledge, he also showed what can happen if you let yourself go a little too much, delivering a line that was so stunning and shocking that it was guaranteed to take attention away from his formalistic arguments. Taking aim at the preeminent Founding Father and a beloved national icon who happened to be the person who had just nominated him to be chief justice, Rutledge said that while "dearly as he loved Washington, he would rather see him dead than see him sign the Treaty" and that, if faced with a choice between war with England and Jay's treaty becoming law, he'd root for war.[20]

Of course, that provocative line was what people remembered—even today, that's the quote that usually gets cited when reading about Rutledge and Jay's treaty. Predictably, Federalists were outraged, and some leading members of the party, including Hamilton, John Adams, and some of Washington's cabinet questioned Rutledge's mental faculties while urging their leader not to go forward with the nomination. Even more embarrassingly for Federalists, Democratic-Republicans, including Jefferson and future Vice President Aaron Burr, had disingenuously embraced Rutledge, using his quotes and analyses to argue against ratification of the treaty.[21]

As a result, when Rutledge's nomination finally reached the Senate in December 1795, he faced an uphill struggle—especially once Hamilton, the intellectual leader of the Federalists, got involved. Hamilton vigorously lobbied senators to reject Rutledge, citing Rutledge's own behavior during his passionate denunciation of Jay's treaty as evidence that he had gone insane. Conveniently, Hamilton produced several letters from observers in Charleston, South Carolina, who attested that Rutledge was losing his mind, and was in poor health overall.[22]

[19] George S. McCowan, "Chief Justice John Rutledge and the Jay Treaty," *The South Carolina Historical Magazine* 62, no. 1 (1961), 10–23, http://www.jstor.org/stable/27566321.

[20] Ibid.

[21] Barry, supra, 356–357.

[22] Barry, 357–358.

Back then, judicial nominees did not appear before the Senate for testimony or hearings, so Rutledge was not able to defend himself or answer the allegations against him. According to Barry, no senator even "talked with Rutledge personally while the question of his confirmation was before the Senate" and "no medical report was asked for or received."[23]

As a result, the Senate rejected a Supreme Court nominee for the first time in its history, turning Rutledge down 14–10. Despondent over his rejection and still not over the recent death of his wife, Rutledge tried to kill himself by jumping into the Charleston Harbor, but was rescued by two slaves. Two days after that suicide attempt, Rutledge resigned from the court, despite the fact his recess appointment would have allowed him to stay on until the Senate term ended. He would be replaced as chief justice by Oliver Ellsworth, a Federalist senator from Connecticut who had been one of the 14 to vote against Rutledge.[24] Other than a single term in the South Carolina House of Representatives, Rutledge lived a private, quiet life until his death in 1800.

While questions over his mental state had proven to be the proximate cause of the Senate vote, most political observers at the time knew the truth. "The rejection of Mr. Rutledge by the Senate is a bold thing, because they cannot pretend any objection to him by his disapprobation of the treaty," Jefferson wrote to William B. Giles.[25]

There were a few tough confirmation battles that involved similar factors that Parker would face. In 1881, outside interest groups nearly torpedoed the nomination of Stanley Matthews. During the dying days of his administration, President Rutherford B. Hayes nominated his longtime friend and fellow Ohioan to replace retiring Justice Noah Swayne. A former U.S. attorney for the Southern District of Ohio and U.S. senator from Ohio, Matthews had represented Hayes before the Electoral Commission to resolve the disputed presidential election of 1876—an

[23] Id.

[24] McCowan, supra, 21.

[25] Joseph P. Harris, *The Advice and Consent of the Senate: A Study of the Confirmation of Appointments by the United States Senate* (New York: Greenwood Press, Publishers, 1968).

engagement that ended successfully as Hayes was awarded all of the electoral votes in question, giving him the White House by one electoral vote over Democrat Samuel Tilden.[26]

However, Democrats held the majority in the Senate at the time and had a long memory. They made clear they weren't inclined to vote for someone they considered a crony of the outgoing president—someone many of them still called "Rutherfraud" because they believed he had stolen the White House.

Others opposed Matthews because of his previous work as a lawyer for the railroad industry, including a representation of Jay Gould, one of the most well-known and controversial train tycoons in the nineteenth century.[27] The Hayes Administration had used federal troops to put down railroad labor strikes in 1877, so the issue was a hot-button one at the time.

Therefore, the Senate refused to act on the nomination before Hayes' term ended. However new president, James A. Garfield, another Ohioan, resubmitted Matthews's name—a move that drew criticism and questions as to why the new president had "repeated one of the most injudicious and objectionable acts of his predecessor."[28] Unlike Hayes, Garfield had not been close to Matthews and, as president-elect, had refused to help or support his fellow Buckeye despite entreaties to do so. When Garfield renominated him, it led to speculation that the president had been pressured by corporate interests, including Gould.[29]

Therefore, Matthews had a gigantic target on his back as he embarked on the confirmation process. For the first time, outside interest groups, in this case organized labor, decided to mount a lobbying campaign against a Supreme Court nomination and almost succeeded.[30] While the Judiciary Committee reported the nomination unfavorably, Matthews was able to

[26] Sheldon Gilbert, "A look at the closest Court confirmation ever," National Constitution Center, October 6, 2018, accessed February 27, 2024.

[27] Ibid.

[28] Ibid., quoting *The New York Times*, March 15, 1881.

[29] Scott H. Ainsworth and John Anthony Maltese, "National Grange Influence on the Supreme Court Confirmation of Stanley Matthews," *Social Science History* 20, no. 1 (1996), 49.

[30] Oona Hathaway, "Review: The Politics of the Confirmation Process," *The Yale Law Journal* 106, no. 1 (1996), 237.

squeak by with the full Senate, winning by a single vote, 24–23. He would serve seven years on the court until his death in 1889.

Geographic concerns and presidential politics nearly took down Melville Fuller. In 1888, after Chief Justice Morrison Waite died suddenly, President Cleveland seemed unsure of whom to nominate. Two complicating factors were that Republicans controlled the Senate, and it was a presidential election year, which meant he had to appoint someone who could win over enough senators who might otherwise be content with running out the clock in the hopes Cleveland lost reelection. The president considered a number of politicians and judges before settling on Fuller, an Illinois attorney and ex-politician.

The move was not well-received. *The Philadelphia Press* called him "the most obscure man ever appointed Chief Justice of the United States."[31] Boasting a long mane of white hair and a bushy white mustache to match, Fuller seemed more qualified to be a Mark Twain impersonator than chief justice. There is a possibly apocryphal story about how, years later, Twain would give out autographs pretending to be Fuller.

Upset that his friend and fellow Vermont native Edward Phelps, a former ABA president who was then serving as ambassador to the United Kingdom, did not get the nod, Senator George Edmunds (R-VT), the chairman of the Judiciary Committee, tried to block Fuller's confirmation.[32] First, he and a couple of his allies dug up stuff from Fuller's previous career as a politician. For instance, Fuller, who had risen through the Democratic Party ranks in Illinois, had been a steadfast ally of Stephen A. Douglas and an ardent critic of Abraham Lincoln. Having previously spoken out against many of Lincoln's wartime policies, particularly the decision to suspend habeas corpus and to issue the Emancipation Proclamation, Edmunds and his allies portrayed Fuller as a disloyal Copperhead (a term for an anti-war Northerner) and sought to rally Republicans, who controlled the Senate, into voting down the nomination.

Fuller, however, had some help—not the least of which came from Lincoln's son, Robert, who argued that Fuller's views did not make him a traitor and, through his actions, had demonstrated his loyalty to the Union. Edmunds then tried another tactic, accusing Fuller of impropriety.

[31] James W. Ely, Jr., *The Chief Justiceship of Melville W. Fuller, 1888–1910* (Columbia, SC: University of South Carolina Press, 1995), quoting *Philadelphia Press*, May 1, 1888.

[32] Henry Abraham, and Edward Goldberg, "A Note on the Appointment of Justices of the Supreme Court of the United States," *ABA Journal* 46, no. 2 (1960), 148.

However, Fuller did not dignify these charges and lawyers involved with the relevant cases filed affidavits with the Judiciary Committee refuting the allegations.

With all else failing, Edmunds tried to stall for as long as possible—preferably until after the 1888 presidential election. However, other Republicans senators, most notably Shelby Cullom and Charles Farwell of Illinois, wanted to confirm Fuller in the hopes of securing their home state for their presidential nominee, Benjamin Harrison. The importance of Illinois in what was shaping up to be a close race between Harrison and Cleveland was so obvious that Fuller even told Cleveland that he wouldn't be devastated if the delay in his confirmation meant the president would win Illinois (the state ended up going for Harrison by a tight margin). Under pressure, Edmunds agreed to refer the nomination to the full Senate without a recommendation from the Judiciary Committee. He then put up one last fight on the Senate floor during the debate over Fuller's confirmation, presciently arguing that Fuller could not be counted on to properly interpret or enforce the Thirteenth, Fourteenth, and Fifteenth Amendments, only for Cullom to discredit him by reading an anti-Lincoln speech given by his friend, Phelps.[33] In the end, Fuller was confirmed by a 41–20 count with 15 senators not voting.[34] As Edmunds warned, Fuller would interpret the Reconstruction Amendments very narrowly—at least when it came to protecting civil rights.

Four decades later, Harlan Fiske Stone's nomination ran into trouble after the nominee was attacked for doing what he believed was his constitutional duty to faithfully execute his job despite others arguing that he could or should have acted differently. Picked by Coolidge to replace Justice Joseph McKenna, Stone, as attorney general, had made a very powerful enemy in Senator Burton K. Wheeler. A Democrat from Montana who had been La Follette's running mate in 1924 with the Progressive Party, Wheeler had been indicted by the Department of Justice in a bribery case initiated under Stone's predecessor as attorney general, the controversial Harry Daugherty. The case seemed like retaliation against Wheeler for his leading role in investigating the Teapot

[33] Ely, supra, 44–45.

[34] Willard L. King, *Melville Weston Fuller—Chief Justice of The United States 1888–1910* (United Kingdom: Read Books Limited, 2013).

Dome Scandal that had taken place during the Harding Administration and had resulted in indictments for several officials, including Daugherty. Wheeler was investigated by the Senate and exonerated. He had also been acquitted in the court of public opinion; even Republican-leaning newspapers called the indictment a frame job.[35]

Stone felt like he had to do his job and let the criminal probe play out, much to Wheeler's chagrin and anger. After the Judiciary Committee voted to recommend the nomination to the full Senate, Wheeler's ally and colleague from Montana, Thomas Walsh, got the nomination referred back to the committee—a move that usually had the effect of killing a nomination and forcing its withdrawal. However, Coolidge refused to nominate anyone else, and Stone took the unprecedented step of appearing before the committee to address his critics. On January 28, 1925, Stone testified for five hours and gave what the *Washington Post* called a "complete and convincing demonstration of [Stone's] high purpose and good faith in dealing with the Wheeler case."[36] The Judiciary Committee re-recommended his nomination unanimously, and Stone was easily confirmed 71–6 by the full Senate.[37]

Tempest

Sandwiched between the Matthews and Stone battles were two other hard-fought nominations that would have ramifications for Parker.

On January 28, 1916, Woodrow Wilson nominated Boston-based lawyer Louis Brandeis, touching off a bitter, four-month confirmation fight. One of the most well-known lawyers in the country, Brandeis had been dubbed "The People's Lawyer" or "The Robin Hood of the law" for his high-profile fights on behalf of consumers against big businesses and powerful corporations, trusts, and monopolies. For instance,

[35] "The Indictment and Trial of Sen. Wheeler," *The Washington Post*, April 23, 1993, www.washingtonpost.com/archive/opinions/1993/04/23/the-indictment-and-trial-of-sen-wheeler/0291e2af-9aa7–4914-a279–8956a8743542/. According to the *Post*, the bribe had been offered by Wheeler's client, not Wheeler, and had taken place after Wheeler had left the case. In fact, Wheeler was in Europe when the action in question occurred.

[36] "Stone Tells Senate Committee He Assumes Full Responsibility for Pressing New Wheeler Case," *The Washington Post*, January 29, 1925.

[37] "Committee Grills Nominee," *Senate.gov.*, www.senate.gov/about/powers-procedures/nominations/committee-grills-nominee.htm.

he took on financier J.P. Morgan when the banking magnate had tried to monopolize the railways in New England by merging New Haven Railroad and Boston and Maine Railroad. Through public pressure, litigation, and political lobbying, including consultation with President Theodore Roosevelt, Brandeis was able to stop the merger from happening.

He also represented the state of Oregon when it tried to limit the hours of women workers. With the *Lochner* era still in full swing, and the Supreme Court regularly siding with businesses or private companies against government intervention or regulation, it was widely expected that the regulation would be struck down. However, Brandeis devised an innovative strategy and cited social science, witness observations, scientific and medical reports, and other evidence that were not of a legal nature but were relevant to the case at hand, in order to prove that the proposed regulation was in the best interests of the female workers' health and well-being. The strategy worked and the court ruled in his client's favor in *Muller v. Oregon* (1908). The "Brandeis Brief" would become a popular and standard tool for lawyers and was used most successfully by the NAACP attorneys in the *Brown v. Board of Education* case.

Mostly, Brandeis stood for the proposition that the Constitution was a living document that should be interpreted based on current needs. In his eyes, courts had failed to protect the most needy and vulnerable, choosing instead to help businesses protect their contracts and property. He argued in his influential law review article "The Living Law" that the Industrial Revolution had resulted in radical changes in our political, economic, and social systems. However, he pointed out that the law had not followed suit. "Courts continued to ignore newly arisen social needs. They applied complacently 18th century conceptions of the liberty of the individual and of the sacredness of private property. Early 19th century scientific half-truths like 'The survival of the fittest,' which translated into practice meant 'The devil take the hindmost,' were erected by judicial sanction into a moral law," he wrote.[38]

Naturally, he made some powerful enemies along the way, many of whom were horrified at the thought of their scourge being elevated to the Supreme Court. For instance, several railroad titans expressed opposition to Brandeis, who had often clashed with them and fought to keep

[38] Louis Brandeis, "The Living Law," *Illinois Law Review* 10, no. 7 (1916), 464.

their rates low. Abbott Lawrence Lowell, president of Harvard University, got 55 influential individuals, including a number of Boston-area elites, to sign onto an anti-Brandeis letter and sent it to Senator Henry Cabot Lodge, an influential Republican senator from Massachusetts and a well-known opponent of Wilson. "It is difficult—perhaps impossible—to get direct evidence of any act by Brandeis that is, strictly speaking, dishonest; and yet a man who is believed by all the better part of the bar to be unscrupulous ought not to be a member of the highest court of the nation," Lowell wrote to Lodge.[39]

Henry Lee Higginson, a Boston-area banker who was famous for founding the Boston Symphony Orchestra, was another implacable foe who had clashed with Brandeis repeatedly over the years. When Wilson had previously tried to name Brandeis to his cabinet, Higginson led and financed the campaign to derail the move. Like Lowell, upon hearing of Brandeis' nomination to the court, Higginson wrote Lodge and urged the Senate to investigate the would-be justice.[40]

Another committed foe was Clarence Barron, owner of the Dow Jones Company and *The Wall Street Journal*, who was committed to defeating the nomination and had compiled a list of perceived misdeeds that Brandeis would have to answer for. They painted him as a radical who lacked the "dispassionate temperament that is required of a judge."[41] Meanwhile, seven former presidents of the ABA, including future Chief Justice William Howard Taft, even sent a letter to the Senate saying that Brandeis was "not a fit person to be a member of the Supreme Court of the United States."[42] The opposition of Taft, who desperately wanted a Supreme Court seat and had somehow convinced himself that Wilson might appoint him in a grand show of bipartisanship, bordered on the pathological. The future chief justice called Brandeis' nomination "one of

[39] David Dalin, "The Appointment of Louis D. Brandeis: First Jewish Justice on the Supreme Court," archived at https://web.archive.org/web/20190412031118/http://bir.brandeis.edu/bitstream/handle/10192/31435/LDB100Dalin.pdf?isAllowed=y&sequence=1. Also: "The Brandeis confirmation a century letter," *Oxford University Press Blog*, https://blog.oup.com/2016/06/the-brandeis-confirmation-a-century-later/, accessed May 25, 2024.

[40] Dalin, supra.

[41] Alden L. Todd, *Justice on Trial: The Case of Louis D. Brandeis* (New York: McGraw-Hill, 1964).

[42] Simon, supra, 236.

the deepest wounds that I have had as an American and as a lover of the Constitution and a believer in progressive conservatism," while calling his future colleague an "utterly unscrupulous" "muckraker," "socialist," and "hypocrite."[43]

There was a clear anti-Semitic undercurrent to much of the opposition that went largely unspoken but hung over the nomination like the Sword of Damocles. As the first Jewish nominee to the Supreme Court (Judah Benjamin of Louisiana had been offered a seat on the court by Presidents Millard Fillmore and Franklin Pierce, but turned them down to serve in the U.S. Senate), there were plenty of people in the country and, most notably, in the Senate, who were anti-Semitic and would never support the confirmation of a Jew. Lowell, for instance, was known to be anti-Semitic and even tried to institute a Jewish student quota at Harvard. A conservative Boston-area lawyer named Arthur Hill wrote a letter to Lodge, which was later submitted to the Judiciary Committee, that summed things up pretty well. "He is a radical and has spent a large part, not only of his public, but of his professional career, in attacking established institutions, and this alone would, in my judgment, account for a very large part of his unpopularity," Hill wrote.[44] "When you add to this that Mr. Brandeis is an outside, successful and a Jew, you have, I think, sufficiently explained most of the feeling against him."

That ended up being one of the few overt mentions of Brandeis' faith. His opponents stuck to attacking his ideology and some even claimed they didn't know he was Jewish.[45] However, the implication was clear—by questioning his ethics and, in some cases, even utilizing tropes and negative stereotypes traditionally associated with Jews, including calling him "money grubbing" and "greedy,"[46] Brandeis' detractors considered him to be an "other" who did not belong in their world, especially in a position of power.

As is often the case with contentious nominations, the fight ended up being about something larger than just the person being voted on. Many of Brandeis' detractors were conservatives who were concerned

[43] Dalin, supra, 3.

[44] Paper, supra, 229–230.

[45] Ibid., 441–442.

[46] Ronald Shafer, "The first Jewish justice was also the first to face confirmation hearings," *The Washington Post*, April 4, 2022. Also: "The Brandeis confirmation a century letter," supra.

that his appointment would signal a shift in the court's long tradition of upholding property rights and protecting big businesses from governmental regulation. "If Brandeis went onto the bench, he would also bring with him a new outlook and different experience from the old-school justices, and if his ideas prevailed, they would topple the old bastion of property-oriented classical thought," Melvin Urofsky wrote in his book, *Louis D. Brandeis: A Life*.[47] "Both his friends and those opposed to the appointment recognized this, and while his career gave both sides ammunition to debate the man, in fact, the real fight involved the future of the Court."

Luckily for Brandeis, he had some powerful allies. Besides the president, two of his cabinet officials, Treasury Secretary William G. McAdoo and Attorney General Thomas Watt Gregory, were admirers and had encouraged the president to name him to the court with the latter calling Brandeis "the greatest lawyer in the United States."[48] Similarly, La Follette had enthusiastically encouraged Wilson to make the nomination and promised he would cross party lines to vote for him. In fact, Wilson was so determined to appoint Brandeis, he didn't even bother to follow the tradition of checking with the senators from Massachusetts, Brandeis' home state, instead talking only with La Follette.[49]

Other influential figures supporting the nomination included national labor leader Samuel Gompers, *The New Republic* and *Harper's Weekly* editor Walter Lippmann, workers' rights activist Frances Perkins, and diplomat Henry Morgenthau Sr. Meanwhile, Charles Eliot, a widely respected former dean of Harvard Law School, wrote a stirring statement in favor of Brandeis, something which a former Brandeis partner later said was the next best thing to a letter of reference from God.[50] Indeed, almost the entire faculty at Harvard Law, led by future Justice Felix Frankfurter, backed Brandeis, their former colleague. Brandeis' allies also pushed back on the forces opposing him, accusing them of fearing

[47] Melvin Urofsky, *Louis D. Brandeis: A Life* (New York: Random House, 2009), 439.

[48] Steve Hunegs, "Realm, reach and influence of Brandeis was reflected in important Minnesota cases," *Minnesota Post*, June 1, 2016.

[49] "Brandeis Names for Highest Court; Will Be Opposed," *The New York Times*, January 29, 1916.

[50] Simon, supra, 236–237.

him as a "militant crusader for social justice"[51] while privately stating the obvious: If his mother hadn't been Jewish, then he would have been easily confirmed.

Nevertheless, they understood what they were in for, with Gregory prophesying that a Brandeis nomination would cause a "tempest."[52] When the nomination was announced in the Senate, it reportedly drew gasps.[53] Overman, who chaired the Judiciary Committee, later said that if the full body had voted on the nomination the day it first came to them, Brandeis would have lost.[54]

Due to the public outcry, the Senate Judiciary Committee took the then unprecedented step of holding public hearings on Brandeis' nomination and allowing witnesses both for and against him to testify (the committee had held hearings in the past, but behind closed doors). Much like what would happen with Parker's nomination, Brandeis did not publicly defend himself, despite his instincts telling him to fight and take on his detractors head-on. Instead, he took on more of an advisory role, coordinating with his allies and helping out behind-the-scenes. For instance, he helped organize a letter-writing campaign on his behalf among prominent lawyers in the country and prepared a list of cases he had argued before the Supreme Court.[55] In the meantime, his law partners would work with Gregory and other administration officials to lobby on his behalf and identify wavering senators to work on.[56]

Some of the witnesses testifying against Brandeis clearly had a personal axe to grind with him. The first witness was Clifford Thorne, chairman of

[51] William O. Douglas, "Louis Brandeis: Dangerous Because Incorruptible," *The New York Times*, July 5, 1964, archived from the original on February 25, 2021, https://web.archive.org/web/20210225234657/https:/www.nytimes.com/1964/07/05/archives/louis-brandeis-dangerous-because-incorruptible-justice-on-trial-the.html.

[52] "Shapiro on Dalin, 'Jewish Justices of the Supreme Court: From Brandeis to Kagan'," *H-Judaic*, https://networks.h-net.org/node/28655/reviews/1488181/shapiro-dalin-jewish-justices-supreme-court-brandeis-kagan, accessed May 24, 2024.

[53] "The Senate Approves Louis D. Brandeis," *Visit The Capitol*, www.visitthecapitol.gov/artifact/senate-resolution-advise-and-consent-appointment-louis-d-brandeis-be-associate-justice, accessed May 24, 2024.

[54] Simon, supra, 236.

[55] Urofsky, supra, 445.

[56] Lewis J. Paper, *Brandeis: An Intimate Biography of One of America's Truly Great Supreme Court Justices* (Secaucus, NJ: Citadel Press, 1983). Also, Harris, supra, 114.

the Iowa Railroad Commission,[57] and, unlike many of Brandeis' critics, Thorne's opposition was rooted in the feeling that Brandeis wasn't radical enough. The Iowan had represented some shippers who were fighting a railroad rate increase before the ICC in 1913–1914, and thought he had it in the bag when Brandeis was hired as an independent expert. After all, not only was Brandeis the foremost opponent of rate hikes, but he had done legal work for the shippers on a different matter. But to his surprise, Brandeis, who had been hired to do an impartial review of the record and make a recommendation based on that unbiased investigation, put aside his relationship with his former clients and backed a rate increase for railroads in the Midwest. Most observers agreed with the decision, but Thorne was not only angry, but felt personally betrayed. During his testimony, he accused Brandeis of "infidelity, breach of faith, and unprofessional conduct in connection with one of the greatest cases of this generation."[58]

Thorne's testimony did not impress the committee too much, and Brandeis' law partner, Edward McClennan called it "less than nothing."[59] However, Barron testified on the second day of hearings and his allegations proved to be much more serious. Picking up on the conflict of interest thread, Barron accused Brandeis of unethically double-dealing in a number of cases.

For instance, after the father of Brandeis' law partner, Samuel D. Warren, passed away in 1888, Brandeis and Warren put the family's paper mill business into a trust so that its profits could be shared by Warren, his mother, and his siblings. One member of the family wasn't happy about the arrangement and accused Brandeis of a conflict of interest.[60]

Similarly, Brandeis had been on the board of directors for United Shoe Machinery Company but resigned. Some years later, one of his clients challenged some of United Shoe's business practices, and Brandeis took the case and accused his old company of being monopolistic. Once again, Brandeis was accused of a conflict of interest and behaving unethically.

[57] Ibid.

[58] Clyde Spillenger, "Elusive Advocate: Reconsidering Brandeis as People's Lawyer," *The Yale Law Journal* 105 (1996), 1514.

[59] Paper, supra, 216.

[60] Ibid., 218–221.

There was also a complaint about how Brandeis had handled a bankruptcy matter as trustee for a company run by the Lennox family. In that case, a member of the Lennox family had erroneously believed that Brandeis had been representing him and his family and not acting as trustee for the bankruptcy estate. When Brandeis prioritized paying off creditors, Lennox got upset because he felt his interests should have been taken care of first.

There were a few other matters that Barron cited, including the New Haven Railroad fight, where Brandeis' opponents had spread rumors that he had been hired by rival railroads to destroy New Haven. Through his allies, Brandeis defended himself by stating that he had behaved ethically and had always communicated his role clearly to the parties involved. If these well-heeled, sophisticated individuals believed that Brandeis would somehow help them, it just showed how self-interested they were and underscored how great his reputation was that they thought they would be in good hands with him on their side.

His opponents inadvertently helped his cause by presenting witnesses who would attack Brandeis' reputation but then, when asked specific questions by senators, would demur.[61] Indeed, for Brandeis' allies this was proof that no one actually had any real evidence against their man and were coming out against him out of a general dislike and discomfort with the nominee's views and ethnicity. Multiple witnesses testifying against Brandeis admitted under questioning that they did not know of any specific instances of impropriety or unethical behavior, just that they had heard things from people. In some cases, they couldn't even name the people they had heard it from. Or, if they did, they couldn't remember what had been said.[62]

Once it was clear that none of the charges against Brandeis would stick, his opponents turned to stall tactics to try and delay the inevitable. The Senate Judiciary Subcommittee in charge of conducting the hearings had approved the nomination on April 3, 1916, on a 3–2 vote. However, Brandeis' opponents continued their obstruction, delaying a full committee vote for nearly two months. During that time, Senator George Sutherland (R-UT), Brandeis' future court colleague, was able to squeeze another day of testimony before the subcommittee by merely

[61] Paper, supra, 228–229.

[62] Ibid.

repeating a rumor that he had heard about Brandeis working for a company judged to be an illegal trust.[63]

In the meantime, Brandeis and his allies worked behind-the-scenes to shore up his support. The nominee met with a couple of members of the committee and won them over. Wilson, Gregory and other administration officials also secured some key votes for their man, with the president going as far as attending a North Carolina party in order to secure Overman.[64] Finally, on May 24, his Senate opponents could stall no longer, and the full committee voted 10–8 along party lines to send the nomination to the Senate floor with a favorable recommendation.

After waiting a then record 125 days since his nomination, including 20 days of hearings, Brandeis was finally confirmed on June 1, 1916, by a 47–22 vote with 27 absent or not voting. Despite the strength of the anti-Semitic Ku Klux Klan, all Southern senators either voted for him or did not vote at all. In a show of partisan discipline and loyalty to Wilson, only one Democrat voted against Brandeis. La Follette, true to his word, voted for him, as did fellow progressive Republicans Miles Poindexter (R-WA) and George Norris.[65]

As his supporters hoped, and his opponents feared, Brandeis did bring his views with him to the court, serving as an anchor for a small faction of justices who opposed the *Lochner* status quo. For most of his tenure, he was unable to sway the court over to his way of thinking. However, his opinions and ideology would eventually prevail, bringing about the demise of *Lochner* and the creation of a more activist court that tried to protect the less powerful. And, to the chagrin of his anti-Semitic critics, Brandeis would blaze a path for other Jewish justices, including Benjamin Cardozo, Felix Frankfurter, and Ruth Bader Ginsburg.

[63] "A Timeline of Louis D. Brandeis' Confirmation, Part 1," *Brandeis and Harlan Watch*, https://brandeiswatch.wordpress.com/2020/08/04/a-timeline-of-louis-d-brandeiss-confirmation-part-1/, accessed June 5, 2024. Also: "A Most Controversial Nominee: Louis Brandeis," https://fascinatingpolitics.com/2022/03/27/a-most-controversial-nominee-louis-brandeis/, accessed June 5, 2024.

[64] Harris, supra, 112–113.

[65] "To confirm the nomination of Louis D. Brandeis, to be an associate justice of the Supreme Court of the U.S.," *Govtrack.us*, https://www.govtrack.us/congress/votes/64-1/s147, accessed June 5, 2025.

"Sons of the Wild Jackass"

There was another confirmation battle—one that occurred immediately before Parker's attempted elevation that, in retrospect, seemed like a clear warning sign that senators were spoiling for a fight.

On February 3, 1930, after months of sharply declining health, Taft resigned his beloved chief justiceship and made his dying wish known to Hoover that Charles Evans Hughes be his replacement. It wouldn't be the first time that Hughes followed in Taft's footsteps.

Having previously served as an associate justice for six years, Hughes resigned from the court in 1916 to succeed Taft as the Republican nominee for president. That year, Republicans had looked for a compromise candidate who would be acceptable to both the progressives who had bolted the party in 1912 to support Theodore Roosevelt and the more conservative members who had stayed behind to back Taft. Hughes was their choice to unify the party, and the move nearly paid off. The judge came within a few thousand votes of defeating the incumbent Wilson—had he won California, a state carried by Roosevelt in 1912, Hughes would have won the election.

After that disappointment, Hughes went into private practice, where he helped build his law firm into one of the biggest in the country (known today as Hughes Hubbard & Reed, the firm is still among the largest firms in the country by gross revenue and lawyer headcount). During that time, Hughes represented several large companies and institutions—as is standard among the major law firms in the country. He had also served as secretary of state for four years under Presidents Harding and Coolidge.

Hughes was widely seen as a good, if not safe, choice for the court. His legal credentials were top notch, and he was well-known with Republicans, many of whom had campaigned for him in 1916. While some were surprised that Hoover had not chosen to elevate his close friend Justice Stone, Hughes' appointment was met with widespread acclaim.[66] "Never

[66] Charles Rappleye, *Herbert Hoover In The White House: The Ordeal Of The Presidency* (New York: Simon & Schuster, 2016), 139–140. At one point, a Hoover aide strode into a room full of reporters in the White House and, in an audible whisper, said that Stone was the choice. When Hughes got the nod, that led to speculation that Hoover had offered the job to Hughes as a courtesy, fully expecting him to turn it down, only to be surprised when Hughes accepted.

was there a clearer case of the office seeking the man," *The New York Times* stated.[67]

When Hughes' nomination was first considered by the Senate, it seemed like it would be another in a long line of rubber stamp confirmations. While Hughes thought that his political career might engender some opposition, Hoover had no such concerns and was supremely confident that the nomination would sail through the Senate.[68] But then Hughes ran into the infamous "Sons of the Wild Jackass."

Perhaps it's stating the obvious, but the term was not exactly one of endearment. Consisting of several western progressive populist senators who could be unpredictable and never shied away from a fight—especially with their own parties—the Sons often served as thorns in the side of the ruling GOP. The bipartisan group included the likes of Wheeler, La Follette, Hiram Johnson (R-CA), who was Theodore Roosevelt's Progressive Party running mate in 1912, and some others. But two senators were seen as the leaders: George Norris and William Borah.

Borah was the senior of the two—at least when it came to service in the Senate. First elected in 1907 by the Idaho legislature, Borah was a colorful figure who had made his name as a lawyer before embarking on a career in politics. Handling a lot of criminal cases, both as a defense attorney and prosecutor, Borah built a successful practice and soon became a well-known, in demand lawyer. In 1907, before heading to Washington, he tried Big Bill Haywood, a labor organizer accused of conspiring to murder former Idaho Governor Frank Steunenberg. Going against the legendary Clarence Darrow, Borah lost the case. However, he made national headlines for his prosecution, which included an eloquent summation that helped set the stage for his political career.

That same year, Borah also found himself on the other end of the law, being indicted for conspiring to defraud the federal government out of 17,280 acres of timber lands. Under the federal Timber and Stone Act, a citizen could buy a limited amount of timber land for their own exclusive and personal use. In this case, a number of individuals then transferred their deeds to Borah's clients, the Barber Company, drawing the ire of the federal government, which indicted Borah along with several others.

[67] Quoted in Rappleye, supra, 139.

[68] James Simon, *FDR and Chief Justice Hughes: The President, the Supreme Court, and the Epic Battle Over the New Deal* (New York: Simon & Schuster, 2012), 178.

Meanwhile, the deceased Steunenberg was also named in the indictment—a move that raised eyebrows considering the Haywood trial was about to start. Indeed, the prosecution reeked of politics, and Borah and his allies believed the true motivation behind it was to prevent him from officially taking his seat in the Senate.[69]

Borah went on the offensive and pushed for a quick trial so that his fate would be resolved, one way or another, before he was scheduled to take his seat in the Senate in December 1907. The gamble paid off and Borah was acquitted after less than 15 minutes of deliberations. People in Boise rejoiced and celebrated while Borah expressed his gratitude to his supporters, vowing that he would always protect their welfare and interests.[70]

Senate Republicans had expected Borah to fall in line when he arrived in Washington. Instead, he bucked the party by staking out progressive positions—especially on labor issues, where he became a strong ally to unions. Perhaps his colleagues should have known that Borah would not be so receptive to party discipline. After all, he had bolted the party in 1896 to support William Jennings Bryan, whose free silver policies were popular in the silver mining state of Idaho.

That was only the start of his spotty record when it came to backing his party's nominee for president, giving life to the phrase "with friends like these, you don't need any enemies." In 1912, he initially supported Roosevelt but, after Roosevelt left to form the Progressive Party, Borah refused to join him and stayed in the GOP. Despite that, he also refused to endorse Taft, staking out an ambiguous middle ground that satisfied followers of neither candidate. After endorsing and campaigning for, ironically enough, Hughes in 1916, Borah would only do that for one other GOP nominee: Herbert Hoover in 1928.

Some of that intransigence was due to personal ambition. Despite his independent streak, Borah had long harbored presidential ambitions and had hoped to be nominated by the Republicans. However, many in the party distrusted him and refused to support him. He ran in 1928, but he quickly realized he could not win and threw his support to Hoover. Finally, in 1936, four years before his death, he made one last attempt to

69 Marian McKenna, *Borah* (Ann Arbor, MI: University of Michigan Press, 1961), 64–69.

70 McKenna, supra, 78–80.

win the presidency and actually won some primaries, but came up short to Kansas Governor Alfred Landon. Borah refused to endorse him as Landon lost in a landslide that fall.

Another reason why he had trouble campaigning loyally for his party's standard bearer was because, in some cases, he was closer to the Democrats. When Franklin D. Roosevelt first ran in 1932, Borah pointedly refused to endorse Hoover, an action that was seen as a quasi-endorsement of the Democratic nominee. Borah also supported aspects of the New Deal, lending credence to the theory that he wasn't all that broken up about seeing FDR in the White House.

When he wasn't focused on the presidency, he made his mark as a legislator. He helped pass the Sixteenth and Seventeenth Amendments, which allowed for income taxes to be levied by the government and the direct popular election of senators respectively. "Borah, thus, secured for himself a life option on a seat in the Senate," Marian McKenna wrote in *Borah*.[71] Indeed, Borah would be elected by the people of the Idaho four times after the enactment of the Seventeenth Amendment in 1913, and never got less than 63% of the vote.

From his perch on the Foreign Relations Committee, Borah argued that the United States should stay out of World War I. After the United States finally entered the war, he supported the effort but helped lead the fight against the League of Nations alongside several other senators in a group that became known as "The Irreconcilables." Believing that membership of the League of Nations would force the country into a never-ending series of foreign entanglements, the Irreconcilables engineered the rejection of the Treaty of Versailles in the Senate and successfully kept the United States out of the League, essentially turning the League into a paper tiger. As World War II drew near, Borah became an implacable isolationist, even hoping to visit Germany and speak to Adolf Hitler directly to see if they could resolve their differences. Even after Germany invaded Poland in 1939, Borah lamented that "if I could have only talked to Hitler—all this might have been averted."[72]

Norris, on the other hand, was a little more low-key than his compatriot. First elected to the House of Representatives in 1902, the Republican Norris established himself as a progressive and reformer—someone

[71] McKenna, supra, 110.

[72] McKenna, supra, 360.

who wasn't afraid to exercise his independence from his party. Norris broke with his party on issues including tariffs, railway regulation, and support for labor unions. Never as popular or powerful within his home state the way Borah was in Idaho, Norris survived a near defeat in 1908, squeaking by his Democratic opponent by a mere 22 votes—a result he attributed to lukewarm support from the national GOP because of said independent streak.[73]

His resistance to partisan discipline caused him to clash with the autocratic Speaker of the House Joseph Gurney Cannon (R-IL). The speaker, who wielded near absolute power to the point where he once simply ignored a voice vote that didn't go his way and unilaterally declared his side the winners, was a conservative who often stymied much of Roosevelt's and Taft's progressive agenda.[74] Both presidents, along with many members of the House and Senate, wanted nothing more than to see Cannon deposed, but they understood they couldn't take him on unless they were certain of winning.

Finally, in 1910, they saw their opening—and it was Norris who led the charge. After Cannon surprisingly lost a vote, demonstrating his weakness, Norris made his move. Cannon's power emanated from his chairmanship of the House Rules Committee, which determined which bills were debated on the floor and how much time representatives would have for debate. Norris introduced a resolution to replace all the members of the Rules Committee and ban the speaker from being an *ex officio* member. Cannon tried to stall the ensuing vote but ended up losing. The speaker was able to defeat a subsequent motion to vacate the chair, but his power had been broken, and neither he nor subsequent speakers ever wielded the same level of control. "I had no personal feeling against the Speaker," Norris said.[75] "My opposition was solely to his frightful abuse of power."

After one more term in the House, Norris was elected to the Senate in 1912, where he would serve five terms, including a victory in 1936 in which he ran as an independent. Norris supported Roosevelt for the GOP

[73] George Norris, *Fighting Liberal: The Autobiography of George Norris* (New York: The MacMillan Company, 1945), 91–92.

[74] "Cannon, Joseph G." In *Congress A to Z*, 6th ed. edited by McCutcheon, Chuck, 78, American Government A to Z Series. Washington, DC: CQ Press, 2014. https://sk.sagepub.com/ency/edvol/congress-a-to-z-6e/chpt/cannon-joseph-g. "The Ayes make the most noise, but the Nays have it," he once ruled.

[75] Norris, supra, 118.

nomination for president in 1912 and, like Borah, refused to bolt for the Progressive Party. After Wilson's election that year, Norris supported some of the new president's agenda, but drew the line at entering World War I. Unlike Borah, who ultimately backed entry into the war, Norris was one of only six who voted against the declaration of war. After Germany's defeat, Norris became one of the Irreconcilables along with Borah and some of their other Progressive colleagues, like La Follette and Johnson.

Norris also had a hand in passing some important pieces of legislation, including a bill to build a dam and an electric power system in the Tennessee River at Muscle Shoals that was vetoed by Presidents Coolidge and Hoover but served as the basis for Franklin D. Roosevelt's New Deal initiative, the Tennessee Valley Authority, in 1933. He also worked with Representative Fiorello La Guardia (R-NY) to pass a law outlawing "yellow-dog" contracts, a practice whereby employers would force prospective employees to agree not to join a union during the pendency of their employment, and prohibiting federal courts from issuing injunctions in nonviolent labor disputes.

"It embodies only matters of simple justice," Norris said of the Norris-La Guardia Act, which was signed into law by Hoover in 1932.[76] "The right of men to organize for the improvement of conditions under which they labor should not be open to question." These yellow-dog contracts (so named because organized labor believed they reduced workers to the same level as a yellow dog) would prove to be pivotal regarding Parker's nomination—had this law been in effect at the time, he might have won confirmation to the court.

Norris and Borah hadn't always been in agreement when it came to Supreme Court nominations. For instance, Norris had supported Brandeis while Borah did not vote on the final roll call, but had voted against the nomination in the Judiciary Committee.[77] As for Stone's confirmation, the roles were reversed, with Norris warning that the nominee would be a tool of big business and special interests, like many of his fellow nominees from the Harding and Coolidge Administrations, and Borah

[76] Norris, supra, 315.

[77] Paper, supra, 238.

supporting a man he considered a leading liberal and a fine attorney general.[78]

For Hughes, though, they were very much on the same page—eventually. At first, Norris seemed fine with the nomination, even saying that he had no objection.[79] But after a week went by and the Senate tried to approve the nomination by acclamation, Norris objected and launched into a lengthy denunciation of Hughes. In fact, Norris took his task so seriously, he claimed it was the only time he ever wrote a floor speech in advance. "I felt the distinction that had come to [Hughes] required that I write what I intended to say so that there could be no possible misunderstanding or misinterpretation of my words," he recounted in his autobiography.[80]

As with Brandeis' contentious nomination, the Hughes fight was about more than the individual being voted on. In this case, Norris, Borah, and their allies were concerned that putting Hughes on the court would strengthen the existing conservative majority that seemingly lived to free businesses from burdensome governmental regulations. "We have reached a time in our history when the power and influence of monopoly and organized wealth are reaching into every government activity," Norris warned. "Perhaps it is not far amiss to say that no man in public life so exemplifies the influence of powerful combinations in the political and financial world as does Mr. Hughes." Norris pointed out that, since going into private practice, Hughes had appeared before his old colleagues at the court 54 times and almost always represented big, wealthy companies.

However, Norris went further, arguing these clients obviously retained Hughes because of his relationships with justices on the court, and this perceived influence allowed Hughes to charge nearly unlimited fees for himself. Norris stopped short of accusing either Hughes or his clients of engaging in any improper or unethical conduct—instead claiming that Hughes' views would, inevitably, become clouded because of his close relationships with wealthy clients. "[I]t is only fair to say that the man who lives this kind of a life, whose practice brings him wealthy clients and

78 Harris supra, 118–119.

79 Rappleye, supra, 140.

80 Norris, supra, 374.

monopolistic corporations seeking special governmental favor, it is reasonable to expect that these influences have become a part of the man," he said.[81]

Borah, meanwhile, cited *United Railways & Electric Co. of Baltimore v. West*, a Supreme Court decision that had come down the previous month, as his reason for opposing Hughes. In that case, United Railways had challenged a rule fixing rates so that carriers would earn a profit of 6.26%. United had sought a higher rate so that it would get a 7.44% profit, and the majority sided with them, finding that the 6.26% rate was confiscatory and a deprivation of property in violation of their substantive due process rights.[82]

"I do not know of a proposition of more concern to all the people of the United States than the relationship which the owners of these properties and these natural resources and means of transportation shall bear to the masses of the people of the United States. It is one of the great unsolved problems yet to be finally settled by the Supreme Court," Borah said during his February 11, 1930, speech.[83]

After citing Brandeis' dissent, Borah then claimed Hughes would have voted with the majority because his views were clear on these types of matters. "Justice Hughes is associated in his views with the contention which is sustained by the majority, and which, in the end, if earned to its logical conclusion, must result in great economic oppression to the people of the United States," he said, adding that such views should not be "incorporated in and made a permanent part of our legal and economic system."[84]

Ordinarily, Norris, Borah, and the other anti-Hughes senators might have been summarily ignored. But thanks to the stock market crash the previous year and the worsening economy, their warnings now resonated. All of a sudden, Hughes' work for big business became an issue and obscured his fairly progressive record from his first stint on the court, including votes to uphold state minimum wage and workers' compensation laws while taking an expansive view of the Interstate Commerce

81 Ibid.

82 *United Railways & Electric Co. of Baltimore v. West*, 280 U.S. 234 (1930).

83 Senator Borah, speaking on the nomination of Charles Evans Hughes to be Chief Justice of the Supreme Court, on February 11, 1930, 71st Cong., 2nd Session, Congressional Record.

84 Ibid.

Clause. He had also joined the majority in *Guinn v. United States* (1915), a case that had outlawed the use of grandfather clauses to determine eligibility to vote. Ironically enough, his progressive streak had caused some Southerners to oppose him, including his future court colleague Hugo Black (D-AL).

Meanwhile, Hughes' concern that his political past might engender some opposition proved to be well-founded. Norris had argued that Hughes' initial resignation from the court to run for president made him a politician, and putting him back on the court would hurt its integrity by making it into a more partisan organization.[85] The argument landed with some of Norris' Democratic colleagues, particularly Carter Glass (D-VA).[86]

Members of the anti-Hughes coalition may have had another big reason for wanting to pick a fight with the White House over the nomination. The previous year, the highly contentious and controversial Smoot-Hawley Tariff[87] had made its way through the House and Senate, and its eventual passage in June 1930 had been rife with bitterness and anger. A similar coalition made up of western and midwestern progressives led by Borah and Norris and a group of Southern conservatives had advocated for more protection for farmers, while accusing some of their colleagues of only caring about industrial tariffs. Indeed, it was during this fight that Senator George Moses (R-NH) first used the "sons of the wild jackass" epithet to describe Borah and Norris and others.[88]

Not helping was Hoover and his vacillating views regarding the tariff. During his presidential campaign, Hoover had called for increasing

[85] Senator Norris, speaking on the nomination of Charles Evans Hughes to be Chief Justice of the Supreme Court, on February 10, 1930, 71st Cong., 2nd Session, Congressional Record.

[86] Simon, supra, 179.

[87] "To Pass H.R. 2667," *Govtrack.us*, www.govtrack.us/congress/votes/71–2/s295, accessed December 5, 2023.

[88] "Sons of the Wild Jackass Remark is Clarified by Senator Moses," *The Baltimore Sun*, November 10, 1929. Apparently, Senator Burton K. Wheeler took offense to the remark, accusing Moses of calling them "sons of wild jackasses." Moses clarified that he said "sons of the wild jackass," which, as the article goes into quite a bit depth explaining, can be interpreted metaphorically and was not necessarily a literal statement of fact alleging that Wheeler, Norris, Borah, and their allies were actually related by blood to wild jackasses. Another theory is that Moses could have referred to the wild jackass, an animal indigenous to parts of Africa and Asia.

protective tariffs on agricultural goods. Once it was clear that the tariff rates for agricultural goods would be smaller than those for industrial goods, the Sons had proposed a compromise known as export debentures. In other words, the government would pay farmers a subsidy on their exports that was about half the tariff rate.

Hoover opposed debenture, likening it to a governmental handout. However, Borah and others claimed Hoover had privately told them he would accept it for the sake of forging a compromise, only for the president to then publicly stab them in the back. Some historians have disputed this. Nevertheless, relations between the progressives and Hoover worsened, with Borah and others feeling frozen out by the White House and turned into fall guys once the Depression hit. "Hoover sided with conservatives and accused Borah's coalition of causing business uncertainty and impeding recovery after the stock market panic in the fall of 1929. Borah bitterly resented this imputation, which steadily widened the gulf between him and Hoover," McKenna wrote in *Borah*.[89]

The bill eventually passed with tariff increases for agricultural goods; however, the rates for industrial goods were higher and seen to be more protective. Therefore, the Sons of the Wild Jackass and their allies ended up voting against passage. The bill was then signed into law on June 17, 1930, by Hoover despite the president's own misgivings about it, as well as against the advice of thousands of economists and business leaders.

Norris and his allies were outraged by the tariff, claiming it had been conceived and written by big business to further solidify their power at the expense of ordinary Americans. Vowing that the tariff would live in infamy, Norris charged that "those who are behind it will see that they have used their own power to bring about their own destruction."[90]

Norris' warnings proved prescient, as the Smoot-Hawley (or Hawley-Smoot) Tariff's legacy has been that of economic destruction and despair. The longtime consensus among economists is that the tariff exacerbated the effects of the Great Depression. Others, including Douglas Irwin, have argued that the tariff's role was fairly minor, and that bank failures and deflation played a much greater role in turning a recession into a depression. Nevertheless, Smoot-Hawley resulted in a trade war as other

[89] McKenna, supra, 265.

[90] Douglas Irwin, "The Hawley-Smoot Tariff and the Great Depression, 1928–1932," in *Clashing Over Commerce: A History of U.S. Trade Policy*, ed. Douglas Irwin (Chicago: University of Chicago Press, 2017).

countries retaliated against the tariffs and is widely seen as a mistake in American history. For decades, it served as a form of shorthand for bad policy, economic myopia, and even outright mockery,[91] as well as a cautionary tale for any politician thinking about bringing back protective tariffs—at least until Donald Trump's presidency.

Borah, Norris, and other anti-Smoot-Hawley progressives had felt abandoned by the White House during the lengthy debate over the bill and were eager to make a point over it. "Charles Evans Hughes was not the monopolists' shill that the Senate insurgents were gunning for, and they knew it. As much as Norris and Borah blasted away at Hughes, the obvious target was the White House. The president had deserted them in the tariff fight, and now they were frustrated with the court appointment," Rappleye wrote in *Herbert Hoover in the White House: The Ordeal of the Presidency*.

In the end, they came up short, and, ten days after he was first nominated, Charles Evans Hughes was confirmed as chief justice by a 52–26 margin.[92] Far from being a rubber stamp for big business, Chief Justice Hughes would compile a fairly moderate-to-liberal record, serving, along with Justice Owen Roberts, as one of two swing votes on a sharply divided court featuring the archconservative Four Horsemen and their ideological foes, the Three Musketeers, consisting of Brandeis, Stone, and Cardozo.

The Hughes vote significantly raised the stakes of Parker's confirmation—and gave disgruntled senators and concerned interest groups more incentive to make a stand. It also previewed some of the tactics that would be used against Parker and made the earlier prognostications of an easy confirmation look like wishful or delusional thinking. "I hope that some of the coalition radicals in the Senate are now beginning to be ashamed at the Pandora's Box of Horrors which they opened up in their unseemly and disgusting assault on Chief Justice Hughes," said Sidney S. Alderman in a letter to Parker following the latter's nomination.[93] "Now that the box has been opened up, it seems that every judicial appointment of one who has previously served on the bench is to be an opportunity for all

[91] Dave Barry, *Dave Barry Slept Here: A Sort of History of the United States* (New York: Fawcett Columbine, 1989), 112–116, 123.

[92] "To Advise and Consent to the Nomination of Charles Evans Hughes to be Chief Justice of the United States," *Govtrack.us*, www.govtrack.us/congress/votes/71-2/s175, accessed December 5, 2023.

[93] Parker Papers, supra, Letter from Alderman to Parker, March 31, 1930.

disgruntled litigants to use the ancient prerogative of cussing the court, and in a very public and prominent manner.”

CHAPTER 5

Beware of Yellow Dog: Organized Labor Mobilizes

On April 2, 1930, a profile of John J. Parker written by Rodney Dutcher for the Newspaper Enterprise Association was published in various papers throughout the country. Designed to help readers learn more about the nominee, the article contained an in-depth description of Parker's character and demeanor. For instance, the story noted that Parker rarely ever smoked or drank alcohol, and his only habit seemed to be that he carried a cane in public. He spoke with a heavy Southern accent and was well-known throughout North Carolina for having a "strong reputation for righteousness and ability." He was also very proud of being a Sunday School teacher at his Episcopalian church in Charlotte and almost never missed the weekly luncheon at the local Kiwanis Club. He was a serious person (the earlier anecdote about how he was referred to as "John" and not "Jack" came from this piece), and while he possessed a politician's gift for the jocular, he was, in actuality, a low-key, cultured man with a deep reservoir of inner strength and resilience.

The article also listed his various accomplishments over the years and noted his status as the workhorse of the Fourth Circuit while casting him as a "middle of the road" type of person and judge who was always well-prepared and knowledgeable. At the end, there was a paragraph that contained information from Henry Horace Williams, a professor of philosophy at UNC and one of his mentors in college. According to the story, Williams had advised Hoover that Parker when it came to

V. Li, *Supreme Pressure*,
https://doi.org/10.1007/978-3-032-07864-3_5

the struggle between human rights and property/contract rights, Parker would "give first consideration to human rights."[1]

Perhaps the story should have started with that instead of burying the lede.

That's because, by the time the story came out, storm clouds were already forming on the horizon that would eventually wash away any chance he had of becoming a Supreme Court justice. Perhaps if the story had made the case more forcefully that Parker was not some *laissez faire* disciple enthralled with maintaining the status quo, it might have undermined at least one major avenue of attack against him.

Of course, not all storms are big ones or capable of doing much, if any, damage. In fact, the first such cloudburst was hardly worth breaking out an umbrella. The day after Parker's nomination was announced, Mary W.F. Speers, president of Speers Sand and Clay Works, Inc., sent a letter to several senators, including Overman. Alleging that oil interests had placed Parker on the circuit court and were now conspiring to get him a promotion, Speers complained that the judge, along with his colleagues, had the temerity to issue an unsigned *per curiam* opinion in a foreclosure case involving her company.[2] While claiming not to question his credentials and ability, Speers, nonetheless, argued that there was no way learned, responsible judges would dare issue an unsigned opinion in such an important case as hers unless they were biased or prejudiced. In her long and rambling letter, Speers also accused Parker of being a "wet" and claimed that how she was treated would not play well with the millions of women voters in the country.[3]

Overman, who would serve as chairman of the Senate Judiciary subcommittee in charge of handling Parker's nomination, was dismissive of Speers' letter, telling Parker that she wrote like "she must be half cracked."[4] Nevertheless, he advised Parker not to take any chances and answer her charges in a letter. Parker did so, stating that her case

[1] Rodney Dutcher, "New Appointee to U.S. Supreme Court Is Called a Middle-of-the-Road Man," *The Reading Times*, April 3, 1930.

[2] A *per curiam* opinion is a ruling issued by a court that is presented collectively by the court as a whole, rather than being authored by a specific judge. Oftentimes, courts will use them to dispense with cases they see as fairly routine and noncontroversial.

[3] Parker Papers, supra, Letter from Mary W.F. Speers to Senator Lee Overman, March 22, 1930.

[4] Parker Papers, supra, Letter from Overman to Parker, March 24, 1920.

had been straightforward and did not involve any complicated applications of the law, which was why they disposed of it with a *per curiam* opinion. He also pointed out that Speers had represented herself, and the judges had given her extra latitude and leeway because they understood she didn't have professional legal training or experience. As for his position on Prohibition, Parker was dumbfounded as to what Speers could have been referring to. He noted that he only took part in one case in which the Eighteenth Amendment was at issue, and the court held that it had been properly ratified.[5]

Speers' objection was not taken very seriously—nor was the next charge levied against Parker. A Virginia lawyer named William Werth, who represented the estate of a West Virginia man in a wrongful death lawsuit against the Appalachian Power Company, filed a protest with the Judiciary Committee. Werth, who had argued the case on appeal before the Fourth Circuit in 1927, took issue with Parker's ruling against his client. Was Werth upset about a matter of procedure, like Speers had been? Or did he allege improper bias or behavior on the judge's part? Did he claim Parker had objectionable political or ideological beliefs that he believed to be incompatible with serving on the High Court?

No. Werth was upset he lost before the Fourth Circuit and advised the committee to look into the matter. That was it. Needless to say, the committee was not impressed. According to the *Greensboro Daily News*, there was a similar grievance filed by another disgruntled lawyer who had come up short in Parker's courtroom. "Presumably the lawyers who were successful in these cases, and collected their fees, are happy, and are persuaded that Judge Parker will honor the Supreme Court by becoming a member thereof," *The Greensboro Daily News* opined.[6]

At around the same time, Overman informed Parker about a protest "sent almost as an anonymous letter" concerning his ruling in *Bluefield Water Works v. Public Service Commission*.[7] Involving the always controversial and contentious issue of public utility rates, Parker explained that the decision was a hyper-technical issue involving an application for an interlocutory, or temporary, injunction against enforcement of a rate

[5] Parker Papers, Letter from Parker to Overman, March 25, 1930.

[6] "Wednesday Selected Tentatively as Day for Parker Hearing," *The Greensboro Daily News*, March 30, 1930.

[7] Parker Papers, supra, Letter from Overman to Parker, March 28, 1930.

fixed by the Public Service Commission of West Virginia. Parker and his colleagues granted the injunction, meaning the fixed rates would not be applied while the case went forward. The judges also ruled that whatever Bluefield charged while the injunction was in effect should not exceed the previous rate by more than 10%. However, the letter protesting against Parker had misstated things, alleging that the judges had ruled that the commission was entitled to a return of at least 10%. Parker pointed out that distinction and also noted to Overman that the parties came to an out of court settlement before any more proceedings occurred—as such, there was no written opinion.[8]

Overman only brought up *Bluefield* because of what had happened during Hughes' recent confirmation fight, where the would-be chief had been heavily criticized in relation to a rate case that he hadn't even taken part in. Nevertheless, the senator was not terribly concerned about the *Bluefield* matter in relation to Parker's chances at confirmation. Helping matters was that he received a letter from the commission's lawyers saying that, while they disagreed with the decision, they felt Parker's conduct in the case was "beyond criticism" and that they were pleased to see his nomination to the Supreme Court.[9]

"I don't think there is any doubt about your being confirmed," Overman predicted to Parker in his March 28 letter, "but we may have to make a fight."[10]

In that same letter—almost as an aside—Overman informed Parker that organized labor was making a stink over an opinion he wrote in 1927 in the case of *International Organization, United Mine Workers of America, et al. v. Red Jacket Coal and Coke Company*.[11] The case involved yellow-dog contracts that Red Jacket Coal and Coke Company had their workers sign promising not to unionize. Union officials had long despised these yellow-dog contracts, arguing that workers had no choice but to sign them or risk losing their jobs and being unable to support themselves and their families. Additionally, they argued that once

[8] Parker Papers, supra, Letter from Parker to Overman, March 28, 1930.

[9] "Statement by Green Relates His Forces Will Wage Struggle," *The Greensboro Daily News*, March 29, 1930. Also: William J. Borah Papers, Letter from F.M. Livezey to Senator Overman, March 26, 1930.

[10] Parker Papers, supra, Letter from Overman to Parker, March 28, 1930.

[11] *International Organization, United Mine Workers of America, et al. v. Red Jacket Coal and Coke Company*, 18 F.2d 839 (4th Cir. 1927).

workers were gainfully employed, they were completely at the mercy of their bosses because they wouldn't be able to collectively bargain or go on strike without being replaced. However, at that point, they were still legal, and Parker and his brethren upheld an injunction against union officials who had tried to organize Red Jacket's workers despite the fact that they had signed the contracts.

As with the other protests, Overman wasn't worried and made another prediction to Parker. "I have read the so-called *Red Jacket* case and am satisfied you decided the case right according to the law," he said.[12] "I think we can satisfy the committee as to all of that."

"Tempted to Strike"

Under normal circumstances, John J. Parker wouldn't have even written the opinion that ended up undoing him.

The *Red Jacket* case originated in 1920, when Parker was running for governor of North Carolina. Union officials had tried to organize coal miners located in the Williamson-Thacker field in Mingo County, West Virginia. The field had always been non-union territory, and the companies working it had required their employees to sign contracts promising not to join unions. When the United Mine Workers of America (UMWA) called for a nationwide strike in the field, union officials in the Williamson-Thacker field tried to organize the non-unionized workers so they would walk out as well. Red Jacket and nearly 300 other companies then sued to enjoin the union from interfering with their operations.

That was only part of the story, though. Miners and union officials had been in conflict with coal companies since 1912, with the disputes often turning violent. In September 1912, for instance, West Virginia's governor had to declare martial law and send in state troops to keep hostilities between miners and companies from reaching a boiling point.

In this case, things came to a head when the companies, including Red Jacket, had fired the workers who had either refused to sign the yellow-dog contracts, joined a union or taken part in the strike. As part of that termination, they were required to vacate company-owned housing located near the mines. Knowing that things could get dangerous, the

[12] Parker Papers, supra, Letter from Overman to Parker, March 28, 1930.

company tasked the Bluefield, West Virginia-based Baldwin-Fetts Detective Agency, whose agents were known as union busters and "fearless mountain gunmen," with the task of physically removing the terminated workers and their families.[13]

On May 19, 1920, when they arrived in Matewan, Mingo County, to carry out the evictions, things went sideways. According to Lon Savage's *Thunder in the Mountains: The West Virginia Mine War, 1920–21*, the agents, who included Lee and Albert Felts, brothers of the agency's co-founder and director, behaved in a heavy-handed manner, throwing women and children out into the street and tossing their belongings and furniture out with them. The stories spread and, like a game of "Telephone," became more and more outrageous with each telling (pregnant women, sick children, newborn infants, all kicked out of their warm, safe homes on a cold and rainy day). Some of the townsfolk got enraged, including Police Chief Sid Hatfield (a member of the famed Hatfield clan) and Mayor Cabell Testerman. The two officials and some miners confronted the agents and questioned whether they had the authority to do this. After some more back and forth, both the police chief and the agents tried to arrest each other, eventually resulting in a gunfight that killed seven agents and three townspeople, including the mayor.[14]

> When the [Battle of Matewan] ended, the streets were lined with dead and dying. Men hid beneath railroad boxcars, behind walls and trees and in ditches. Both Felt brothers, five other detectives, and two miners had been killed, and Mayor Testerman lay dying on a cot, ministered to by his wife. Five others had been wounded.
>
> Moments later, the five o'clock train, No. 16, pulled into Matewan, and the engineer and passengers looked out, wide eyed, at the bodies lying in a row on the street before them. Sid, his guns back in their holsters, walked among them, searching the bodies. As he stood over the remains of Al Felts, he brandished the warrant for the detective's arrest and said, "Now, you son of a bitch, I'll serve it on you."[15]

[13] Peter Graham Fish, "Red Jacket Revisited: The Case that Unraveled John J. Parker's Supreme Court Appointment," *Law and History Review* 5, no. 1 (1987), 60–62.

[14] Lon Savage, *Thunder in the Mountains: The West Virginia Mine War, 1920–21* (Pittsburgh: University of Pittsburgh Press, 1990), 20–22.

[15] Ibid., 24.

That wasn't the end of the violence. Sid Hatfield was killed by a group of Baldwin-Felts agents in August 1921, months after he was acquitted of murdering Albert Felts. Later that month, miners started arming themselves and organizing in Logan County, West Virginia. Not to be outdone, the county's anti-union, politically connected sheriff, Don Chafin, began building up his forces and placed them throughout Blair Mountain. By the end of the month, armed fighting broke out between miners and Chafin's forces, with the latter even utilizing World War I surplus poison gas and bombs. The federal government sent in troops in early September, after which the fighting petered out.

The Battle of Blair Mountain ended up having huge repercussions for the UMWA—mostly bad ones. The union's membership in the state declined from 50,000 in 1920 to about 600 in 1929, while nationwide, it went from 600,000 to 100,000 by the end of the 1920s.[16] There were also criminal charges for the people involved, as Logan County grand juries handed down over 1,200 indictments, including over 300 murder charges and two dozen indictments for treason. Hundreds of union miners went to jail; however, some West Virginia counties were more favorable to their cause and defendants there saw plenty of acquittals or dismissals. For his part, Sid Hatfield, who helped cause the Battle of Matewan and whose murder helped spark the Battle of Blair Mountain, ended up being memorialized as a martyr and defender of workers' rights.[17]

"No backward step was taken but the ground lost by the union became a landslide into the gutter for the union," Fred Mooney, a Mingo County union organizer later recounted, playing off UMWA President John Lewis' confrontational motto "no backward step."[18]

So, it was against that backdrop that Red Jacket's lawsuit made its way through the courts. First, it went before Judge McClintic. Long known as an anti-labor judge who had once called union officials "enemies and

[16] Abby Lee Hood, "What Made the Battle of Blair Mountain the Largest Labor Uprising in American History," *Smithsonian Magazine*, www.smithsonianmag.com/history/battle-blair-mountain-largest-labor-uprising-american-history-180978520/, August 25, 2021, accessed: July 9, 2024. Also, Robert Shogan, *The Battle for Blair Mountain: The Story of America's Largest Labor Uprising* (New York: Perseus Books Group, 2004).

[17] Savage, supra, 165–167.

[18] Shogan, supra.

traitors to America"[19] McClintic issued a sweeping temporary injunction in 1922 that forbade union officials from doing anything that would "interfere with the right of such employees and those seeking employment to work," including "counseling and advising that these plaintiffs should in any way or manner be injured in the conduct and management of their business and in the enjoyment of their property and property rights."[20] The case was finally tried in 1923 and McClintic ruled in favor of Red Jacket and the other companies. Two years later, he issued a final judgment that included a permanent injunction against union officials that, among other things, prohibited them from interfering with the companies' employees in any manner, whether it be through violence, threats of abuse or even peaceful means, that could affect their employers' ability to conduct and manage their business and enjoy their property and property rights.[21]

The Fourth Circuit finally heard the appeal in 1926. Consisting of Parker, Waddill and Rose, union officials had reason to hope the appellate court might vacate or limit McClintic's injunction. Parker, after all, had expressed strong support for organized labor during his political career, saying during his 1920 campaign: "Laboring men have a right to organize. They have a right to strike. They have a right collectively to enter into agreements with their employers. These rights are fundamental and should not be abridged by the state." Waddill had also expressed prolabor sentiments during his prior political career, which included one term in the U.S. House of Representatives as a Republican.[22]

Meanwhile, Rose was seen as the most progressive judge on the court and the most sympathetic towards organized labor, having expressed support for a national child labor ban, employer liability legislation and other issues. Also seen as the intellectual powerhouse on the court—at least in the years prior to Parker's arrival—Rose was an expert on federal civil procedure and jurisdiction, issues that were relevant to the *Red Jacket*

[19] Fish, "Red Jacket Revisited," supra, 65–66.

[20] *International Organization, United Mine Workers of America, et al. v. Red Jacket Coal and Coke Company*, supra.

[21] Ibid.

[22] Fish, "Red Jacket Revisited," supra, 67–68.

case. He had also written a prior opinion delicately handling a railway strike, making him the natural choice to handle this one.[23]

Unfortunately for everyone involved, Rose's health was failing and his ability to take part in the case was in question. The elderly judge had been stricken with a heart attack in the spring of 1926 and was still recovering when he sat for oral arguments on the *Red Jacket* case that November. After the arguments, Parker, as was his *modus operandi* at the time as the youngest, healthiest member of the court, circulated a memorandum summarizing the key legal points of the *Red Jacket* case to his colleagues, what he thought the result should be and what the opinion should say. Parker's habit of doing this often led to him being assigned to write the actual opinion, since he would have already done much of the heavy lifting. It was a major reason why he had written so much more than his colleagues at the time.

In this instance, though, he made it clear that Rose should write the opinion if he were healthy. In a letter to Waddill, who as senior judge was in charge of assigning the opinion, Parker opined that, since the three of them saw eye-to-eye on the issues and outcome, it would be a good idea to let Rose write the opinion "if he wants to write it and is able to do so."[24]

Waddill, however, decided to assign the opinion to Parker. For one thing, Waddill was battling his own health issues and was not looking to create more work than necessary. For another, Rose had indicated he wanted to dismiss the case as to three of the union officials—something neither Waddill nor Parker believed was warranted.

More ominously, Waddill was perturbed by a letter Rose sent about the case stating that he did not "like the *Hitchman* case" and believed the Supreme Court knew it had gone too far. Rose went even further, saying that he hoped to limit "injunctions against peaceful persuasion to join the union"—at least as far as *Hitchman* would allow them to do so.[25]

So, what was this *Hitchman* case and why was Waddill so alarmed that Rose was expressing doubts about it? Decided by the Supreme Court in 1917, *Hitchman Coal & Coke Co. v. Mitchell* dealt with a similar set of facts as *Red Jacket*: A coal and coke company utilized non-union workers

[23] Ibid.

[24] Parker Papers, supra, Letter from Parker to Waddill, March 10, 1927.

[25] Parker Papers, supra, Letter from Rose to Parker, March 8, 1927.

in a West Virginia field who were bound by yellow-dog contracts, and the UMWA tried to unionize them. The court, in a 6–3 decision, upheld the legality of yellow-dog contracts and held that Hitchman Coal and Coke were entitled to an injunction forbidding UMWA officials from trying to induce their employees to break their contracts in order to unionize them. Union officials had made the case that, as long as their efforts were peaceful and nonviolent, then they were legal. But the court responded with a resounding defense of Hitchman's property rights. "In our opinion, any violation of plaintiff's legal rights contrived by defendants for the purpose of inflicting damage, or having that as its necessary effect, is as plainly inhibited by the law as if it involved a breach of the peace," wrote Justice Mahlon Pitney for the majority.[26]

With its near-identical set of facts, Parker and Waddill saw *Hitchman* as directly controlling for *Red Jacket* and felt obligated to follow it. As lower court judges, it wasn't their place to try to limit it, express disapproval of it or carve out exceptions to it. As Waddill told Parker, if the Supreme Court wanted to limit *Hitchman* and carve out an exception for peaceful activity, then "they should do it, not us."[27]

Nevertheless, Rose tried to warn Parker that the situation was not as cut and dried as which precedent controlled and how closely it should be followed. Perhaps understanding the level of emotion and anger felt by organized labor and cognizant of the recent spate of violence, Rose stated that the case may have been straightforward from a legal perspective, but not when looking through the lens of "ultimate justice." "The peculiar facts of the situation in these mining hamlets make impossible the doing of real justice or at all events the preservation of the neutrality of the Courts in the industrial pursuit," Rose wrote in his March 8 letter to Parker.[28]

So, with that in mind, Parker got to work. Balancing *Red Jacket* with a complex patent case, he worked diligently and painstakingly to finish both opinions. The opinion turned out to be quite an ordeal for Parker, who told Rose that he was "tempted to strike" from the assignment. He also told his senior colleague: "You are the only man that I know who

[26] *Hitchman Coal & Coke Co. v. Mitchell*, 245 U.S. 229 (1917).

[27] Parker Papers, Letter from Waddill to Parker, March 12, 1927.

[28] Letter from Rose to Parker, supra.

can handle the questions involved in this case as they really ought to be handled."[29]

It's not known whether Rose ever saw that letter, which was dated March 24, 1927. Two days after that listed date, Rose passed away at the age of 65. When it came to the *Red Jacket* decision, Parker and Waddill opted not to have the case re-argued since Rose's death did not change the outcome—a ruling in favor of Red Jacket and other companies and against the union by upholding McClintic's injunction. Parker and Waddill had been adamant that *Hitchman* controlled the case, and Rose's doubts or negative feelings about the case were immaterial.

For Parker, the main issue in the case centered on whether the district court had jurisdiction to issue its injunction in the first place. McClintic had taken it as an article of faith that the union had illegally engaged in a conspiracy in violation of the Sherman Antitrust Act to "monopolize and control all labor in the United States and on the American continent engaged in the work of mining and producing coal," which would have the effect of restraining or restricting the production, trade, and shipment of coal in interstate commerce.[30]

Writing in his usual economic, straightforward style (Parker even assured Waddill in a letter dated April 7, 1927, that his opinion was only 18 pages in length and was about "as short as is expedient"[31]), Parker felt McClintic had overreached in portraying unions as engaging in illegal activities per se—especially when it was well-established that workers had the right to organize. Instead, Parker noted that the Supreme Court had long held that labor organizations were legitimate and that "such an organization shall not be held in itself—merely because of its existence and operation—to be an illegal combination or conspiracy in restraint of trade."[32]

That didn't mean Parker was sympathetic to the union's main argument as to why the district court lacked jurisdiction. The union's lawyers had argued that coal mining did not constitute interstate commerce and

[29] Parker Papers, Letter from Parker to Rose, March 24, 1927.

[30] Fish, Red Jacket Revisited, supra, 77, n. 157.

[31] Parker Papers, Letter from Parker to Waddill, April 7, 1927.

[32] *International Organization, United Mine Workers of America, et al. v. Red Jacket Coal and Coke Company*, supra, quoting *Duplex Printing Press Co. v. Deering*, 254 U.S. 443 (1921).

cited two recent Supreme Court precedents, including *UMWA v. Coronado Coal Co.* (aka "First *Coronado*") from 1922, which held that, even if unions prevented some coal from moving across state lines, it did not necessarily constitute an illegal restraint or restriction of commerce.[33]

As can probably be deduced by that case's nickname, there was a "Second *Coronado*." In that case, the Supreme Court ruled three years later that the first case had relied on erroneous facts and had severely understated the sheer volume of coal produced by the mines and earmarked for export. Therefore, the court found that coal mining could be interstate commerce if a substantial amount of coal was being blocked or hindered from moving out of state.[34]

In the *Red Jacket* case, Parker noted that the 316 companies named in the case produced 40 million tons a year, with over 90% of it going into interstate commerce. Therefore, Parker followed the reasoning of "Second *Coronado*" to determine that the union clearly intended to interfere with the shipment of coal to other states. "Interference with the production of these mines as contemplated by [the] defendants would necessarily interfere with interstate commerce in coal to a substantial degree," Parker wrote.[35] "Moreover, it is perfectly clear that the purpose of [the] defendants in interfering with production was to stop the shipments in interstate commerce."

With the Sherman Act violation established, Parker held that Red Jacket was clearly entitled to an injunction under the Clayton Antitrust Act. Ordinarily, this is where Parker would have relied on *Hitchman*, stating that the case was clearly binding precedent and following it without disapprobation or hesitation—as he and Waddill had spoken about in their letters to each other. This time, however, Parker stopped short of that. Maybe it was out of deference to his fallen colleague, or his own doubts about *Hitchman*.

Or maybe Parker was trying to square *Red Jacket* with a similar case that the Fourth Circuit had heard the previous year. In *Bittner v. West Virginia-Pittsburgh Coal Co.*, the UMWA were accused of using violence, threats, and coercion to unionize coal miners in West Virginia. The

[33] *United Mine Workers v. Coronado Co.*, 259 U.S. 344, 42 S. Ct. 570 (1922).

[34] *Coronado Co. v. U.M. Workers*, 268 U.S. 295, 45 S. Ct. 551 (1925).

[35] *International Organization, United Mine Workers of America, et al. v. Red Jacket Coal and Coke Company*, supra.

lower court issued a wide-ranging injunction forbidding the UMWA from trying to unionize the company's workers, enticing them to break their yellow-dog deals, using threats, coercion, or violence to get employees to leave the company, interfering with the company's employees in any way, and picketing or trespassing on company property.

In October 1926, Waddill wrote an opinion on behalf of himself, Rose, and Parker upholding the injunction by citing *Hitchman*. However, Waddill's opinion carved out an exception allowing unions to utilize peaceful persuasion to advocate for their cause. Waddill justified his limitation of *Hitchman* by citing several recent Supreme Court cases, most notably *American Steel Foundries v. Tri-City Central Trades Council*, which was handed down in 1921. That case did not involve a yellow-dog contract but did cover a strike and what unions could and could not do under federal law. Writing for a unanimous court, Chief Justice Taft held that unions could use peaceful persuasion to advocate for their cause and try and augment their numbers. Taft even waxed poetic about the importance of unions and how they were necessary to help single employees who were "helpless in dealing with an employer" and were "essential to give laborers [the] opportunity to deal on equality with their employer."[36]

In that vein, Waddill held that "in view of what was said by that court in *American Foundries Company v. Tri-City Council*, there can be no doubt as to the right of defendants to use all lawful propaganda to increase their membership."[37] Therefore, Waddill modified the injunction to allow for activities from unions that were "free from threats and other devices to intimidate."[38]

Perhaps in an effort to try and square away what Waddill had done in *Bittner* while still following *Hitchman*, Parker ended up citing *Tri-City* and several other cases to show that the court clearly believed unions were allowed to engage in certain types of conduct no matter what. "To make a speech or to circulate an argument under ordinary circumstances dwelling upon the advantages of union membership is one thing," Parker

[36] *American Steel Foundries v. Tri-City Central Trades Council*, 257 U.S. 184, 42 S. Ct. 72, 66 L. Ed. 189.

[37] *Bittner v. West Virginia-Pittsburgh Coal Co.*, 15 F.2d 652 (4th Cir. 1926).

[38] *Bittner*, supra.

wrote.[39] "To approach a company's employees, working under a contract not to join the union while remaining in the company's service, and induce them, in violation of their contracts, to join the union and go on a strike for the purpose of forcing the company to recognize the union or of impairing its power of production, is another and very different thing."

Ultimately, the distinction was academic since Parker found that the union had tried to induce workers to breach their yellow-dog contracts, which meant *Hitchman* applied and the injunction was justified. Despite reiterating at the very end that the court did not agree with all of McClintic's findings, Parker nevertheless upheld the injunction and ruled in favor of Red Jacket.

Predictably, UMWA lawyers appealed to the Supreme Court and argued that Parker had ignored the series of cases defending unions and their right to organize peacefully. Thanks to their new powers of discretionary review, the court passed on hearing the case. According to Fish, Justice Van Devanter, the court's expert on jurisdictional issues, did read Parker's opinion and thought it was correct.[40] Parker, himself, took the denial of certiorari to mean that the court agreed with his reasoning and did not see the need to step in. "Application for certiorari was denied, which in view of the importance of the case, meant not only that the Supreme Court thought that the decision was right but that the principles were so well settled as not to justify further discussion," he would argue in 1930 during his confirmation battle.[41]

"A Thunderbolt Out of a Clear Sky"

It may have been well settled to Parker, but William Green certainly begged to differ.

An Ohio coal miner by trade and blood (his father had been a coal miner as well), Green had steadily risen up the ranks of organized labor over the last decade. In 1911, he became the UMWA's international statistician, followed by promotion to UMWA secretary-treasurer two years later. He joined the executive council of the American Federation

[39] *Red Jacket*, supra.

[40] Fish, Red Jacket Revisited, supra, 100–101.

[41] Parker Papers, Letter from Parker to W.P. Stacy, April 11, 1930.

of Labor the following year and, in 1924, became president of the AFL, succeeding famed leader Samuel Gompers.

Unlike his predecessor, Green advocated a strategy of cooperation over confrontation. Green despised yellow-dog contracts and referred to *Hitchman* as the "*Dred Scott* decision to labor,"[42] invoking the infamous Supreme Court case that, essentially, upheld slavery and consigned all Blacks, free and enslaved, to second-class citizenship. However, he decided to fight his battle in the halls of Congress. Forging close relations with pro-labor politicians, Green advised on a number of important laws and reforms in the 1930s, including the Norris-LaGuardia Act, which outlawed the yellow-dog contracts he hated so much. He also helped get the National Labor Relations Act of 1935 passed, as well as the Fair Labor Standards Act of 1938.

When it came to judicial nominations, his strategy of cooperation only went so far. When Hughes was nominated for chief justice, Green and the AFL were concerned about the direction of the court and its tendency to protect businesses and property owners while upholding damaging injunctions against unions. Nevertheless, they decided to stay officially neutral after Green came to the conclusion that he felt Hughes could be a fair judge.

After Sanford passed, however, the AFL and Green felt the stakes had risen dramatically and decided to make their views clear to the president in the hopes of convincing him to nominate someone who would be more acceptable to organized labor. "I said our interest had increased; the fact they were placed there for life, that they rendered decisions that deeply affected the life of the people impelled me to come to see him," Green said.[43]

Shortly after Sanford's funeral, Green and other members of the AFL's executive committee met with Hoover and tried to advocate for William S. Kenyon, a U.S. circuit judge for the Eighth Circuit Court of Appeals, a former Republican U.S. senator from Iowa who, at one point, was considered as Calvin Coolidge's running mate in 1924. Appointed to the bench in 1922, Kenyon was seen as someone who would appeal to progressives and liberals—especially the ones in the Senate still upset about the Hughes

[42] Hearing Before the Subcommittee of the Committee on the Judiciary, United States Senate, April 5, 1930.

[43] Minutes of the Meeting of the Executive Council, American Federation of Labor, Washington, D.C., May 5–12, 1930.

confirmation battle.[44] For instance, as a senator, Kenyon had sponsored a 1914 bill to outlaw child labor.[45] Kenyon, who was also endorsed by the Iowa Farmer's Union,[46] had the added advantage of being known to and respected by the president, serving on Hoover's National Commission on Law Observance and Enforcement, which consisted of several well-regarded lawyers and academic figures tasked with a broad mandate to find ways to reform the criminal justice system.

Instead, Parker got the nod, something a blindsided Green likened to "a thunderbolt out of a clear sky." Green seemed to remember Parker's name being connected to an injunction case but wasn't sure. After having his record examined, the *Red Jacket* case came up and Green and the AFL were sufficiently outraged over the prospect of Justice John J. Parker that they immediately mobilized their opposition.

On March 25, 1930, a few newspapers carried a story about the AFL gathering material for a brief to be filed with the Judiciary subcommittee protesting Parker's nomination.[47] The following day, Green sent a telegram to other union leaders, including Frank Duffy of the United Brotherhood of Carpenters and Joiners of America, T.A. Rickert of the United Garment Workers of America, and several members of the AFL executive committee, calling for labor to "vigorously oppose" Parker's nomination due to his opinion in *Red Jacket*.[48]

"The officers and members of the American Federation of Labor believe the attitude shown by Judge Parker in this injunction case reveals a judicial state of mind which totally unfits him for service as a member of the Supreme Court," Green said in a public statement, adding that Parker demonstrated a clear preference for "property rights above human rights"

[44] "Contest Expected Over Sanford Seat," *The Buffalo News*, March 11, 1930.

[45] "Start Campaign to Stop Child Labor; Senator Kenyon's Bill in Congress Is Backed by International League," *The New York Times*, January 9, 1914.

[46] "Farmer's Union Backs Kenyon for High Scout," *The Des Moines Register*, March 14, 1930.

[47] "Mine War Case May Block Path of Judge Parker," *The Evening Sun*, March 25, 1930.

[48] *American Federation of Labor Executive Council Vote Books, July 1929–Feb. 1931*, Telegram from Green to Other Labor Leaders, March 26, 1930.

by approving an injunction that "reduced the conditions of the miners in West Virginia to a point approximating industrial servitude."[49]

Green then sent letters to Borah, Norris, and Overman, all members of the Senate Judiciary Committee, making it clear that Parker's appointment meant "another injunction judge will become a member of the Supreme Court of the United States" and that "the broad minded, humane, progressive influence" exercised by the likes of Holmes, Brandeis, and Stone in the minority would be "correspondingly weakened."[50]

In his letter, Green laid out the AFL's opposition in detail, arguing that Parker's opinion in *Red Jacket* upholding the sweeping and draconian injunction issued by "petty tyrant" and "arrogant despot" Judge McClintic had "served to make serfs of the miners." "Their condition is hopeless. Their wages are below a subsistence level, and their conditions of employment are un-American and intolerable," Green wrote in his April 4 letter.[51]

He also took on yellow-dog contracts, arguing they were not only socially and morally wrong but indefensible under the law because they were completely one-sided in favor of employers. Freedom of contract went both ways, and there could be no valid contract when one side, in this case the workers, had no choice but to sign or face unemployment, starvation, poverty or all of the above, Green maintained. Moreover, yellow-dog contracts completely hamstrung unions and defeated their core purpose which, in the words of Chief Justice Taft in *Tri-City* and other cases, was to help the helpless from being exploited by companies and businesses. Anyone who worked to maintain their legality was, in the eyes of labor, unfit for the Supreme Court.[52]

Green also amplified arguments made by UMWA's lawyers during their unsuccessful appeal of the *Red Jacket* case to the Supreme Court that Parker had ignored these pro-union sentiments from Taft and others. Therefore, there was no validity to the notion that Parker had little discretion to do anything other than follow the *Hitchman* precedent. Instead,

[49] "A.F. of L. To Fight Confirmation of Judge J.J. Parker," *The Springfield Daily Republican*, March 29, 1930.

[50] Herbert Hoover Papers, supra, Letter from Green to Borah, Norris and Overman, April 4, 1930.

[51] Herbert Hoover Papers, supra, Letter from Green to Borah, Norris and Overman, April 4, 1930.

[52] Ibid.

it must have been a conscious choice on his part. "[H]e has shown in the opinion he wrote and through his judicial attitude that he is in entire sympathy and accord with the legal and economic policy embodied in the injunction issued by Judge McClintic," Green wrote in his April 4 letter.[53] "There has never been a more glaring example of a judicial disregard of human rights, and a corresponding regard of property rights as transcendent over human rights than is shown in the judicial attitude of Judge Parker as expressed in the written opinion he rendered in the *Red Jacket Consolidated Coal and Coke Company* case."

Green was not the only labor leader who came out against Parker. Max Dyer, secretary and business manager of the Kansas City Central Labor Union, called Parker a menace to the liberty of the people and the well-being of the republic and warned that workers' rights and welfare would be harmed if he were confirmed.[54] H.W. Gross, general chairman of the Brotherhood of Railroad Trainmen, sent a telegram to Senator Henry Allen (R-KS) making clear his union's opposition to Parker on similar grounds.[55] The Conference for Progressive Labor Action also wrote to Borah, endorsing the AFL's protest and adding that "judges who uphold on technical grounds the right of corporate wealth to impose such bondage upon workers show themselves to utterly lacking in knowledge of modern conditions, [and] are attempting to apply standards of the horse and buggy era to the era of the automobile and airplane."[56] Meanwhile, Leo Shook, a union official for hosiery workers in Nazareth, PA, pointed out that they had also been victimized by yellow-dog contracts and echoed Green's comparison of opinions like *Red Jacket* to *Dred Scott*.[57] Socialist newspaper *The Oklahoma Weekly Leader* went even further, charging that Parker was a tool of electric utility company Duke Power and that energy lobbyists like GOP national chair Claudius Huston were behind his nomination.[58]

[53] Ibid.

[54] "Wednesday Selected Tentatively As Day for Parker Hearings," *The Greensboro Daily News*, March 30, 1930.

[55] Herbert Hoover papers, supra, Telegram from Gross to Allen, April 4, 1930.

[56] William J. Borah Papers, Letter from A.J. Muste to Borah, March 27, 1930.

[57] "State Labor Leader Opposed to Parker, Explains His Stand," *The Greensboro Daily News*, April 3, 1930.

[58] "Negro, Labor, Protest May Stop Parker," *The Oklahoma Weekly Leader*, April 25, 1930.

Meanwhile, the UMWA's Lewis also came out strongly against Parker. Lewis, whose later feud with onetime subordinate and ally Green would help set the stage for Lewis and his allies to split from the AFL and found rival labor organization the Congress of Industrial Organizations (CIO), was on the same page as his future counterpart when it came to Parker. Conceding that lawyers might not care much about what non-lawyers think about case law and precedent, Lewis emphasized the human toll and cost of yellow-dog contracts on mine workers, who slave away in dangerous, near-lethal conditions where they could be hurt or killed by any number of factors, including faulty equipment, unstable mines, toxic fumes, diseases, and inadequate safety regulations. "Why lay another lash across the tortured shoulders of the struggling mine workers by placing in a position of vastly increased power a man who regards them as industrial bondmen?" Lewis wondered.[59] "Why should any consideration of politics or statecraft impel any Senator to vote for the confirmation of a man who would operate American industry with bonded men-servants?".

North Carolina labor leaders were in a tough position. Should they follow their national executives and go against Parker? Or should they stick with their fellow Tar Heel so that they could finally get one back on the Supreme Court bench? On March 25, 1930, the same day news broke of the AFL's opposition, T.A. Wilson, president of the North Carolina branch of the AFL, wired Green and told him that "labor as a whole in this state is satisfied with Judge John J. Parker."[60] A little over a week later, however, Wilson reversed himself. Saying that he had not been aware of Parker's decision in *Red Jacket*, Wilson said that, upon learning of it, he and the members of the North Carolina Federation of Labor decided to back Green and oppose Parker's nomination.[61] Meanwhile, a former president of the North Carolina Federation of Labor, *Brevard News* editor James Barrett, decided to back Parker, saying that, while he understood the contempt Green and others had for the yellow-dog contract, he felt the judge did the only thing he could have done and followed established Supreme Court precedent. Barrett also pointed out that Parker had been very pro-labor during his 1920 gubernatorial

[59] "Green Says Count Defeats Parker," *The New York Times*, April 21, 1930. Also, William Borah Papers, Letter from Lewis to Borah, April 19, 1930.

[60] "North Carolina Labor Back Of Parker for High Post," *The Greensboro Daily News*, March 26, 1930.

[61] "State Labor Leader Opposed to Parker," supra.

campaign and stated that many of his votes that year had come from laborers. "Had the American Federation of Labor known Judge Parker as labor in North Carolina knows him, we believe this protest would not have been made," he added.[62]

As the storm clouds darkened over him thanks to his *Red Jacket* opinion, Parker, nevertheless, was fairly sanguine about it. "Anyone who will read the opinion and the authorities cited therein will see that our Court followed the law as laid down by the Supreme Court of the United States," Parker said.[63] "I do not think that the Senate will be impressed with criticism directed at a Judge because he follows the law as laid down by the Supreme Court."

"It All Looked Hopeless"

On the morning of April 5, 1930, Senators Overman, Borah, and Felix Hebert (R-RI), gathered in room 212 of the Senate Office Building to begin considering Parker's nomination to the Supreme Court. The stakes had changed considerably in the two weeks since Hoover announced Parker's nomination—the subcommittee noted that it had received communications from nearly two dozen individuals expressing their support of Parker and nearly twice as many statements from labor unions, civil liberties, and civil rights groups in opposition.[64]

Parker's allies seemed to understand how much the terrain had shifted under their feet over the last fortnight. After submitting a pre-written biography prepared by Parker, Overman, who was the chairman of the subcommittee, entered into the record a letter of support written by North Carolina Governor O. Max Gardner. Despite their political differences, the Democratic governor extolled his fellow 1920 gubernatorial candidate's character and abilities and underscored his deepest respect for his fellow Tar Heel.

His words, however, went beyond broad platitudes. Understanding that Parker was being attacked for, among other things, being hostile to labor and overly sympathetic to businesses and their property rights, Gardner made clear that he knew of no one who possessed a higher

[62] Hearing Before the Subcommittee of the Committee on the Judiciary, supra, 5–6.

[63] Parker Papers, supra, Letter from Parker to Thomas G. Bradley, March 31, 1930.

[64] Hearing Before the Subcommittee of the Committee on the Judiciary, supra, 58–59.

sense of justice than his old college classmate and stated he would treat everyone the same, regardless of whether they were rich and powerful or poor and penniless. "I have never known any man whose concern for the upholding and protection of what we know in a democracy as human rights, as distinguished from property rights, excelled Judge Parker's," Gardner said.[65]

Overman then admitted a written statement from Plummer Stewart, Parker's old law partner, reiterating the judge's fairness and expressing disbelief that someone could seriously be in trouble for following Supreme Court precedent.

After Overman entered several news articles, letters, statements, and editorials into the record, both for and against Parker, Green then took center stage. Stating that he was there on behalf of the AFL and its affiliates, as well as several other major unions that had authorized him to speak for them, Green laid out his case as to why he believed Parker was wrong for the Supreme Court. "Labor firmly believes that those who are appointed to serve as members of the Supreme Court of the United States should possess a knowledge and understanding of modern-day economic questions, of human relations in industry, and should possess a trained mind sympathetic toward the hopes and aspirations of the masses of the people," Green said in his testimony.[66]

Green then went through his problems with the *Red Jacket* opinion and yellow-dog contracts. Reading from the same text that he wrote in his April 4 letter to Borah, Overman, and Norris, Green made clear he was not questioning Parker's integrity or academic qualifications. Instead, Green spoke of the plight of laborers and how cases like *Hitchman* and *Red Jacket* hamstrung their abilities to organize and improve their lives and livelihoods. He condemned yellow-dog contracts and argued that they were immoral and unfair, but also illegal under the law since they were borne of coercion and lacked mutuality. Therefore, he reiterated his disdain for McClintic and his injunction, which he argued made "criminals out of law-abiding honest, loyal American citizens" and argued that Parker's decision to uphold it meant that he had a "judicial and mental bias in favor of powerful corporations and against the masses of people."[67]

[65] Hearing Before the Subcommittee of the Committee on the Judiciary, supra, 2–3.

[66] Ibid., 24.

[67] Ibid., 25, 33.

To illustrate his point, Green noted that Parker's spartan, straightforward opinion lacked any indication that he was in any way critical of *Hitchman*. To Green, the issue was less about Parker executing his duties as a lower court judge and following Supreme Court jurisprudence and more about how he failed to show even the slightest bit of inner conflict, turmoil or doubt about *Hitchman*. Due to his failure to throw in even a few words or phrases expressing some sort of skepticism or disapproval of, or desire not to have to follow, *Hitchman* showed Parker was fully in agreement and harmony with the ruling and would bring that frame of reference with him to the Supreme Court, Green argued. Judges were well within their rights to do this, he stated pointing out Parker's would-be predecessor, Justice Sanford, who had done just that in a 1927 decision in which he wrote that he had tried to distinguish a case deemed binding precedent only to come to the conclusion that he could not do so.[68]

Green's argument didn't seem to carry much water with the senators on the panel. "It all looked hopeless," he recalled.[69] "There did not seem to be much interest, even Borah, by his line of questions, indicated we could make no case against Parker because he had followed the *Hitchman* case in the ruling of the Supreme Court."

Instead, Borah and Hebert steered the discussion towards the validity of yellow-dog contracts in general. Borah showed his hand by making it clear that he believed the contracts were against public policy. Whereas Parker, in his position as judge, had focused on the jurisdictional question, Borah, instead, framed *Red Jacket* as being a case where the central issue was whether union men could persuade non-union workers to break an "illegal contract." At one point, he even teed up Green by asking whether workers receive any consideration for giving up their right to organize. "None whatsoever," Green responded.[70]

Borah seemed fixated on whether the validity of the yellow-dog contract had been questioned or tested during *Red Jacket*, and whether any other courts were examining this issue.

"What possible consideration can flow to a man for agreeing not to join a union? What mutuality?" Borah asked.

[68] Ibid., 28–29.

[69] Minutes of the Meeting of the Executive Council, American Federation of Labor, supra, 14.

[70] Hearing Before the Subcommittee of the Committee on the Judiciary, supra, 30–33.

"I can not see any," Green responded.

"The question is why wasn't that point tested? Judge Parker, taking the 'yellow-dog' contract as valid, sustained the injunction to the effect that union men could not ask non-union men to break their contract, but it seems to me the way to have reached that question was to test the validity of the contract upon which they were basing such an injunction. I am speaking without full investigation," Borah wondered.

"That might have been the proper procedure, and that point may have been raised in some of these cases. I have not gone into that. It may have been raised. I am not sure," Green replied.[71]

Green had left the legal arguments to others. He submitted a memo drafted by one of his organization's lawyers that sought to take apart the argument that Parker had just been following precedent. The memo argued that *Red Jacket* was distinguishable from *Hitchman* on the facts because the latter involved allegations that union officials were using fraud and deception to sign up workers who were under a yellow-dog contract, whereas that was not the case in *Red Jacket*, in which union officials had relied on peaceful persuasion. "From the foregoing it is perfectly apparent that Judge Parker in his opinion and decision in *the Red Jacket Coal* case has gone far beyond the doctrine laid down either by the Supreme Court of the United States or by the Circuit Court of Appeals of the Fourth Circuit," the memo stated.[72]

Overman tried to step in and rescue Parker, pointing out that the Supreme Court could have granted certiorari but declined to hear an appeal of the *Red Jacket* case. "That is another reason why we should like to see the Supreme Court liberalized," Green responded, underscoring his ultimate aim.[73]

The senators directed a few more questions towards Green, including Overman asking whether he had threatened Wilson, the North Carolina labor leader who had previously expressed support for Parker only to reverse himself a week later. "That is not true, Senator. I am not made that way," Green responded before offering to turn over all of his correspondence with Wilson to the committee.[74] Green also condemned Barrett,

71 Hearing Before the Subcommittee of the Committee on the Judiciary, supra, 29.

72 Ibid., 44.

73 Ibid., 52.

74 Ibid., 57.

the other high-profile North Carolina labor leader to go on the record in favor of Parker, stating that he does not speak for labor and had been kicked out for violating rules.[75]

The senators then turned to the next witness, E.C. Townsend, the tax commissioner of the state of West Virginia. Townsend had represented the UMWA in *Red Jacket* and, before he could even make an opening statement, Overman and Borah immediately peppered him with questions about whether he had challenged the validity of the yellow-dog contracts in court.

"Did the question of the yellow-dog contract come up directly in this case?" Overman asked.

"I never so considered, Senator. I think the major question involved in the *Red Jacket* case was a question of jurisdiction. Of course, the question of the yellow-dog contract was incidentally in the case," Townsend responded, explaining that the case was mainly about whether the coal mining in question constituted interstate commerce, and that issue had to be resolved before anything else could be considered. Therefore, he added that he focused on jurisdiction more than anything else, and that, even though he questioned the validity of the yellow-dog contract, he admitted that he believed the issue had been settled by *Hitchman*. Borah, however, dismissed that argument, stating that he believed the yellow-dog contract was the main issue.

Ultimately, Townsend gave a lawyer's response when asked about Parker's qualifications for the Supreme Court. Reiterating his personal opposition to yellow-dog contracts, Townsend, nevertheless, felt Parker had followed precedent and came to the decision he was obligated to. When asked if putting him on the court would only reinforce the validity of yellow-dog contracts under the law since justices would have to follow existing precedent, Townsend conceded that it probably would. "I think this whole question of the yellow-dog contract, so far as it affects the Federal courts, is one for legislation, under its present status, and not a court decision," he said to Borah.[76]

Borah retorted that such legislation could always be struck down by the Supreme Court, underscoring just why this nomination was so important

[75] Ibid., 55.

[76] Ibid., 61–70.

to him and others who believed that the justices had skewed too far in favor of property rights.

"I Might Have Attempted Some Criticism of the Hitchman *Decision"*

One wonders whether, if Parker had simply thrown in a sentence to the effect of "this court has *reluctantly* come to the conclusion that *Hitchman* controls the instant matter," that would have been enough to satiate Green and the rest of his opponents in labor. Then again, given Parker's utilitarian writing style and commitment to not wasting time or ink on *obiter dicta*, doing something like that not only would have been out of character but gone against his principles. Green, however, wasn't interested in any of that. He just wanted to see something, anything, that would indicate Parker wished he did not have to do what he ultimately did. Parker, however, gave him no such acknowledgment.

In fact, Parker didn't say a word during his confirmation process—at least not publicly. Unlike Stone, Parker chose not to testify before the subcommittee and maintained the same state of dignified silence that he did when he was up for the circuit court judgeship and that Brandeis did when he faced his confirmation battle. For one thing, Parker had long considered it unseemly to actively pursue a judicial appointment and saw no reason to change his thinking now. Another was that he believed judges should not publicly comment or declare their position on questions likely to come before them.[77]

Like Brandeis, he took an active behind-the-scenes role in his nomination, relaying his views and instructions via private correspondence with his allies and surrogates, particularly his law partner, Plummer Stewart, prominent Republicans David H. Blair, Charles Jonas, and Marion Butler, fellow North Carolina federal judges Edwin Y. Webb and Elliott Northcott and nationally known attorney Thomas W. Davis. Parker drafted a memorandum aimed at refuting labor's charges against him and reiterating that he followed the law and did his job. Parker argued that the *Red Jacket* case was not about the validity of yellow-dog contracts and was actually a pro-union opinion because it ultimately upheld the right to organize and strike.[78]

[77] Parker Papers, supra, Letter from Parker to Blair, April 3, 1930.

[78] Parker Papers, supra, Red Jacket memorandum, undated.

He also wrote a long letter to Overman answering his opponents and explaining his actions. He reiterated his duty to follow the Supreme Court and pointed out that the court chose not to revisit the matter, thereby validating him. He also stated that the main question had been a jurisdictional issue and not the validity of the contracts. "To conclude, we followed in the *Red Jacket* case, the law as declared by the Supreme Court," he stated matter-of-factly.[79] "This I understand to be the duty of judges."

Privately, he was upset with the attacks on him. "The only thing that I can do is to maintain an attitude of dignified silence, but it is very galling to one who has helped to fight the fight of real democracy to hear himself branded as placing property rights above human rights," Parker said in a letter to his old philosophy professor at UNC, Henry Horace Williams.[80] He added that, had he done what Green and others had wanted him to do, he would have been "rebuked by the Supreme Court." Parker also pointed out that only the Supreme Court could have given Green what he wanted and declared yellow-dog contracts invalid—and they chose not to do it by declining certiorari.

Understanding that his nominee had been caught in deep waters and was in danger of going under, Hoover got involved, engaging with Green personally. After receiving a letter from the labor leader expressing his disappointment in Parker's nomination and asking that it be withdrawn, Hoover responded in kind and enclosed a memorandum from the U.S. Department of Justice defending Parker's actions in *Red Jacket*. "It is evident that you have been entirely misled and are doing a great injustice," Hoover responded in a letter dated April 14, 1930.[81] "I cannot but believe that if you will peruse the enclosed digest of the matter in question, you will agree that he should be confirmed."

The DOJ's memo maintained that Parker and his fellow judges were bound by the *Hitchman* precedent and had ruled correctly. Moreover, in examining the history of the case and the available record, the DOJ pointed out that the union's own lawyers did not raise the issue of validity when it came to the yellow-dog contract. Therefore, the DOJ inferred

[79] Parker Papers, supra, Letter from Parker to Overman, April 22, 1930.

[80] Parker Papers, supra, Letter from Parker to Williams, April 7, 1930.

[81] Minutes of the Meeting of the Executive Council, American Federation of Labor, supra.

that the union lawyers must have accepted that these contracts were legal and that the matter was settled under the law. "There does not appear to be a point decided in the *Red Jacket* case on which Judge Parker assumed to exercise any independent judgment or opinion," the brief stated.[82] "The question is not whether the Supreme Court was right or wrong in its conclusion. The question is whether Judge Parker was dealing with points which had been settled by the Supreme Court, which he was bound, under his oath of office, to follow." The brief even argued that a judge with true animus towards labor would have tried to extend *Hitchman's* ruling beyond what the majority had intended. Parker did not do that, which clearly showed that he was not anti-labor, the DOJ concluded.

Green was unmoved by the DOJ memo. Once again invoking *Dred Scott*, Green argued that no respectable or enlightened judge in their time would follow that infamous decision considering what it stood for and what it resulted in. For Green, that extended to *Hitchman*, a decision he maintained forced millions of laborers into a state of modern-day servitude. And, unlike Parker and his supporters, who focused on legal and procedural arguments to justify his actions, Green focused on the human and economic costs of yellow-dog contracts. "As a result of the decision of Judge Parker the employees of more than three hundred coal companies, thousands of working-men parties to the Yellow Dog Contracts are living in a most degrading economic and social condition in Southern West Virginia," Green said.[83] "This has had a deleterious effect upon the entire bituminous coal industry."

The law can be a powerful weapon for change, but it can be an even more powerful shield to preserve the status quo. Sure, Parker behaved as a proper judge, examining the facts and applying the law with dispassion and detachment and delivering an opinion that was on solid, legal ground. But what he and his allies failed to grasp was that, to Green, Borah and others, this was not something that could be handled without passion or, in this case, compassion. They were moved by the actual, human costs of the injunctions and the yellow-dog contracts and questions over jurisdiction or legal procedure were secondary, at best. They understood the

[82] Hoover Papers, Department of Justice memorandum on the opinion of Circuit Judge John J. Parker in International Organization, *United Mine Workers of America v. Red Jacket Consolidated Coal and Coke Co.*, April 13, 1930.

[83] Minutes of the Meeting of the Executive Council, American Federation of Labor, supra, 20–21.

background and context behind these fights and, when they saw a judge like Parker not consider them because they weren't immediately relevant to the case in front of him, they did not see a responsible judge; they saw someone who was out of touch at best, and a potential Fifth Horsemen at worst.

Most importantly, they were sick and tired of a Supreme Court that refused to do anything to help the people who needed it. In a speech delivered at Amherst College in 1950, Parker condemned the *laissez faire* theory of government and noted that it had only come about because people ignored the "social element in human life." He added: "Free men will no more submit to economic tyranny than to political tyranny. The Government is their creation and it is the only agency that they have with sufficient power to deal with the economic forces that threaten them."[84]

As pointed out earlier, Parker had made strong pro-labor and pro-union statements during his 1920 gubernatorial campaign, so the sentiments expressed in his Amherst speech were consistent with his long-held views. It does raise the question as to why neither Parker nor his surrogates thought to trumpet those statements to inoculate him from labor's attacks. But, as we'll see in the next chapter, Parker had a reason not to want to draw attention to his 1920 race.

Had he been more open about his views, especially after he became a judge, would he have mollified organized labor and neutralized any possible opposition from them? Then again, making a speech like this so early in his career and during a time when *laissez faire* government was still in effect, might have undermined his effectiveness as a judge and placed a gigantic bullseye on him—especially given all of the labor, mining, and shipping cases he heard. Perhaps a happy medium would have been to do what Green and others had wanted him to do and express some sort of disagreement with *Hitchman* while still upholding it. "Had I been longer upon the bench I might have attempted some criticism of the *Hitchman* decision," Parker reflected in 1941.[85]

Of course, it wouldn't have done anything to address the concerns of the other major group that had decided to oppose his nomination based on something he had said in the past.

[84] John J. Parker, "Liberty and Law: The Role of Law in a Free Society," *American Bar Association Journal* 36, no. 7 (1950), 523–526, 591–594.

[85] Fish, "A Freshman Takes Charge," supra, 89.

CHAPTER 6

Raising Hell: The NAACP Makes Its Move

There was one other person in the room ready to give testimony before the Senate Judiciary subcommittee considering Parker's Supreme Court nomination. The good news for Parker and his allies was that he wasn't a representative of organized labor and he wasn't there to talk about *Red Jacket*, the dangers of yellow-dog contracts, or even Parker's performance as a circuit court judge.

The bad news was he wasn't any happier than the others at the prospect of seeing Parker become an associate justice of the Supreme Court.

Born in Atlanta, GA in 1893, Walter White probably could have lived a life where he benefited from Jim Crow instead of choosing to fight it. White was mixed-race and had African and European ancestry on both sides of his family. His parents were very light-skinned, and he looked very much like a white man, something that could have allowed him to pass for white had he chosen to do so.

Despite that, Walter White identified as Black and not just because he was considered to be Black under the unofficial "one-drop" rule that was in place in the Jim Crow South at the time.[1] Both of his parents had been born into slavery, and White later claimed, without evidence, that

[1] Under this rule, any person with even a single Black ancestor—or "one drop" of Black blood—was considered Black, regardless of their appearance or how distant that ancestry was.

V. Li, *Supreme Pressure*,
https://doi.org/10.1007/978-3-032-07864-3_6

his grandmother had been a slave mistress to William Henry Harrison and had given birth to six illegitimate children with the ninth president of the United States. Additionally, one of his formative memories from childhood was a race riot in Atlanta during which a white mob nearly burned down their family home because they knew his father was a Black man. Years later, his father needed emergency medical attention and was mistakenly transported to a white hospital. When they found out his race, they shipped him to a Black hospital rather than try and save his life. By the time he got to the Black hospital, it was too late. As he described himself in the opening line in his autobiography, *A Man Called White*: "I am a Negro. My skin is white, my eyes are blue, my hair is blonde. The traits of my race are nowhere visible upon me."[2]

The dichotomy between White's appearance and his identity would lead to newspapers and media organizations at the time calling him "Negro by choice."[3] It would also serve as ammunition for his critics in the Black community—if he did something that some of them found objectionable they could accuse him of being a race traitor, which is something that happened later in his life when he married editor and writer Poppy Cannon, a white woman born in South Africa.

However, his appearance also had advantages. White joined the NAACP shortly after graduating from Atlanta University in 1916 and helped establish a local chapter of the association in the Georgian capital. His work caught the attention of famed NAACP founder W.E.B. DuBois and executive secretary James Weldon Johnson, and White relocated to New York, where he worked as an assistant secretary at the association's headquarters. He then made his name as an undercover agent in the South investigating a series of lynchings, where his looks allowed him to pass for white. For instance, while looking into a lynching in Georgia of a pregnant Black woman who was close to childbirth, White managed to get a local business owner to spill the beans simply by looking and acting like a racist white man. "Little by little he revealed the whole story. When he told of the manner in which the pregnant woman had been killed, he chuckled and slapped his thigh and declared it to be 'the best show, Mister, I ever did see. You ought to have heard the wench howl when we

[2] Walter White, *A Man Called White: The Autobiography of Walter White* (Athens, GA, and London: Brown Thrasher Books: 1948), 1.

[3] Jennifer Latson, "The Surprising Story of Walter White and the NAACP," *Time*, July 1, 2015.

strung her up.' Covering the nausea the story caused me as best I could, I slowly gained the whole story, with the names of the other participants. Among them were prosperous farmers, businessmen, bankers, newspaper reporters and editors, and several law-enforcement officers."[4]

White's undercover exploits could have made for an epic Hollywood film. According to White, he was recruited to join the Ku Klux Klan as a state organizer in Georgia until they started digging into his past and realized who they were dealing with.[5] He once had a close shave in Arkansas when word got out that there was a Black man passing as white—an offense often prosecuted and punished by lynch mob. Worried that his cover had been blown, he got on a train in order to get out of town. According to White, he got nervous when the conductor looked at him funny and told him "the fun" was about to start. But then, he breathed a sigh of relief after the conductor said he heard a Black man was trying to pass for white and when the lynch mob found him, "he won't pass for white no more!"[6] During the infamous Tulsa race massacre in 1921, law-enforcement agents mistook White for a white man, deputized him and gave him legal authority to shoot Black people on sight.[7]

White didn't just dig up information on lynchings and race massacres. Often posing as a journalist, White wrote up his accounts and published them in various newspapers and magazines throughout the country. Ultimately, thanks to the South's lax attitude towards lynchings and the inability of the federal government to pass meaningful anti-lynching laws, exposing these crimes to the public was all the NAACP and White could hope for.

White's travels also brought him into contact with Herbert Hoover. Then U.S. secretary of commerce, Hoover was a smart, efficient bureaucrat who expanded the power of his department and was so influential within the Coolidge Administration that he was referred to as "Secretary

[4] Walter White, "I Investigate Lynchings," *National Humanities Center, The Making of African-American Identity*, Vol. III, 1917–1968, https://nationalhumanitiescenter.org/pds/maai3/segregation/text2/text2read.htm.

[5] White, *A Man Called White*, supra, 14–15.

[6] White, *A Man Called White*, supra, 50–51.

[7] Chris Messer, "The Tulsa Race Riot of 1921: Toward an Integrative Theory of Collective Violence," *Journal of Social History*, no. 4 (2011), 339.

of Commerce and Undersecretary of Everything Else."[8] One of the many things in his portfolio was overseeing the administration's response to the Great Mississippi Flood of 1927—an effort that led to tons of positive press and media attention and helped catapult him to the 1928 Republican nomination for president despite never having won elected office up to that point.

White, however, was no fan of Hoover's efforts and reported on widespread mistreatment of Black Mississippians. According to White, these Black refugees were being hoarded into concentration camps and confined there and, in some cases, were forced to pay for relief that the Red Cross had provided for free. If they could not pay, their "debt" would be assumed by a landlord and they would be forced to work off what they "owed" in the field.[9] Hoover heard about these claims and appointed a civilian committee consisting of Black Americans, but not a single member of the NAACP, to look into the matter.

The situation was such that DuBois wrote in the November 1927 issue of *The Crisis*, the NAACP's official magazine: "[W]e have grave suspicions that the colored committee recently appointed by Mr. Hoover to investigate flood conditions and peonage in the Mississippi Valley will be sorely tempted to whitewash the whole situation, to pat Mr. Hoover loudly on the back, and to make no real effort to investigate the desperate and evil conditions of that section of our country. Slavery still exists in the Mississippi Valley and this Committee knows it."[10] Ultimately, Hoover's commission made its findings. However, commission chair Dr. Robert R. Moton, principal of the Tuskegee Institute, agreed to keep them quiet so as not to hurt Hoover's presidential aspirations.[11]

His experiences with Hoover left a bad taste in White's mouth. So much so that, when he became president in 1929, White referred to him as "The Man in the Lily-White House."

[8] "Secretary of Commerce, Undersecretary of Everything Else," *U.S. Department of Commerce*, https://library.doc.gov/digital-exhibits/hoover-digital-exhibit, accessed: July 31, 2024.

[9] White, *A Man Called White*, supra, 80–81.

[10] Richard M. Mizelle, Jr. "Black Levee Camp Workers, The NAACP, and the Mississippi Flood Control Project, 1927–1933," *The Journal of African American History* 98, no. 4 (2013), 523.

[11] "Robert Moton and the Colored Advisory Commission," *PBS*, www.pbs.org/wgbh/americanexperience/features/flood-moton-cac/, accessed July 31, 2024.

"Separate But Equal"

At around the same time that Hoover ascended to the presidency, White rose to a position of power within the NAACP, becoming acting executive secretary in 1929. Two years later, he would assume the job permanently and, in that position, he would lead the NAACP for the next quarter century, serving as an important bridge between the founding years of the organization and the Civil Rights Movement of the 1950s and 1960s.

The Supreme Court played a pivotal role during the Civil Rights Movement, ordering the desegregation of public schools, banning segregation of interstate and intrastate transportation facilities, striking down anti-miscegenation laws, and prohibiting racial discrimination in real estate transactions, among other things. That was a radical change from the previous century, during which time the Supreme Court routinely ruled against expanding, protecting, or enforcing civil rights.

The ratification of the Thirteenth, Fourteenth and Fifteenth Amendments after the Civil War was supposed to guarantee equal rights for all and to protect the newly freed slaves from having their newfound freedoms repressed or denied by their former masters. The Supreme Court, however, took a narrow view of the "Reconstruction Amendments" and seemingly shirked its duties to enforce them—particularly the Fourteenth Amendment.[12] The 1873 *Slaughter-House* cases ruling limited the Fourteenth Amendment's scope to rights specifically related to U.S. citizenship, and did not restrict states' plenary powers. Writing for the majority, Justice Samuel Miller differentiated between federal and state citizenship, confining the amendment's protections to privileges or immunities specifically enumerated in the Constitution. Justice Stephen Field's dissent argued this interpretation rendered the amendment into a "vain and idle enactment."[13]

Later rulings further narrowed the Fourteenth Amendment's impact. In 1876, the court ruled in *United States v. Cruikshank* that the Fourteenth Amendment did not apply the Bill of Rights to states or private

[12] Eric Foner, *The Second Founding: How the Civil War and Reconstruction Remade the Constitution* (New York: W.W. Norton, 2019).

[13] Victor Li, "The 14th: A Civil War-era amendment has become a mini Constitution for modern times," *ABA Journal*, May 1, 2017. Also, *The Slaughterhouse Cases*, 83 U.S. 36 (1873).

actors.[14] Seven years later, the court handed down a decision in the *Civil Rights* cases striking down the 1875 Civil Rights Act, which had guaranteed equal access to public accommodation, transportation and theaters, holding Congress had no power to enforce the Thirteenth and Fourteenth Amendments against states and private actors. Worried that they were giving Blacks special privileges and protections, Justice Joseph Bradley wrote for the majority that, once a person has been freed from slavery and has benefited from laws that have helped remove the associated conditions of that state, they should be considered an ordinary citizen rather than someone requiring special legal protection.[15]

The lone dissenter, Justice John Marshall Harlan, warned that, without federal protection, Black Americans would be subject to widespread, state-sanctioned discrimination. Harlan's words soon came true in the form of Jim Crow laws throughout the South. "Today it is the colored race which is denied, by corporations and individuals wielding public authority, rights fundamental in their freedom and citizenship. At some future time, it may be that some other race will fall under the ban of race discrimination," Harlan warned.[16]

Harlan was, once again, the lone dissenter in *Plessy v. Ferguson*, the 1896 case that had the effect of enshrining "separate but equal" accommodation throughout the country, but especially in the Jim Crow South. Harlan argued that the legislation at issue in *Plessy* would give states wide license "to interfere with the full enjoyment of the blessings of freedom to regulate civil rights, common to all citizens, upon the basis of race" and would "place in a condition of legal inferiority a large body of American citizens." In his now famous and widely quoted passage, Harlan maintained that "in view of the Constitution, in the eye of the law, there is in this country no superior, dominant, ruling class of citizens. There is no

[14] *United States v. Cruikshank*, 92 U.S. 542 (1876).

[15] *The Civil Rights Cases*, 109 U.S. 3 (1883). Bradley served as the swing vote on the 1877 Electoral Commission awarding disputed electoral votes in the 1876 presidential election to Republican nominee Rutherford B. Hayes and making him the president. Some historians argue that the vote was part of a deal between Republicans and Democrats to withdraw federal troops from the South and end Reconstruction, but others dispute this.

[16] *The Civil Rights Cases*, supra.

caste here. Our Constitution is color-blind, and neither knows nor tolerates classes among citizens. In respect of civil rights, all citizens are equal before the law."[17]

There were some instances of the court striking down racially discriminatory laws during this era. Perhaps the most notable example was *Yick Wo v. Hopkins*, which the court handed down in 1866. At issue was a San Francisco ordinance that made it illegal for laundromats to operate inside wooden buildings without a permit. The law did not mention race, but it was overwhelmingly enforced against Chinese-owned laundromat owners. Justice Stanley Matthews, writing for a unanimous court, held the Equal Protection Clause of the Fourteenth Amendment forbade discriminatory application of a race-neutral law.[18]

However, 12 years later, the court basically ignored that precedent in ruling that states could use poll taxes and literacy tests that had the effect of disenfranchising Black voters because the statutes in question were not discriminatory on their face and were not necessarily applied in a way to hurt a particular race, only that they could have been.[19]

That's not to say that the Supreme Court did not believe in enforcing, protecting, or expanding civil rights. During this era, which largely fell under the chief justiceships of Morrison Waite and Melville Fuller, who between them served from 1874 to 1910, most of the action was in the area of economic liberties, where it was good to be a corporation or business. As mentioned earlier, the *Lochner* era of jurisprudence dominated this period—all thanks to an offhand comment made by Waite prior to oral arguments in *Santa Clara County v. Southern Pacific Railroad Co.* in 1886. The case involved railroad companies challenging a California tax, claiming they were "persons" under the Fourteenth Amendment and entitled to equal protection. Before arguments began, Waite declared: "The court does not wish to hear argument on the question whether the provision in the Fourteenth Amendment to the Constitution, which forbids a state to deny to any person within its jurisdiction the equal protection of the laws, applies to these corporations. We are all of the opinion that it does."[20]

[17] *Plessy v. Ferguson*, 163 U.S. 537 (1896).

[18] *Yick Wo v. Hopkins*, 118 U.S. 356 (1886).

[19] *Williams v. Mississippi*, 170 U.S. 213 (1898).

[20] Li, "The 14th," supra.

As mentioned earlier, in the ensuing decades, the Supreme Court frequently protected corporations and employers and regularly ruled against state and federal business regulations, including laws on minimum wage and child labor. The Court was also hostile to civil rights, often ruling against minorities and groups challenging discriminatory laws. The Court's antipathy to civil rights was such that when faced with a state law prohibiting integration in educational institutions chartered as corporations, the Fuller Court issued a rare opinion departing from its otherwise robust defense of corporate civil rights, holding that states could prohibit private schools from admitting both Black and white students.[21]

That being said, the NAACP actually had some success arguing civil rights cases before the Supreme Court in the 1910s and 1920s. In 1913, the NAACP filed a brief in a Supreme Court case for the first time in its then four-year history in a case challenging the legitimacy of grandfather clauses. In that case, *Guinn v. United States*, a unanimous court struck down an Oklahoma law that required literacy tests for voters, but provided an exception for voters who could prove they had a grandfather who had voted or had served in the army before 1866, which had the practical effect of allowing illiterate whites to vote while excluding illiterate Blacks.[22]

The NAACP then represented a Black man challenging a Louisville, Kentucky ordinance banning the sale of real estate to Blacks in white-majority neighborhoods or buildings. Arguing that the ban violated freedom of contract, the NAACP convinced the Supreme Court to strike down the ordinance on Fourteenth Amendment grounds in 1917. Perhaps it helped that the court did not see the case as a civil rights matter. Instead, the more pertinent issue was whether a man, in this case a white man, could dispose of property in a manner he saw fit rather than be constrained over who he could sell it to.[23]

Six years later, the NAACP represented several defendants who were convicted of murder during a race riot in Arkansas—the case White was investigating when he thought he was going to get lynched for trying to pass as white. Arguing that they did not get a fair trial because of the actions of a white mob that did everything from decide who would

[21] *Berea College v. Kentucky*, 211 U.S. 45 (1908).

[22] *Guinn v. United States*, 238 U.S. 347 (1915).

[23] *Buchanan v. Warley*, 245 U.S. 60 (1917).

be indicted, coercing testimony and arming themselves and surrounding the courtroom during the trial, the defendants filed for a federal writ of habeas corpus despite being charged on state crimes. The NAACP managed to convince the Supreme Court to vacate the convictions and established a precedent whereby criminal defendants could file for a writ of habeas corpus in state court cases if defendants could prove their federal constitutional rights were violated.[24]

During this time, the NAACP would also have success striking down a Texas law barring Blacks from voting in primary elections.[25] On the other hand, the association came up short when it challenged racially restrictive covenants forbidding the sale of land to Black people, as a unanimous court found these deals to be constitutional and enforceable.[26]

There was another major case pending before the Supreme Court during the time Parker's nomination was being considered—and it happened to be one in which he had taken part in. The case involved Richmond, Virginia's use of zoning laws to prohibit sales of real property to mixed-race families or couples. In *City of Richmond v. Deans*, the Fourth Circuit issued a short, *per curiam* opinion ruling that the ordinance was unconstitutional, citing prior Supreme Court cases that had held that zoning laws could not be used to deny sales or rentals to nonwhite people. Lawyers for the city had tried to distinguish Richmond's law by pointing out that it was not targeted at nonwhites, but intermarriage. Parker and his two fellow judges, however, did not buy it, pointing out that bans on intermarriage were still a form of racial discrimination.[27]

"The publicity the [NAACP] received for its efforts provided it with another victory by showing that some progress in extending civil rights for Black people and others could be attained through the courts," Kenneth Goings wrote in his 1990 book, *The NAACP Comes of Age: The Defeat of John J. Parker*.[28] Therefore, they would be very interested in the makeup of the court and wary of any attempts to swing the court further away from the cause of civil rights—especially now that the man White had

[24] *Moore v. Dempsey*, 261 U.S. 86 (1923).

[25] *Nixon v. Herndon*, 273 U.S. 536 (1927).

[26] *Corrigan v. Buckley*, 271 U.S. 323 (1926).

[27] *City of Richmond v. Deans*, 37 F.2d 712 (4th Cir. 1930).

[28] Kenneth Goings, *The NAACP Comes of Age: The Defeat of John J. Parker* (Bloomington: Indiana University Press, 1990), 18.

referred to as the occupant of the "Lily-White House" would be the one making the appointments.

"I Was Rendering a Service"

Immediately after Justice Sanford died, White got a tip that Senator Walter George (D-GA), an ardent segregationist, and Henry W. Anderson, the lily-white Republican from Virginia who had gone against Parker in the "par clearance" case, were being considered for the vacancy. Concerned, White reached out to Elliott Thurston, a Washington, D.C. correspondent for the *New York World*, to see if there was any truth to the rumors. Thurston didn't put too much stock in either man getting the nod, but did acknowledge that Hoover wanted to pick a Southerner. Thurston then suggested that Parker would be the most likely pick, although he hedged his bet by pointing out the judge's relative youth.[29]

White had never heard of John J. Parker, so he wrote to several allies in North Carolina, including H.L. McCrorey, president of Johnson C. Smith University in Charlotte and A.M. Rivera of the North Carolina Mutual Life Insurance Company, asking them if they knew anything. "We want to be in position to work against his confirmation in the Senate if there is any reason for such action," White wrote in his March 22 letter.[30] "Of course, if he is all right and is looked upon favorably by the colored people of North Carolina, we will not act."

Rivera immediately responded, dashing off a letter to White recounting the 1920 gubernatorial election and Parker's speech accepting the Republican nomination about Black people not wanting to vote and the Republicans not wanting their vote. In his letter to White, he recalled that Parker had said: "The Negro does not desire the ballot. Furthermore, he is incompetent, and the Republican Party does not desire him to participate in the political life of the State."[31] Rivera also told White

[29] Papers of the National Association for the Advancement of Colored People, Part 11, Special Subject Files 1912–1939, Letter from Elliott Thurston to Walter White, March 19, 1930.

[30] Papers of the National Association for the Advancement of Colored People, supra, Letter from Walter White to H.L. McCrorey, March 22, 1930 and Letter from White to A.M. Rivera, March 22, 1930.

[31] Papers of the National Association for the Advancement of Colored People, supra, Letter from Rivera to White, March 24, 1930.

that Parker had vowed he would rather be defeated by white votes than victorious via Black votes. "[I]t is very obvious he is not of the proper judicial temperament, so far as the Negro electorate is concerned, unless he has changed his opinion," Rivera said in his letter dated March 24, 1930.[32]

The actual portion of the speech did not contain a reference to losing with whites instead of winning with Blacks. It also didn't mention "incompetence," as Rivera alleged. This was the full text of Parker's remarks:

> The Republican Party in North Carolina has accepted the amendment in the spirit in which it was passed and the Negro has so accepted it. I have attended every State convention since 1908 and I have never seen a Negro delegate in any convention that I attended. The Negro as a class does not desire to enter politics. The Republican party of North Carolina does not desire him to do so. We recognize the fact that he has not yet reached that stage in his development where he can share the burdens and responsibilities of government. This being true, and every intelligent man in North Carolina knows it is true, the attempt of certain petty Democratic politicians to inject the race issue into every campaign is most reprehensible. I say it deliberately, there is no more dangerous or contemptible enemy of the State than men who for personal or political advantage will attempt to kindle the flame of racial prejudiced or hatred … the participation of the Negro in politics is a source of evil and danger to both races and is not desired by the wise men in either race or by the Republican Party of North Carolina.[33]

The "amendment" Parker referred to in his speech was the so-called "Suffrage Amendment," a 1900 addition to the North Carolina constitution enshrining the use of literacy tests, poll taxes, and grandfather clauses to determine who was eligible to vote. Similar to the suffrage laws enacted in other parts of the South, North Carolina's were drafted to be race-neutral. However, when it came to enforcement, they were mainly used as a tool to disenfranchise millions of Black voters in North Carolina and keep the Democratic Party in power.

White was alarmed and asked Rivera for documentation of his claims. In the meantime, he got a different response from McCrorey, saying he

[32] Ibid.

[33] Hearing Before the Subcommittee of the Committee on the Judiciary, supra, 74.

had a positive impression of Parker and that he was considered "fair-minded irrespective of race." McCrorey also warned that Parker was probably the best they could hope for if Hoover was determined to appoint a Southerner. "I am of the opinion that Judge Parker, if his appointment is confirmed, will fill the position as well, so far as the Negro is concerned, as any other man who may be appointed from the South," he wrote in a letter dated March 26, 1930.[34]

With these two diametrically opposed reactions in his mailbox, White figured he would try and hear it straight from the horse's mouth. On March 26, White sent Parker a telegram asking him for an explanation of his quote and whether he still believed it. "May I inquire on behalf of the National Association for the Advancement of Colored People if you made his statement or if it is indicative of your attitude so far as the Negro is concerned in the enforcement of the Fourteenth and Fifteenth Amendments to the Constitution," White wrote.[35]

White had decided to give Parker a couple of days to respond.[36] Nevertheless, the NAACP head, perhaps anticipating what the end result was going to be, sent a letter to Washington, D.C. Municipal Court Judge James A. Cobb the day after contacting Parker making it clear that the NAACP would oppose the judge. White also started drafting letters to senators known to be supportive of civil rights, including progressives like Norris, Robert La Follette, Jr. (who had replaced his celebrated father in the Senate in 1925), Wheeler and Hiram Johnson. Eventually, he wrote to 46 senators informing them of Parker's 1920 speech and urging them to reject his nomination. Parker never responded to White's telegram.

Indeed, Parker was dismissive of the NAACP's campaign against him—much like he had been of labor's opposition to him when it was first starting to take shape. "I saw in yesterday's papers that the Society for the Advancement of Colored People is making criticism of a speech which I made in Greensboro when I was a candidate for Governor in 1920, but I do not think that this protest will be seriously received by any of the

[34] Papers of the National Association for the Advancement of Colored People, supra, Letter from McCrorey to White, March 26, 1930.

[35] Parker Papers, supra, Telegram from White, March 26, 1930. Also Papers of the National Association for the Advancement of Colored People, supra.

[36] Papers of the National Association for the Advancement of Colored People, supra, Letter from White to Cobb, March 27, 1930.

Senators," Parker wrote in a March 31 letter to Representative Charles A. Jonas (R-NC), one of his most prominent surrogates and backers.[37]

After all, Parker genuinely believed that he had been doing everyone—Blacks, whites, Democrats and Republicans—a favor by trying to address the issue and remove it from the election. As he had said in 1920, Parker saw how Democrats relied on race-baiting in order to keep voters scared and in line—and distracted from the fact that they had not actually accomplished much during their decades in uncontested power.

He reiterated his views in 1925—right before he assumed his place on the federal bench. When asked about the then nascent Southern States Republican League, comprising of insurgents and reformers looking to take on the lily-whites and align the Southern GOP with the national party,[38] Parker drafted an August 11 letter to Oliver D. Street, Republican National Committee member representing Alabama, stating that the league could be useful in terms of helping build the GOP in the South, but not if was just a collection of "disgruntled office seekers." He then opined on the league's rule restricting membership to whites only, saying he did not find it objectionable. "If Negroes are admitted to membership in it, its usefulness in the Southern states will be at an end," Parker said.[39] "I believe that the only hope of enlisting the South as a factor in the cause of militant Republicanism is through the organization of white voters in the South and this organization cannot be effected if Negroes are permitted to join these political organizations which have social as well as political features." Parker ultimately did not send the letter—perhaps because his stealth campaign for the circuit court seat was already underway, and he did not want any controversies that could derail his nomination.

Despite his views on Blacks staying out of politics, he was happy to have the support of a couple of high-profile Black surrogates who were willing to go to bat for him against the NAACP. James Shepard, president of North Carolina College for Negroes, frequently defended Parker against attacks from civil rights groups and others who questioned his attitude towards Blacks and maintained that he would be fair and impartial

[37] Parker Papers, supra, Letter from Parker to Jonas, March 31, 1930.

[38] "Southern States Republican League Will Be Organized at Memphis on February 12," *The Arizona Republic*, February 3, 1925.

[39] Parker Papers, supra, Letter from Parker to O.D. Street (not sent), August 11, 1925.

towards nonwhite parties. "His decisions will be fair both to labor and all races," Shepard said.[40] "He will endeavor to interpret laws for the best interest of the people. Instead of widening, he will endeavor to promote peace between the races." Shepard sent letters on Parker's behalf to various senators and was frequently cited in newspaper stories at the time vouching for Parker—in one instance he told Carl Murphy, editor of *The Afro-American*, that Parker had always been personally friendly with him and other Black people and believed he would bring that attitude with him to the court. "I do not take the campaign utterances as being the true test of the man," he said.[41] Other prominent Black supporters of Parker included Dr. Simon Green Atkins, first president of Winston-Salem State University and founder of the North Carolina Negro Teachers' Association, E.H. Copeland, president of the North Carolina Elks Association, and D.M. Epps principal of the Industrial School at Greenville.[42]

Meanwhile, National Executive Secretary for the National Association of Negro Tailors, Designers, and Dressmakers M.K. Tyson went even further, stating that Parker's statements and sentiments about Black North Carolinians were completely accurate. "The reason that the Negro is out of politics in North Carolina is because he brought it upon himself. If the Negro had acted right, he would have been in politics in North Carolina this very day. In some respects this condition has benefited the Negro," Tyson wrote in a letter to Overman.[43]

White was apoplectic when he heard this, dismissing Tyson as a nonentity and sycophant.[44] He and others were also angered at Shepard. The *New Pittsburgh Courier*, for instance, wondered if Shepard was only backing Parker out of obligation because his school was reliant on funding from the state of North Carolina, which was solidly behind its native son.[45] Another Black paper, *The New York Amsterdam News*, remarked that "it was not expected that a Negro of intelligence could be found in all

[40] Parker Papers, supra, Telegram from Shepard to Judge Jonathan Hayes, April 12, 1930.

[41] Parker Papers, supra, Letter from Shepard to Murphy, April 5, 1930.

[42] "Protests Pour In Against Anti-Negro Judge," *The Afro-American*, April 19, 1930.

[43] *Congressional Record*, Proceedings and Debates of the Second Session of the Seventy First Congress of the United States of America, Vol. LXXII—Part 7, April 10–28.

[44] Papers of the National Association for the Advancement of Colored People, supra, Telegram from White to R.G. Randolph, April 28, 1930.

[45] "Our Shepard of Durham," *New Pittsburgh Courier*, April 26, 1930.

America willing to come to the defense of Judge John J. Parker" and that Shepard was unfit for his position if he really thought Parker could be a fair and impartial judge after what he said in 1920.[46] Shepard didn't help matters when he later downplayed any personal relationship with Parker and said he was doing this because he was a loyal Republican.[47]

Others argued Parker was just saying what he needed to in order to run a credible campaign. Joseph R. Pollard, a Richmond lawyer who represented the NAACP in the *City of Richmond v. Deans* case, asked White to withdraw his opposition to Parker. Citing his decision striking down the anti-miscegenation zoning ordinance at issue in his case, Pollard chalked up Parker's 1920 rhetoric as "the usual political claptrap of white Southerners."[48] Meanwhile, the *St. Luke Herald*, a Richmond-based Black newspaper, published an editorial arguing Parker's vote in *Deans* should be given more weight than something he said ten years ago to try and win office.[49]

White was dismissive of Pollard's argument. Unlike how Green and other labor leaders had felt about *Red Jacket*, White argued that Parker had been boxed in by Supreme Court precedent and had no choice but to rule the way he did. As for the politics-as-usual argument, White was even more dismissive. In a letter, White threw some of Pollard's own rhetoric back at him, saying that the court deserved the best and if someone needed to stoop to "political claptrap" then they were clearly not fit for such an honor and privilege.[50]

"Nothing Except This Statement Here"

White may have been invited to give live testimony before the Judiciary subcommittee considering Parker's nomination, but it doesn't mean the senators or the other witnesses made him feel welcome. White recalled

[46] "Bitter Negro Attack on Parker Scares Senators," *The News and Observer*, April 12, 1930.

[47] "Four Speakers 'Cut' Durham Fact Finding Conference," *The Afro-American*, May 3, 1930.

[48] Papers of the National Association for the Advancement of Colored People, supra, Telegram from Pollard to White, March 30, 1930.

[49] "Makes Parker Plea," *The New York Times*, April 28, 1930.

[50] Papers of the National Association for the Advancement of Colored People, supra, Letter from White to Pollard, March 31, 1930.

that, despite having met and spoken with him before, Green gave him the cold shoulder—most likely so that senators, reporters or spectators would not get the impression that he agreed with White's views on civil rights.[51]

When it was White's turn to speak, the reception did not get any warmer. Green later recalled that no one in the room really paid much attention to White nor seemed terribly interested in what he was saying.[52] Starting off with the usual introductory information, White got right down to business, quoting the offending portion of Parker's 1920 speech that had resulted in the NAACP's decision to oppose him:

"Do you know anything in the career of Judge Parker to indicate that he is unfriendly to the Negro?" Borah asked White.

"Nothing except this statement here," White responded.

"Do you know of anything in his career that you have heard of, where he has been in any way unjust?" Borah asked.

"Frankly, we never heard of him until he was nominated by President Hoover," White said. The NAACP leader then revealed that he and others within the organization then conducted a background investigation of Parker and concluded that the 1920 speech was the only objectionable thing they found in his record.[53] White had even asked one of his colleagues to scrutinize Parker's judicial record for any evidence of racial prejudice, bias or animus and had come up completely empty.[54] Nevertheless, White had made clear that this one statement from 1920 was enough for him to wholeheartedly oppose Parker because it reflected his social and political views—qualities that would inevitably inform his opinions as a Justice.

At this point, Overman then jumped in and steered the conversation back to the Suffrage Amendment. It was obvious to White and others that the purpose of the amendment was to disenfranchise millions of Black voters in the state, allowing Democrats to hold onto power permanently.

It wasn't obvious to Overman, though—at least not that he could admit. The senator denied that the amendment was used against any

[51] White, *A Man Called White*, supra, 106.

[52] Minutes of the Meeting of the Executive Council, American Federation of Labor, Washington, D.C., May 5–12, 1930.

[53] Hearing Before the Subcommittee of the Committee on the Judiciary, supra, 77–78.

[54] NAACP Papers, supra, Memo from Andrews to White, April 25, 1930.

particular race and challenged White to prove that Black voters in North Carolina had really been denied the franchise.

"Do you know, Mr. White, that most of the intelligent, educated, colored people vote in North Carolina?" Overman asked. After White responded that that had been the case in recent years, but that Blacks were largely disenfranchised throughout the South, Overman claimed that he was talking just about North Carolina, and that when Parker ran for governor, he got more votes than any other GOP candidate in history—something he attributed, in part, to Black votes.

"He was supported loyally, was he not, but these colored men, who could vote and by some who could not?" Overman asked, while pointing out that the grandfather clause had been gone since 1915.

"Some of them can vote in the larger cities of North Carolina," White said. "But it is still not a safe matter for Negroes, even in North Carolina, Senator Overman, to talk too much about voting in the rural districts."

"Not if he can read and write," Overman retorted.

"Even some of those who can read and write," White maintained.[55]

Overman then challenged White to produce evidence of Black voters who were not allowed to vote even if they could read and write and were otherwise qualified under the law. White demurred and said he didn't have the facts in front of him but that he could send Overman the information at a later time. "I don't think you can find much of that sort," Overman remarked confidently.[56]

Overall, the senators did not seem very interested in talking about civil or voting rights—at least not compared to yellow-dog contracts. Borah barely asked White more than a few questions, while Hebert was almost completely silent. However, Overman and Borah became much more active when questioning the next and final speaker at the hearing, Mercer Johnson, director of the People's Legislative Service. Johnson was there for similar reasons to Green, opposing Parker because of *Red Jacket*. In his testimony, he spoke of the yellow-dog contract in even starker terms than Green, positing whether Parker would have upheld such a contract forcing laborers to sign away their right to marry, vote, or worship.

"The committee is inclined to believe what you say, so if it believes this is an unconscionable contract, why argue it?" Overman asked.

[55] Ibid., 78–79.

[56] Ibid., 78.

"Because of the Egyptian darkness of the mind of Judge Parker, when he confronted those conditions in West Virginia," he responded.[57]

Overman then fired back with a defense of Parker that may not have actually helped his man's cause. "He was not a resident of West Virginia. He was a judge that came from another State. What did he know about the conditions in the coal mines?" Overman asked, not realizing that judges are supposed to educate themselves on these matters and not hide behind their ignorance.

Sure enough, Johnson was ready to pounce. "If he was as ignorant as that, sir, in 1922, he was incapable of ever learning enough to sit on the Supreme Court Bench, because it was common knowledge throughout the United States," Johnson responded.[58]

"Since the Civil War"

After a few more questions, Overman gaveled the hearing to a close. White later recalled that he believed the subcommittee did not take him seriously and were not interested in treating him with respect. "When I did speak, Senators Borah and Overman, particularly the latter, became incensed at the temerity of a Negro organization presuming to voice an opinion on a nomination to the Supreme Court," White later recalled.[59]

More importantly, he realized that the NAACP would have to do most of its work behind the scenes, putting direct pressure on senators and warning them of the consequences of voting for Parker—for the country and for themselves. "I do not know whether or not Parker's confirmation can be defeated," White admitted to Rivera, the person who initially tipped him off about Parker, in a letter dated April 7, 1930.[60] Nevertheless, White expressed optimism that, even if they ended up coming up short, their actions would be well worth it. Maybe Justice Parker would think twice if a case involving civil rights came before him and his brethren

[57] Ibid., 82. The "Egyptian darkness of the mind" is a figurative expression that draws on the biblical reference to "Egyptian darkness"—a term symbolizing intense darkness or ignorance. This reference comes from the ninth plague in the Book of Exodus, where Egypt was covered in a profound and oppressive darkness.

[58] Ibid., 82.

[59] White, *A Man Called White*, supra, 106.

[60] Papers of the National Association for the Advancement of Colored People, supra, Letter from White to Rivera, April 7, 1930.

on the High Court. And maybe it would put other Southerners with national ambitions on notice that they needed to tread carefully when it came to how they treated Blacks.

Immediately after his testimony, White telegrammed every NAACP branch office, particularly those located in the North and in border states where Blacks could vote, and urged them to contact their senators individually and on behalf of their churches, unions, schools and other organizations, to encourage them to reject Parker. NAACP leadership also churned out form letters for their followers to send to their senators and prepared op-eds and fact sheets for newspapers to use. The National Association of Colored Women, which had 250,000 members, also signed on to the effort, as did hundreds of Black newspapers, organizations, churches and individuals across the country.[61]

White also solicited leading newspapers and magazines, both Black and white, and cast the fight in fairly stark terms. The NAACP had finally started making headway in the courts—the last thing they needed was another anti-civil rights judge on the court, especially one who had publicly expressed support for disenfranchising Black voters. How could Parker have approached a case like *Guinn* with any semblance of impartiality when he was already on record defending the type of grandfather clauses that were being challenged, White asked Oswald Garrison Villard of *The Nation*.[62]

In mid-April, the NAACP organized a meeting in Harlem consisting of more than 100 white and nonwhite area churches to protest Parker's nomination and put pressure on New York's two senators, pro-labor Democrat Robert F. Wagner and conservative Democrat Royal S. Copeland and New Jersey's two GOP senators, Hamilton Fish Kean and David Baird, Jr. Meanwhile, on the same day as the Harlem meeting, a large NAACP-led delegation from West Virginia traveled to D.C. to meet with Senators Guy D. Goff and Henry Hatfield, the latter a relative of Sid Hatfield, the police chief killed in the Battle of Matewan.

The enthusiasm among the NAACP membership was almost unprecedented. Daisy Lampkin, who coordinated the association's efforts in Indiana, Ohio and Pennsylvania, said she had never seen anything that

[61] Patricia Sullivan, *Lift Every Voice: The NAACP and the Making of the Civil Rights Movement* (New York: The New Press, 2009), 139–140.

[62] Darlene Clark Hine, "The NAACP and the Supreme Court: Walter F. White and the Defeat of John J. Parker, 1930," *Negro History Bulletin* 40, no. 5 (1977), 754.

"has attracted such wide attention to it as this fight" while DuBois remarked that the campaign was "conducted with a snap, determination and intelligence never surpassed in colored America and seldom in white."[63]

The pressure campaign was starting to yield results. On April 12, the *New York Times* reported that Republican senators, particularly those from states with large Black populations, were starting to abandon Parker—so much so that Vice President Charles Curtis and Senate Majority Leader James Watson (R-IN) expressed their concerns to Hoover.[64] The *Times* also reported that protests were underway by Blacks and civil rights groups in West Virginia, Kentucky, Ohio, Indiana and Kansas and, as a result, Senator Arthur Robinson (R-IN) was leaning towards voting no.[65] Meanwhile, Senator Wheeler wrote White on April 14 telling him he opposed Parker's nomination. Three days later, White received a letter from Senator Smith W. Brookhart (R-IA), a progressive who had bolted the Republican Party in 1924 to support La Follette's third-party presidential bid, informing him that he planned to vote against Parker unless the charges against him were disproven.[66] Parker, who was doing his own head count, believed that Arthur Vandenberg (R-MI) had been swayed by the NAACP into opposing him.[67]

Others would follow as the combined labor and NAACP-led opposition campaigns started to yield results. Borah made his opposition known when the Judiciary subcommittee voted on April 14 to recommend Parker's nomination to the full committee (Overman and Hebert voted in favor). Norris, the Judiciary Committee chair, also came out against Parker, telling the White House that he was unhappy with the direction of the Supreme Court and wanted to see more liberal judges there. Norris also expressed his disappointment with Parker for not dissenting in the *Red Jacket* case and vowed to oppose all "reactionary appointments"

[63] Sullivan, supra, 140.

[64] "Fight Over Parker Laid Before Hoover," *The New York Times*, April 12, 1930.

[65] "President is Firm in Backing Parker in Face of Attacks," *The New York Times*, April 13, 1930.

[66] Papers of the National Association for the Advancement of Colored People, supra, Letter from Brookhart to White, April 14, 1930.

[67] Parker Papers, supra, Letter from Parker to Earl J. Davis, April 25, 1930.

that the White House might make.[68] *The New York Times* reported that Judiciary Committee members John Blaine (R-WI) and Clarence Dill (D-WA) were also opposed to Parker and were poised to help lead the fight against him. The *Times* also reported that a group of 17 GOP Senators led by Majority Leader Watson and asked Hoover to withdraw the nomination.[69] John Robsion (R-KY) confided to others that he was scared of losing the Black vote in his upcoming reelection bid.[70]

In fact, things got so bad that Parker's allies on the committee actually had to request a one-week delay, ostensibly to study his record but mainly to put off the vote until all of his Senate allies on the panel could be present.[71] A source in D.C. had told White that the NAACP was "raising hell in Washington,"[72] and the executive secretary had even started privately expressing confidence that Parker could either be defeated in a vote or be withdrawn by Hoover.[73]

White even tried his luck at forcing Hoover's hand, writing a letter to the president encouraging him to withdraw the nomination. White argued that the 1920 quote was disqualifying for two reasons. If Parker meant it, then he couldn't be impartial and fair. If he didn't mean it and was just saying it for political expediency, then he was "all the more unfit in that he descended to an unbecoming appeal to race prejudice and urged violation of the Fourteenth and Fifteenth Amendments to the Federal Constitution for political advantage."

"All thinking Negroes and all persons of other races who feel that those who are entrusted through position on the nation's highest court with the

[68] Hoover Papers, supra, Hoover memo of telephone call with Willebrandt, April 18, 1930.

[69] "17 Senators Join Move to Recall Name of Parker," *The New York Times*, April 17, 1930.

[70] Watson, Richard Jr., "The Defeat of Judge Parker: A Study in Pressure Groups and Politics," *The Mississippi Valley Historical Review* 50, no. 2 (1963), 233.

[71] "Friends of Parker Help Delay Report From Committee," *The New York Times*, April 15, 1930.

[72] Sullivan, supra, 140. Papers of the National Association for the Advancement of Colored People, supra, Memorandum from White to Ludwell Denny, April 18, 1930.

[73] Papers of the National Association for the Advancement of Colored People, supra, Letter from White to Rivera, April 14, 1930.

upholding and enforcement of the laws are opposed to Judge Parker's confirmation," White added in his April 15 letter.[74]

Unlike when Green wrote Hoover to make the same request, the president did not respond to White's letter. Then again, it's not like White or Green were going to change Hoover's mind. The president was resolute that Parker deserved the job based on his judicial achievements and his legal ability and believed that opposition against him was "based chiefly upon extraneous matters."[75]

What might those "extraneous matters" have been? For Hoover and others in the administration, there were undoubtedly political reasons why certain senators and outside groups were opposing Parker. Willebrandt told the president that she had information that the whole thing was being planned by "Smith Democrats" in North Carolina and a "Negro research bureau in Harlem" and that it was all aimed at Furnifold Simmons, who was in a tough reelection fight that year. FBI Director J. Edgar Hoover went further, sending over information about Joel Elias Spingarn, the NAACP's treasurer and former chairman of the board. The FBI rated him as a longtime socialist who was connected to what they considered to be a radical book publisher: Harcourt, Brace & Company. The FBI chief even suggested that Spingarn be called before the Senate's Lobby Investigation Committee to explain his political actions.[76]

Regardless of what they thought was motivating the anti-Parker crowd, the judge's allies weren't about to roll over and give up. So, they did the thing that Parker had been so adamant about not doing when he was running for governor: they played the race card. The Hoover Administration reportedly put pressure on Black Republican federal office holders to make public declarations of support for Parker.[77] Meanwhile, Hoover personally asked longtime supporter Moton to endorse Parker, only to be rebuffed. For Moton, the 1920 remarks, assuming they were true, were a bridge too far and he told the president that the only position he could

[74] Papers of the National Association for the Advancement of Colored People, supra, "Negroes Ask Hoover to Withdraw Nomination of Judge Parker," April 15, 1930.

[75] "President is Firm in Backing Parker in Face of Attacks," *The New York Times*, April 13, 1930.

[76] Hoover papers, supra, "In reference to his man Spingarn," undated.

[77] Sullivan, *Lift Every Voice*, supra, 140. Papers of the National Association for the Advancement of Colored People, supra, Memorandum from White to Ludwell Denny, April 18, 1930.

take and still respect himself was one of "unyielding opposition to his confirmation."[78]

Simeon Fess (R-OH), a major Parker backer, called Shepard into action, asking him to make a public statement refuting the allegations made by "people of your race."[79] Shepard sent telegrams to senators, including Majority Leader Watson. He also released a statement of support that was picked up by major newspapers throughout the country.[80] The statement was cited by newspapers as evidence that leading Blacks were divided on confirmation.[81] *The Charlotte Observer* made that very argument in an editorial, citing the support of Shepard and fellow academic Atkins as proof that not all Blacks in the state were against Parker and that, if anything, the backing of these educators mattered more since they were "in a position to know what is best for their people."[82]

Overman went so far as to claim, according to the letters he had received, a large majority of Blacks were in favor of Parker's confirmation.[83] White and other NAACP leaders took umbrage at this suggestion. Responding to an article with the headline: "Negroes Divided Over Confirmation of Parker" published in the *St. Luke Herald* on April 19, 1930, White accused Overman and others of trying to show there was division when there was not. "I have never in my life seen Negroes so united as they are on this issue and they are united because the issue is so very fundamental," White said.[84] He went even further, later writing in *Harper's Monthly Magazine* that "on no issue have Negroes worked so unitedly since the Civil War."[85]

On the flip side, the memories of the Civil War and the ensuing fallout from Reconstruction was used by some of Parker's allies to try and

[78] Hoover Papers, supra, Letter from Moton to Walter H. Newton, April 18, 1920.

[79] Parker Papers, supra, Letter from Fess to Shepard, April 14, 1930.

[80] "Upholding Judge Parker," *The Columbia Record*, April 17, 1930.

[81] "Negroes Divided Over Confirmation of Parker," *The St. Luke Herald*, April 19, 1930.

[82] "Standing By Parker," *The Charlotte Observer*, April 15, 1930.

[83] Papers of the National Association for the Advancement of Colored People, supra, Letter from Overman to White, April 18, 1930.

[84] Papers of the National Association for the Advancement of Colored People, supra, Letter from White to Claude Bennett, April 21, 1930.

[85] Walter White, "The Negro and the Supreme Court," *Harper's Monthly Magazine*, January 1931.

galvanize support from certain senators, particularly those from the old Confederacy. According to White, they targeted archconservatives and ardent segregationists like Pat Harrison (D-MS), "Cotton" Ed Smith (D-SC) and Coleman Blease (D-SC), basically asking them what they were going to do about Blacks dictating the terms of who could and could not serve on the Supreme Court, especially a Southern white like Parker.[86] Blease, in particular, was such a virulent racist that he was known to do celebratory dances in public after lynchings and once proposed a resolution to proclaim that the "white" in "White House" shouldn't be limited to a physical descriptor.

Hoover and Parker had been counting on many of these Southern Democrats to support the judge, either out of sectional pride or in sympathy with his lily-white views. However, White and others went to work trying to sway less demagogic Southerners by convincing them that supporting Parker would lead to a resurgence of the Republican Party in the South—a process Hoover started with the 1928 presidential election and something he clearly hoped to make progress on for his reelection campaign. White noted that this tactic managed to get Southerners J. Thomas Heflin of Alabama, Tom Connally of Texas, Joseph Robinson of Arkansas and Kenneth McKellar of Tennessee to oppose Parker.[87]

White also heard reports that Blacks in North Carolina were being coerced into signing endorsements for Parker. In a telegram to Governor Gardner demanding answers, White said that the lives and property of prominent Blacks in the state were being threatened by North Carolina lily-white Republicans if they did not sign. Gardner responded that the charges were "utterly without foundation," and *The News and Observer* quoted a Black Winston-Salem lawyer as saying there was "not a word of truth in the charges."[88] Charles T. Ross, a GOP official from Forsyth County, called the allegations "a malicious falsehood" and an attempt to stir up racial animosity in a city where "there is no ill feeling between

[86] White, *A Man Called White*, supra, 108.

[87] Ibid.

[88] "Governor Denies Threat Charges," *The News and Observer*, April 25, 1930.

the races."[89] White took satisfaction in claiming that only two such endorsements were filed.[90]

White used another controversy to his advantage. On April 20, nearly ten years to the day *The Greensboro Daily News* originally reported on Parker's 1920 speech, the paper published a story hoping to clarify those remarks, while calling out others for distorting them for their own ends. Under the headline "Story That Stirred up Negro Attack Against Parker Given In Full," the paper claimed his words had been taken out of context and, in some cases, completely fabricated. At issue was a *Baltimore Sun* story published the previous day that reported on Black civil rights activists circulating pamphlets and affidavits alleging that Parker had claimed in his speech that, if he were elected governor by one Negro vote, he would resign.[91]

The Greensboro Daily News angrily denied that part, saying "it does not appear by any contemporaneous record available yesterday that Judge Parker ever made the statement about resigning or if so when and where he made it."[92] The paper then reprinted the article from 1920, which contained the oft-quoted passages about Black North Carolinians not wanting to be part of the political process and Republicans not wanting them there, and how demagogues who used racism as a way of stirring up voters and staying in power were the worst. There was nothing in the original article about resigning the governorship though.

Meanwhile, Parker categorically denied saying anything about resigning, reiterating to Blair that the words he did say about Blacks not wanting to be part of the political process had been designed to keep race out of the campaign. He also argued that things had been great in North Carolina ever since 1900, when Blacks started "quietly attending to their own business, under the advice of some of their wisest leaders, and were letting politics alone."[93] He then repeated his oft-used line about performing a service to the state by taking race out of the campaign.

[89] Papers of the National Association for the Advancement of Colored People, supra, Telegram to White from Ross, April 25, 1930.

[90] White, *A Man Called White*, supra, 108.

[91] "New Parker Move Reported Made," *The Baltimore Sun*, April 19, 1930.

[92] "Story That Stirred up Negro Attack Against Parker Given In Full," *The Greensboro Daily News*, April 20, 1930.

[93] Parker Papers, supra, Letter from Parker to Blair, April 11, 1930.

His old ally and mentor Marion Butler backed him up, sending a letter to Senator Wesley Jones (R-WA) that, as someone who was in attendance at the North Carolina GOP convention in 1920, Parker made no such vow to resign if he were elected by one Black vote. Butler added that the sentiments Parker actually did express in his 1920 convention speech were common themes he emphasized throughout the campaign, and that he never said anything resembling the resignation comment that others were accusing him of making. Butler also noted that, as two of the leading Republicans in the state at the time, he and Parker had been on the same page when it came to the party's strategy of pursuing white voters and not appealing to Blacks—a move that paid dividends in 1920 when Parker garnered the most votes of any GOP candidate in the history of the state up to that point.[94]

Butler added that the GOP in North Carolina was stronger than it had been in decades and claimed it had a real shot at winning a Senate race in the fall. "If a Republican Senate shall repudiate and condemn such a policy by refusing to confirm Judge Parker, then obviously the growth and success of the Republican Party in North Carolina will be seriously checked," he warned.[95]

Even though the *Daily News* reprinted Parker's quotes about Blacks not wanting to be part of the political process and the GOP not wanting them in the fold, White took the paper's actions as a dirty trick and an attempt to rewrite history by denying Parker had even made the speech in the first place.[96] After hearing a senator cite the revised *Daily News* story on the floor, White sprang into action, copying the original article and sending it to every senator, as well as to Hoover, so there could be no denying that Parker said what he had said.

Of course, the fact that he had a copy of the original article was another point of contention. In their updated story, the *Daily News* contained a curious tidbit about how it had tried to find the original story in its archives, but discovered it had been illegally cut out and removed without consent. In his memoir, White admitted that a Black man in North Carolina sent a light-skinned man into the offices of the *Daily*

[94] Parker Papers, supra, Letter from Marion Butler to Wesley Jones, April 19,1930.

[95] Ibid.

[96] White, *A Man Called White*, supra, 107. Also: Papers of the National Association for the Advancement of Colored People, supra, Letter from White to Herbert Lehman, April 26, 1930.

News to find a copy of the original. The man was supposed to copy it but ended up cutting it out with a penknife. "One of the photostats we had sent to Washington had been rushed to Greensboro. It had fitted perfectly into the mutilated copy of the paper," White recalled.[97] "Fortunately, the episode was soon forgotten."

Ultimately, Parker's and his allies' full-throated denials about the threat to resign highlighted the bind he was in. As the *Baltimore Sun* article pointed out, Parker may have denied making the resignation threat but "other statements he made on the race issue which are considered just as bad are matters of newspaper record and would be difficult to deny." The *Sun* then immediately cited that now infamous "the Negro as a class does not desire to enter politics" quote while positing that, even if Parker wanted to repudiate it, he could end up alienating Southern Democrats whose votes he needed for confirmation. Indeed, the *Sun* reflected on the absurdity of the situation, namely a president "elected by the party of Abraham Lincoln, forcing through an appointment obnoxious to the Negroes with the aid of those whom the Negroes regard as their political enemies."[98]

"I Shall, of Course, Be Glad to Come"

As the month of April wore on, one thing was clear: the halcyon days when it seemed like Parker's nomination would engender no serious opposition and he would be easily confirmed were long gone. Instead, Parker was now in the fight of his life, and he knew it.

So entrenched was his opposition that Parker could no longer afford to stay above the fray or issue general platitudes about following the law. White was so dug in that he doubted that "any perfunctory statement by Parker at this late date that he 'would live by his oath to support, defend and interpret the Constitution irrespective of race, creed or color,' would be sufficient." "Resentment against Parker by Negroes is so widespread that I am convinced that no general statement will satisfy them or the NAACP," White wrote in an April 16 letter to Cobb.[99]

[97] Ibid., 107–108.

[98] "New Parker Move Reported Made," supra.

[99] Papers of the National Association for the Advancement of Colored People, supra, Letter from White to Cobb, April 16, 1930.

Understanding that he had to engage with his detractors, but still unwilling to do it directly or publicly, Parker sent Senator Hatfield a telegram answering some of the NAACP's charges against him. Repeating his line about how he was simply trying to fight against the injection of race into the campaign, Parker also waxed poetic about racial relations, saying he was trying to make "an honest effort to place myself side by side with those whom I considered to be the best men of both races who for twenty years have been seeking to create friendly sentiment and peaceful relations between the races." He also assured Hatfield that, as a judge, he had always been fair and equitable to everyone before him and intended to bring that level of impartiality to the Supreme Court.[100]

Parker also worked on a wide-ranging letter to Overman rebutting the charges made against him by organized labor and the NAACP. In his initial draft, Parker went through the history of Reconstruction and the Fusion Era, talking about racial strife in the state and region and how politics had exacerbated it. Taking a fairly idyllic view of things, Parker argued that, after ending the Fusion government and adopting the Suffrage Amendment, "all racial trouble in the state subsided" and an "era of good feeling" ensued, benefitting both Blacks and whites. Parker also agreed with what Overman had said during the hearing that educated, literate Blacks could vote in North Carolina. "The danger lies in the illiterate voter," he wrote, not differentiating between Black and white.[101] "Such voters might be controlled by irresponsible leaders who might organize them and vote them in blocks; and the evil of block voting in such case would be complicated by the fact that it would inevitably arouse racial prejudice."

In his final draft, however, Parker removed those passages and stuck with his usual arguments about wanting to remove race from the 1920 campaign. He toned down the feel-good rhetoric of his first draft by simply noting that "the best men of both races in the state had been seeking to create friendly sentiments and peaceful relations between the races," and he was trying to stop racist demagogues from ruining that for

[100] Papers of the National Association for the Advancement of Colored People, supra, Copy of Telegram from Parker to Hatfield, April 19, 1930.

[101] Parker Papers, supra, Letter from Parker to Overman, first draft, April 22, 1930.

political purposes. He also obliquely addressed the resignation controversy by issuing a general refusal to dignify statements made against him that were "so obviously absurd and untrue."[102]

"In conclusion let me say that I have no prejudice whatever against the Colored People and no disposition to deny them any of their rights or privileges under the Constitution and the laws," he wrote.[103] "I think that my record as a Judge of the United States Circuit Court of Appeals, in a circuit where many of them reside, shows that I have no such prejudice or disposition."

Perhaps the biggest change he made from his first draft to the version he sent to Overman was the order in which he addressed his critics. In the first draft, his answer to the NAACP came before labor, but in the final version he flipped them. Without reading too much into it, it's possible that he was more concerned about the attacks from Green and organized labor and wanted to make sure that defense was front and center. Or he didn't want it to look like he was trying to mollify the NAACP because he needed to court Southern Democrats. In preparing his letter, Parker had consulted some of his allies and surrogates and, in one exchange with Blair, Parker noted that he did not want to include that he denied supporting the Suffrage Amendment for fear of alienating some Southern senators.[104]

Parker's statement to Hatfield had an effect on one of the major groups opposing him. The Committee on Race Relations for the Society of Friends wrote a letter to Hoover approving of Parker's words to Hatfield and withdrawing its opposition. The committee also made a practical argument, noting that they understood that Parker came from the South and had different views on civil rights than they did and that, assuming the Supreme Court vacancy was always going to go to a Southerner, Parker was probably the best available choice.[105]

The NAACP, however, was unmoved. Herbert Seligmann, publicity director for the association, sent a letter to White encouraging him to hold the line. Calling Parker a longtime leader of lily-whitism in North

[102] Parker Papers, supra, Letter from Parker to Overman, April 24, 1930.

[103] Ibid.

[104] Parker Papers, supra, Letter from Parker to Blair, April 24, 1930.

[105] Parker Papers, supra, Copy of letter from Committee on Race Relations to Hoover, April 19, 1930.

Carolina and claiming he was "admittedly not of the first rank in the legal profession," Seligmann warned that the NAACP would be making a "disastrous mistake" if they withdrew their opposition.[106] Robert Bagnall, national director of branches, was similarly unimpressed by Parker's statement, pointing out that he could have tried to clear the air earlier but chose not to until he started feeling the heat.[107]

Parker still had one card he could have played had he chosen to do so. Remembering how Stone had volunteered to testify before the Judiciary Committee and ended up bolstering his cause, some of Parker's allies began to lobby the judge to make a similar play. Parker could confront his *Red Jacket* critics who wanted to punish him for doing his job the way Stone had with the Wheeler probe. As for the 1920 remarks, Parker could make a personal appeal that he had always been fair and impartial and would continue to be so on the court, and that should give cover to enough senators to vote for him.

Hoover and certain members of his administration thought this was the way to go. Willebrandt argued that Parker should appear before the committee, noting that his opponents had successfully painted him as someone who was "unjudicial." Parker's appearance and testimony could go a long way towards dispelling that notion, while proving he was thoughtful and open-minded and possessed the requisite temperament to be an associate justice.[108] Majority Leader Watson even jumped the gun and announced on April 17 that Parker would be called before the committee.[109] He also suggested to Overman that Hoover and Attorney General Mitchell wanted Parker to be called before the committee, a sentiment Overman then conveyed to the judge.[110]

Parker, himself, was starting to come around to the need to testify. With his nomination in clear trouble, his long-held view that publicly pursuing judicial office was unseemly and that prospective judges should not opine or comment on issues that they were likely to face on the

[106] Papers of the National Association for the Advancement of Colored People, supra, Memorandum from Seligmann to White, April 19, 1930.

[107] Papers of the National Association for the Advancement of Colored People, supra, Memorandum from Bagnall to White, April 19, 1930.

[108] Hoover Papers, supra, Memo from Willebrandt to Hoover, undated.

[109] "Senators to Quiz Parker on Charges," *The Baltimore Sun*, April 18, 1930.

[110] Hoover Papers, supra, Copy of Western Union Telegram from Overman to Parker, April 18, 1930.

bench had started to bend towards pragmatism. In the end, he offered to testify before the Judiciary Committee but stopped short of asking or even demanding a hearing, stating: "If the Judiciary Committee of the United States Senate desires my presence and requests it, I shall, of course, be glad to come."[111]

By putting the ball in their court, Parker essentially gave the committee an out—one that it happily took. Norris and Borah and others on the committee did not see the point in having Parker testify,[112] since, unlike the situation with Stone, there were no ambiguities when it came to Parker. The judge believed his *Red Jacket* opinion was correct, and no amount of argument or clarification would sway his pro-labor critics who saw yellow-dog contracts as modern-day slavery. As for his 1920 speech, Parker was no less clear that he considered those words to be just as right then as they were in the present day. Appearing in person would simply cause both Parker and his opponents to dig into their respective positions.

So, on April 21, 1930, Overman made a motion to summon Parker before the Judiciary Committee, but got voted down 10–4, with only Hebert, Charles S. Deneen (R-IL) and Hubert Stephens (D-MS) voting with the North Carolinian. Then the committee dropped the hammer, voting 10–6 to forward Parker's nomination to the full Senate with an adverse recommendation. Joining Overman, Hebert and Stephens in favor of Parker were three Republican senators: Frederick H. Gillett (MA), Charles Winfield Waterman (CO) and Daniel O. Hastings (DE). Despite wanting to hear from him, Deneen joined with five of his fellow Republicans: Norris, Borah, Arthur Robinson (IN), John Blaine (WI) and Frederick Steiwer (OR), as well as four Democrats: Dill, Henry Ashurst, Thomas Walsh and Thaddeus Caraway (AR) to report the nomination unfavorably.[113]

Hoover was said to be surprised at the result. However, the president made it plain he would not be withdrawing Parker's nomination and was confident the judge would prevail in the Senate vote. Parker, meanwhile, resisted entreaties to take the initiative and withdraw and, along with his close allies, remained convinced that he would win. Perhaps the judge in

111 "Parker Is Willing to Testify, He Says," *The New York Times*, April 20, 1930.

112 Ibid.

113 "Report Unfavorably on Judge Parker," *The Streator Daily Times-Press*, April 21, 1930.

him honestly believed that, as long as he promised to be fair and impartial to people of all races on the bench, then it didn't matter what he had said in the past. Or maybe he imagined that the NAACP, like organized labor, were making mountains out of molehills and the Senate would see through it.

Or maybe he believed that he had to win, because otherwise it would violate his own sense of justice. In the *Red Jacket* case, he maintained that he had done the right thing and upheld his duty as a circuit court judge by following established Supreme Court precedent, putting whatever personal or political views he had aside in order to follow the law. When it came to the 1920 remarks, he believed that he had done the right thing by not only following the law as it existed in his state but putting the best interests of society ahead of his own political gain. The idea that he could be punished for his righteousness was something he could not bring himself to fathom, let alone accept.

But what Parker failed to understand was that his vision of what was right and wrong was drastically different than that of the NAACP, White and other civil rights groups, to say nothing of Green and organized labor. For Parker and his allies, it was unfair that a qualified judge like him be denied the highest position in his profession. For White and his constituents, it was unfair that they couldn't vote, be protected from lynching, go to desegregated schools, eat at the same lunch counters and stay in the same hotels as white, and enjoy true equality under the law—the law that Parker and others were in charge of upholding. For Green and his followers, it was unfair that they couldn't make livable wages, work a reasonable schedule, be protected from dangers on the job, collectively bargain, and enjoy true equality under the law—again, the same law that Parker and others were in charge of upholding.

Cast in these stark terms, it's no wonder that these groups went all out to try and make sure Parker did not get on the Supreme Court. Nevertheless, Parker still believed he had a shot and, as his nomination went before the full Senate, he thought, perhaps naively, that he would still end up on top. After all, he was a judge and dealt with precedent. Interest groups had tried to take down nominees before and they had all failed. Individual senators had succeeded in blocking nominations, but that hadn't happened since 1894. "A hard fight is being made upon me,"

Parker said in advance of the full Senate debate into his nomination, "but I think that there is a good chance of my winning out."[114]

[114] Parker Papers, supra, Letter from Parker to Earl J. Davis, April 25, 1930.

CHAPTER 7

"An Incident": The Senate Decides Parker's Fate

As the Senate began formally debating John J. Parker's confirmation to the Supreme Court on the afternoon of Monday, April 28, there were a few things that were beyond doubt.

The increasingly bitter and nasty fight had captured the imagination of the country and had become one of the hottest tickets in town. On any given day, the galleries would be packed with luminaries and power players, including Oscar De Priest and Alice Roosevelt Longworth, Theodore Roosevelt's daughter, who was married to Speaker of the House Nicholas Longworth III but had carried on an affair with Borah and had even given birth to his love child.[1]

The stakes were high—Parker was young and had the potential to serve on the court for decades. On a closely divided court, he could be the difference between maintaining the status quo and radical change.

The battle had become more than just about one man's qualifications to be an associate justice of the Supreme Court. Progressives were fed up with decades of jurisprudence from the Supreme Court that seemingly gave businesses more rights than individuals. Civil rights leaders

[1] "Senators Assail Parker as Lacking Courage for Post," *The New York Times*, April 30, 1930. For more on Alice Roosevelt Longworth and her affair with Borah, see Thomas Mallon, "Hissing Cousins," *The Washington Post*, April 24, 2015. The affair was an open secret in D.C., so much so that Longworth toyed with naming their daughter Deborah (as in De-Borah). She went with Paulina.

V. Li, *Supreme Pressure*,
https://doi.org/10.1007/978-3-032-07864-3_7

were tired of the Supreme Court turning a blind eye to states intent on relegating entire races of people to second-class citizenship. Southerners, meanwhile, were struggling with partisan identity, with some willing to overlook Parker's party affiliation in order to have a one of their own on the court, while others were worried that supporting a Republican might lead to a weakening of the Democratic monopoly on power in the former Confederacy. As an op-ed that ran in the *Washington Daily News* on April 22 shortly after the committee vote put it, "Parker is an incident. The Supreme Court is the issue."[2]

And no one had any idea which way the vote was going to go. Indeed, his chances for winning or losing depended on whom you asked.

William Green of the AFL confidently predicted the anti-Parker forces had enough votes to defeat the nomination and cited the Judiciary Committee's actions as proof. "It remains to be seen whether or not sufficient pressure can be brought to bear upon members of the Senate to cause them to change their attitude," Green said.[3] "I am confident this cannot be done because the masses of the people have become so thoroughly aroused in their opposition to the appointment of Judge Parker."

Parker allies, on the other hand, believed they had the upper hand and would just about prevail. Groner predicted to Parker that he would be confirmed by five votes and promised that it would be a distant memory once he was on the High Court. "The fight on you will not leave any marks, and you will have the satisfaction of knowing that in spite of every effort on the part of many evil men, you have come through the fire unsinged," Groner said to Parker in a May 5 letter.[4]

Walter White of the NAACP wasn't sure what the result would be, but thought it might come down to one or two votes[5]—so much so that he even sent a telegram to Vice President Curtis encouraging him to vote against Parker in case the vote ended up being tied and required him to break it.[6] Meanwhile, Hoover administration officials kept a running

[2] "The People's Victory," *The Washington Daily News*, April 22, 1930.

[3] "Green Says Count Defeats Parker," *The New York Times*, April 21, 1930.

[4] Parker Papers, supra, Letter from Groner to Parker, May 5, 1930.

[5] NAACP Papers, supra, Telegram from White to Harry Davis, May 1, 1930.

[6] NAACP Papers, supra, Telegram from White to Charles Curtis, May 7, 1930. No vice president has broken a tie against their own president's nominee since John C. Calhoun

tally of where individual senators stood, and this showed a tight race—although it wasn't clear who was in the lead, since the list had plenty of names crossed out or with question marks next to them.[7]

"I Feel Sure That He Would Get No Votes for Confirmation"

As the Senate geared up to debate Parker's nomination, his opponents had four clear lines of attack: his *Red Jacket* opinion, his 1920 remarks about Blacks in North Carolina, his relative youth and inexperience, and his perceived conservatism. His supporters had clear arguments to address each of those issues. In *Red Jacket*, he was doing his duty as a judge. His 1920 remarks were politically necessary for him when he was a politician and bore no weight on his performance as a judge. He was young and relatively inexperienced, but he had distinguished himself as a first-rate circuit judge. As for his ideology, it was hard to pin down where he stood on issues since he was constrained by the Supreme Court, but he had always been more identified with the progressive wing of his party when he was in politics—in other words, he was hardly a reactionary.

Each of those arguments would be repeated at length during the pendency of the Senate debate—as well as some curveballs and unexpected developments that even surprised the participants of the Kabuki theater that the Supreme Court confirmation process was about to become known for.

In the weeks leading up to the commencement of the full Senate debate over Parker's nomination, Overman had diligently taken to the floor of the chamber to submit into the record articles, letters, editorials, and statements in favor of his fellow Tar Heel. Occasionally, he would be joined on the floor by others—both for and against Parker—who likewise would submit material that was both for and against Parker, all in the interests of building an accurate and complete record. In fact, Overman was the one who entered Green's letter into the record while Dill, an anti-Parker senator, submitted an editorial entitled "In Defense of Judge Parker."

voted against Martin Van Buren's nomination to be Ambassador to Great Britain in 1832. Calhoun, who had been embroiled in a feud with his president, Andrew Jackson, ended up being replaced on the ticket later that year by Van Buren.

[7] Hoover Papers, supra, "Against/Doubtful/For," undated.

When the full Senate debate started, Overman seemed like the natural choice to lead the charge for the pro-Parker forces. The Hoover Administration and Senate Republican leadership certainly thought so and had originally been willing to outsource management of Parker's confirmation to Overman and the Democrats, in part, to avoid the prospect of pro-Parker Republicans taking on intraparty colleagues like Borah and Norris. Instead, on April 27, newspapers reported Overman had been sidelined in favor of Senators Fess and Hebert, two Republicans. Evidently, partisan politics had won out and Republicans felt they needed their own out there to help get Parker over the line—relying on Democrats to do the job for them would be problematic.[8]

Despite that, when the debate commenced in the Senate on the afternoon of Monday, April 28, it was Overman who was standing at the dais on behalf of Parker's proponents. Knowing that the vote was going to be close and needing every "yes" possible, Overman asked for unanimous consent that the debate be postponed until May 1 because his colleague, Simmons, had been called back to North Carolina on business. At least he tried to do so. After reading into the record a letter from his son-in-law complaining about trying to borrow from North Carolina banks, Overman realized he had read the wrong statement. After some laughter from the gallery and senators present, Overman then read Simmons' letter asking for a delay.[9]

The moment of levity did not lead to one of comity. Borah objected to the delay, noting that Simmons had plenty of time to return to Washington to cast his vote.[10] In fact, Simmons' absence probably had less to do with pressing business in the state and more to do with giving him time to figure out how to handle a rapidly growing political problem. Already unpopular with certain segments of the Democratic Party over his refusal to endorse Al Smith in 1928, Simmons had drawn a tough primary opponent in the form of 1924 gubernatorial candidate Josiah W. Bailey. The Parker nomination added another hurdle, as Simmons clearly

[8] "Overman Will Not Lead Fight for Confirmation of Judge John J. Parker," *The News and Observer*, April 27, 1930.

[9] "Parker Confirmation Debate Opens in Senate with Flood of Oratory from Spokesmen," *The Greensboro Daily News*, April 29, 1930.

[10] *Congressional Record*, Proceedings and Debates of the Second Session of the Seventy First Congress of the United States of America, Vol. LXXII—Part 7, April 10–28, 7807–7808.

wanted to do whatever he could to get his nomination over the line, but could not afford to alienate labor if he wanted to have any chance of prevailing in the primary.[11]

Therefore, it was left to Overman alone to present his fellow Tar Heel's credentials and biography. The senator spoke of how the Fourth Circuit had not had a justice on the Supreme Court bench in a century and that, while he had hoped Hoover might appoint Stacy, a Democrat, he told the president that Parker was a good and worthy choice. "I said, 'Mr. President, if you are determined in your own mind to appoint a Republican to this position, I cheerfully say to you that I do not believe you could find a better man among the Republicans of the South than Judge Parker,'" Overman said.[12]

While he emphasized that he wasn't there to make an argument but to simply present Parker before the Senate, like Antony at Caesar's funeral, Overman could not help himself and launched into a stirring defense of the judge. First, he acknowledged the work of the AFL and other major labor groups organizing against Parker, admitting he had been overwhelmed by all of their letters, telegrams and communications. He did not mention the NAACP by name during his opening remarks, but referred to "socialists, communists and a large number from the colored population of the country."[13] At the time, it was common for their opponents to refer to the NAACP as a communist front or one with socialist ties, so Overman's implication was unmistakable.

But that was nothing compared to the support Parker had which, according to Overman, included many messages from "leading colored men, the most intelligent men in my state," naming Shepard and three others.[14] He also pointed out that many lawyers, judges, intellectuals, academics, and businessmen were in favor of Parker, adding that those who lived and worked in the Fourth Circuit were near-unanimous in their support for him.[15]

[11] "Attitude of Simmons of Interest in Fight," *The Greensboro Daily News*, April 28, 1930.

[12] Ibid., 7808.

[13] Ibid., 7808.

[14] Ibid.

[15] Ibid.

After submitting biographical information on Parker, as well as numerous statements and letters in favor of him, Overman finally addressed the NAACP and their charges against the judge. Taking White's words out of context, Overman claimed that the secretary had agreed with him that North Carolina was "ahead of every other State in the Union in their advancement and progress" when it came to race relations and treatment of Blacks, and that the literacy test requirement for voting in the state was not discriminatory since Black voters who could read could vote. "There is no trouble, no intimidation, no strained feeling between the white people and the colored people of our State," Overman claimed.[16]

He referenced the contentious 1920 election comments and chalked it up to people saying things in the heat of a campaign that they don't necessarily mean or will be seen as water under the bridge once they win. "[O]ne time I made a political speech in which I made severe castigation of the President then running, and a Republican came to Washington and told the president what I had said. He said: 'Why, I don't care a damn what Overman said in a political speech,' and I never had a better friend than that President," the senator said.[17]

At that point, a few senators interrupted Overman to ask questions. David Walsh (D-MA) asked a few general questions about Parker's background, including what years he ran for office and when he became a federal judge. Overman responded that Parker became a judge at the recommendation of the attorney general, who had been impressed at the way he had handled prosecuting war fraud cases on behalf of the Department of Justice. That opened the door for Senators Wheeler and Hugo Black, who previewed a new angle of attack centering on an issue that had been largely forgotten about.

"What was the result of the war fraud case? Did he win the case?" Wheeler asked.

"No, sir; he did not," Overman responded. "Judge Bailey has written a letter, which the senator probably has seen, saying that Judge Parker conducted the trial with great ability; that he amassed well; it took 10 weeks to try the case, but the jury found in favor of the defendants."

[16] Ibid., 7810.

[17] Ibid.

Of the two war fraud cases Parker had handled, Overman had referred to the *Lumber* case, which had been handled by Justice Jennings Bailey.

Black then jumped in. The former Ku Klux Klan member and future Supreme Court justice had been seen as a potential vote for Parker, and both the pro and anti-camps had been working on him. In a move that was, no doubt, alarming to the pro-Parker forces, Black brought up a recent editorial published in the *New York Telegram*, and reprinted in various papers throughout the country, including *The News & Observer*, that was critical of Parker's handling of the *Harness* case, accusing the then special prosecutor of engaging in unethical and incompetent lawyering. Black was especially troubled over allegations that Parker withheld exculpatory evidence from the defendants, prompting Overman to respond that the presiding judge and several of the defense lawyers in the case had gone on record stating they thought Parker had tried it ably.

Black claimed that how well Parker tried the case was immaterial—what concerned him was whether or not Parker had withheld exculpatory evidence. "If it be true that as a prosecutor he had in his possession evidence which tended to show the innocence of a defendant, and at the same time prosecuted him, I feel sure that he would get no votes for confirmation," he said, adding that he would vote against Parker unless this charge was disproven.[18]

Overman was shaken and said he would try to disprove it, but admitted he wasn't sure if he would be able to. He later reached out to Parker and suggested he explain the circumstances around the *Harness* case to address Black's concerns. Parker did so and sent a copy of his response to Black. Parker categorically denied the allegation that he had withheld exculpatory evidence and went further, saying he had never prosecuted anyone while having evidence that they were innocent. Parker noted that many of the witnesses they put on the stand were hostile and many of the documents those witnesses had relied on had never been shared with the prosecution and had taken them by surprise. "I know of no document that established the innocence of defendants, but I do know that no document tending to establish their innocence was withheld or suppressed by me," he wrote in his letter.[19]

[18] Ibid., 7811.

[19] Parker Papers, supra, Letter from Parker to Overman, April 29, 1930.

A couple of days later, on April 30, the issue came up again, as Thomas Walsh (D-MT) moved the transcript of Groner's lengthy jury instructions from the *Harness* case into the record. Walsh cited a passage in which the judge criticized the government for having four documents in their possession that had not been produced.[20]

Carter Glass, however, diffused the situation by asking Walsh about what Groner had said on the record concerning Parker and this team when it came to how well they had tried the case. "My friends who represent the Government earnestly contend in this case for a verdict. Their conduct has been characterized by fairness; I think by great ability," Groner was quoted as saying.[21]

Walsh countered, arguing one little compliment to the prosecutors was not the be all and end all. The bottom line, he argued, was that the prosecutors still behaved unethically and did something so antithetical to the notion of fairness, justice and presumption of innocence that he could not imagine how they could have looked themselves in the mirror afterwards. "If I were a prosecuting attorney and found myself subject to comment of this character from the judge on the bench, I should be so humiliated as to prompt me to abandon the practice of the law," Walsh said.[22]

Overman then pointed out that Groner's compliment was not some throwaway line that didn't mean anything. He was complimenting the government's handling of the entire case—not the kind of thing you would say if you were just trying to be polite or taking the sting out of things. At this point, Walsh started to move onto other issues—something the rest of the Senate seemed ready to do as well.

[20] *Congressional Record*, Proceedings and Debates of the Second Session of the Seventy First Congress of the United States of America, Vol. LXXII—Part 8, April 29–May 16, 1930, 8023.

[21] Ibid., 8026.

[22] Ibid., 8106.

"No Place in Any Defensible System of Social Justice"

Overman closed his introductory remarks by confirming reports that he would, indeed, be stepping aside as manager of Parker's confirmation in favor of administration-loyal Republicans. He made clear, though, that his decision had no bearing on his feelings for his fellow Tar Heel. Overman was unequivocal—Parker had his support and vote.[23]

On the other hand, there was little controversy or doubt over who would lead the line against Parker. Borah was the obvious choice, given his role scrutinizing Parker's record and examining the witnesses who had testified before the Judiciary subcommittee. Moreover, the battle had become a personal crusade for the charter member of the "Sons of the Wild Jackass"—at least when it came to the issue of yellow-dog contracts, which he claimed had "no place in any defensible system of social justice."[24] Borah also took umbrage at the notion that laborers were not entitled to more rights than others just because they had large numbers of voters and superior organization. Instead, the senator flipped it around, saying that "labor has no rights because of its votes, great or small, but it has rights, regardless of its votes." And for Borah, one of those rights was to be free from onerous, one-sided contracts that they had no choice but to sign that took away their rights and forced them to function as quasi-slaves.

Borah took to the podium and launched into a lengthy speech—so long, in fact, that it began on Monday afternoon and continued the following day. The Idaho Republican spent the entirety of his opening speech railing against yellow-dog contracts, injunctions, *Hitchman*, Parker's actions in the *Red Jacket* case and the plight of the American laborer. Uttering nary a word about the war fraud cases or Parker's 1920 gubernatorial race, Borah's speech could not have made Green and others in organized labor prouder. Indeed, it could have been ghost-written by any one of them.

Arguing that Parker had become synonymous with the term "yellow-dog contract," Borah excoriated him for going further, in his opinion, than any other judge in sustaining and enforcing them. Accepting that

23 "Overman Loses Plea to Postpone Action on High Court Post," *The News and Record*, April 29, 1930.

24 Borah Papers, supra, Letter from Borah to Rignal Baldwin, April 26, 1930.

businesses had the right to stop union organizers from recruiting through illegal activities such as threats, violence and coercion, Borah could not fathom how peaceful methods could be enjoined. Borah also pointed out that, whatever legal or historical basis there may have been to uphold yellow-dog contracts, whether it be common law or Supreme Court jurisprudence, conditions for laborers had changed dramatically over the last century, usually for the worse, and required more modern solutions.

But mostly he railed against what he saw was the blatant unfairness and basic inequality of yellow-dog contracts. Echoing arguments he made during the subcommittee hearing, Borah argued that these contracts were entirely one-sided and procured under duress, since workers had to choose between giving up their rights or giving up their ability to provide for themselves and their families. "Where is the mutuality of this contract? The employee gives up his right to join a labor union. What does the employer give up?" Borah wondered.[25]

He also criticized the courts' fealty to liberty of contract, arguing that the right was hardly absolute and there were plenty of reasonable restrictions—especially if there was a conflict with public policy or clearly established law. For instance, a company could not enter into a slave contract with workers, nor could it exempt itself from any and all legal exposure or liability. Additionally, Borah cited several Supreme Court cases that stood for this proposition, including a 1915 case in which the majority held that liberty of contract was "subject to conditions in the interest of the public welfare."[26]

In Borah's mind, the yellow-dog contract easily fit this criteria of violating the public welfare. "Can there be anything of more concern to the State, to the Government, to the public generally, than that which is calculated to undermine, destroy, or build up, to render fit or unfit for citizenship, men and women who toil?" Borah wondered.[27]

Borah also argued that ***Hitchman*** did not necessarily control ***Red Jacket***. Echoing Green's arguments, Borah maintained that Parker had

[25] *Congressional Record*, Proceedings and Debates of the Second Session of the Seventy First Congress of the United States of America, Vol. LXXII—Part 8, April 29–May 16, 1930, 7932.

[26] Ibid., 7932–7933. See also: *Coppage v. Kansas*, 236 U.S. 1 (1915).

[27] *Congressional Record*, Proceedings and Debates of the Second Session of the Seventy First Congress of the United States of America, Vol. LXXII—Part 8, April 29–May 16, 1930, 7931.

ignored pro-union sentiments from the Taft court in cases like *Tri-City* and others that stood for the proposition that peaceful activities from unions were lawful. He also claimed that Parker would have been within his rights to modify the injunction to proscribe acts that the *Tri-City* court had held were unlawful. There was no way the court would have rebuked or overruled him for doing that, Borah stated.

Labor had made the case that Parker should have tried to distinguish *Hitchman* or even express some sort of disapproval of it in *obiter dicta*. By pointing out that Parker could have explicitly carved out an exception in the injunction for legal activities consistent with *Tri-City*, Borah undercut Parker's claim to have been merely following Supreme Court precedent. But ultimately, Borah admitted that it didn't matter. Even if Parker had done so, Borah was never going to support someone who recognized the legality of yellow-dog contracts. "I think this is so fundamental, so righteous in and of itself that I could not get my consent to put upon the Supreme Court a man who has already declared his position upon the question," he said, adding that, if the Senate voted for Parker, it amounted to a wholehearted endorsement of yellow-dog contracts.[28]

Borah then wrapped up his opening speech in typical politician fashion—listing the brilliant and ingenious qualities and features of American Constitutional government. In doing so, he found one last avenue of attack on Parker. Acknowledging that faith in democratic institutions, especially the courts, was low, Borah argued that it was imperative to find men of courage and conviction who were not just there to maintain the status quo and hide behind precedent or hierarchies. "The fault is not in the Government, the fault is not in the form of our institutions; the fault, if any may arise, will be in the failure to find men with the intelligence to appreciate the obligations imposed and the courage to execute the powers of the Government," Borah said.[29] "Those who say to us here that we are to approve *pro forma* are teaching those doctrines of cowardice and betrayal, the very things which rot out and destroy government. It is not the performance of duty, but the shirking of duty which destroys free institutions."

Several senators took issue with Borah's speech. Frederick Gillett, who had voted for Parker in the Judiciary Committee, argued Borah had

[28] Ibid., 7938.

[29] Ibid., 7939.

misapplied *Tri-City* because that case had involved an injunction against unions using peaceful persuasion to get workers to leave their jobs and not to break their contract, while *Hitchman* and *Red Jacket* had covered breach of contract. "The illegal persuasion on which the injunction is founded was to persuade them to break a contract. That is illegal," Gillett said about *Red Jacket* and *Hitchman*.[30]

Other senators took issue with Borah's call for courage. Fess resented the pressure that outside interest groups were putting on the courts by enlisting senators to fight judicial nominations, believing it undermined judicial independence. He also went through a long discussion of the history of the Supreme Court and the Senate's "advice and consent" power, invoking such notable names throughout history such as Henry Clay, Daniel Webster, John Calhoun, John Marshall, Joseph Story, and others.

Citing the current battle, as well as the previous one involving now Chief Justice Hughes, Fess argued that judges demonstrated their courage by being independent and not being easily swayed by public pressure. "If they were other than independent they would not be fit to be on the bench," Fess stated.[31] He then quoted from the *Washington Daily News* op-ed, saying that "Parker is an incident. The Supreme Court is the issue." The op-ed had actually been against Parker and the above-quoted line was meant as a rallying cry against the status quo—particularly "injunction judges" "yellow-dog contracts" "Supreme Court reactionaries" and "judges inclined toward unfair racial discrimination."[32] Nevertheless, Fess co-opted it to underscore his point that not only was the direction of the Supreme Court at stake but the entire concept of an independent judiciary.

Daniel Hastings (R-DE) questioned Borah's insistence on using the yellow-dog contract as a litmus test, arguing that it turned the court into a subordinate, partisan organization subject to the whims of the president and Senate. "I am wondering whether we are about to adopt a new attitude with respect to the Supreme Court," Hastings wondered.[33] "Can it be said that the Senate of the United States ought to adopt as a policy a

[30] Ibid., 7940.

[31] Ibid., 7949.

[32] "The People's Victory," *The Washington Daily News*, April 22, 1930.

[33] *Congressional Record*, Vol. LXXII, supra, 8032.

plan to put on the Supreme Court only persons who have certain fixed ideas as to the interpretation of the law? Shall that be the policy of the United States Senate? Shall that be the policy of the President of the United States?".

Borah, however, had help. Dill argued it was absurd to say that all judges had to have independence, but then deny inferior court judges any discretion when it came to following the dictates of the Supreme Court, even if they believed the court had acted wrongly. Ashurst, meanwhile, went even further than Borah when denouncing the yellow-dog contract, stating that any judge who would do that, regardless of the circumstances, was unfit for the Supreme Court. And if that sentence was a bit too anodyne for anyone, Ashurst made sure there was no doubt about how little regard he had for the nominee. "Now, when a nominee who has neither great character nor great courage nor great learning is set before us, and we are asked to put the seal of our approval upon him for that high place, it is suggested by the Senator [Fess] that we are trying to destroy the United States Supreme Court because we do not swallow weaklings," Ashurst said.[34] When asked a few days later if he really meant what he had said, Ashurst not only refused to retract of modify his comments but doubled down on calling Parker a "weakling," adding that his nomination was an "injustice to the American people."[35]

Robert Wagner (R-NY) also gave a lengthy speech in opposition of Parker. Echoing Ashurst, Borah and others, he opened by denouncing yellow-dog contracts and arguing that Parker's failure to express even the slightest disapprobation over them disqualified him from serving on the High Court. "That failure to be aware of the fact that he was in the presence of an important problem shows a lack of statecraft which is the *sine qua non* of the high judicial office to which he has been nominated," Wagner stated.[36]

Furthermore, Wagner argued that Parker did not have to rule the way he did in *Red Jacket*, noting that judges in his home state had come to the opposite conclusion on a similar set of facts. In addition to being against public policy, Wagner argued that the yellow-dog contracts at issue in *Red Jacket* did not make sense since the employees were "at will"—in

[34] Ibid., 7952.

[35] Ibid., 8343.

[36] Ibid., 8035.

other words, they could be fired for no reason and they could quit for no reason. Therefore, they were perfectly within their rights to quit their jobs in order to join a union and the union could not have been acting unlawfully by inducing them to do so. "The one and only inference that can be and must be logically drawn from the Parker decision is that he holds it unlawful for a union to organize workers in a trade and persuade them to go on strike–contract or no contract," Wagner argued.[37]

Meanwhile, the other main Son of the Wild Jackass had been fairly quiet during the first few days of debate. That changed when George Norris took the floor on May 1 and debated Hebert and Allen. At one point, he even admitted that "of course," he wanted to see people on the Supreme Court who agreed with his own views. The next day, he gave a speech and launched into a condemnation of Parker. Quoting Theodore Roosevelt, Norris underscored the stakes of this nomination, pointing out that "[m]uch of the future of this country depends upon the direction from which the judges of the Supreme Court approach the great constitutional questions that they will have to decide."

In that regard, the Judiciary chair agreed with Borah and the others that, while Parker had a right to follow *Hitchman*, he also had a right to express his own personal disagreement with it, if he had felt inclined. Judges do it all of the time. By not doing so, Norris argued, it showed Parker was completely in agreement with the principles of *Hitchman*. Moreover, based on the principle articulated by Roosevelt, it showed that Parker had approached this great constitutional question from the side of affirming the injunction and upholding the yellow-dog contract. "I believe we ought to put more humanity into the courts. We ought to have judges who would have the humanitarian viewpoint," Norris said before responding to Fess' citation of what the *Washington Daily News* had said about Parker's confirmation and adding his own flair to it. "Judge Parker is only an incident. The Supreme Court is only an incident. Human liberty is the issue. The preservation of our government is the issue," Norris said, raising the stakes even more.[38]

[37] Ibid., 8036.

[38] Ibid., 8103, 8192.

"An Insufferable and Unjustified Affront to Millions of American Citizens"

Considering how large a role the NAACP had played behind the scenes in marshalling opposition to the nomination, it might be a surprise that there was hardly any mention of Parker's 1920 comments in the opening days of the debate.

Or maybe it was appropriate, considering how dismissive many senators had been towards White and the NAACP—at least compared to Green and other labor leaders.

It also exposed some uncomfortable fault lines between senators who were, purportedly, on the same side. On April 29, Gillett briefly brought up Parker's 1920 comments—the first time they had been addressed since the formal debate over his nomination began. Making it clear that he did not agree with his statement about Black voters in North Carolina, Gillett, nonetheless, reasoned that no Southern politician at the time with any kind of ambition could reasonably be expected to hold the opposite viewpoint. Plus, Gillett stated that he believed Parker was "a man of such breadth of vision, and such broad humanity and such character" that if he were to face a case involving a Black party, he would "treat them with justice and with fairness and without any proscription of any race."[39] Because of that, despite his disapproval over his 1920 comments, Gillett announced he would support Parker, something Parker later expressed gratitude to the senator for.[40]

Even this slightest of rebukes was a bridge too far for Carter Glass. The influential Democrat from Virginia had been one of the architects of that state's disenfranchisement laws—and, unlike others who would pretend that they were not racially motivated, Glass had no such recalcitrance. "Discrimination!" he said plainly when asked what the purpose of the state's voter eligibility laws were.[41] "Why that is exactly what we propose. To remove every voter who can be gotten rid of, legally, without materially impairing the numerical strength of the white electorate." Glass, who ultimately voted in favor of Parker's confirmation, pointed out that

[39] Ibid., 7943.

[40] Parker Papers, supra, Letter from Parker to Gillett, April 30, 1930.

[41] "Senator Carter Glass 1858–1946: The Good and the Bad," *Notes from Under Grounds*, https://smallnotes.library.virginia.edu/2021/09/01/senator-carter-glass-1858-1946-the-good-and-the-bad/, accessed September 10, 2024.

Gillett's home state of Massachusetts also had a literacy requirement for voting before taking on a more confrontational tone.

"I say, why does the Senator assume to know more than Judge Parker about those people in North Carolina?" Glass wondered.

"I do not assume to know more," Gillett responded. "I am sure I do not know as much."

"I am sure the Senator does not," Glass retorted to laughter in the gallery.[42]

The issue of Parker's 1920 remarks did not come up again in debate until Wagner took the floor the following day. After spending most of his time talking about *Red Jacket* and yellow-dog contracts, the New York senator called Parker's now infamous speech "an insufferable and unjustified affront to millions of American citizens." Wagner added that in his state men and women of all races and creeds were able to take part in the democratic process freely and that everyone was better for it.

Wagner also tied Parker's racial comments to what he and others saw as his bias against laborers and workers suffering under yellow-dog contracts, arguing that the judge was "incapable of viewing with sympathy the aspirations of those who are aiming for a higher and better place in the world." He added that Parker was naturally sympathetic to and aligned with the elite and powerful and accused him of using "the authority of his office and the influence of his opinion to keep them on top and to restrain the strivings of the others, whether they be an exploited economic group or a minority racial group."[43]

Wagner's speech angered Southerners, some of whom walked out of the Senate chamber.[44] A few days later, Senator Hubert Stephens (D-MS) responded and called Wagner's speech the "grossest insult to the people of the South that has been offered in a generation."[45] Stephens went even further, stating that there was not an "honest, decent, respectable white

[42] *Congressional Record*, Proceedings and Debates of the Second Session of the Seventy First Congress of the United States of America, Vol. LXXII—Part 8, April 29–May 16, 1930, 7943.

[43] Ibid., 8037.

[44] "Dixon Urged Hoover to Nominate Judge Parker as Political Maneuver," *The News & Observer*, May 1, 1930.

[45] *Congressional Record*, Proceedings and Debates of the Second Session of the Seventy First Congress of the United States of America, Vol. LXXII—Part 8, April 29–May 16, 1930, 8348.

man in the South who does not hold the same views on that question that Judge Parker does" and that should not disqualify any person from the South from being on the Supreme Court. Stephens then brought up former Justice L.Q.C. Lamar, who had served in the Confederate army, and current Justice James McReynolds, a Wilson appointee from Tennessee, as examples of fair-minded men from the South who had never been anything but fair and unbiased on the bench. Stephens did not bring up the fact that McReynolds was known to be a virulent anti-Semite and racist who refused to hire Blacks, Jews, or women as law clerks and almost never spoke with Brandeis on account of his religion. Stephens closed by saying that Southerners had to vote for Parker—or else they might never get another one of them on the court again.

Other Parker allies joined in and tried to help out. Hebert, Hatfield, Henry Allen, Wesley Jones and Roscoe McCulloch (R-OH) pointed out Parker's ruling in the recent *City of Richmond v. Deans* case as evidence of the judge's fairness, while Fess decried DuBois and other NAACP leaders as Bolsheviks and socialists. Jones and Samuel Shortridge (R-CA) went out of their way to point out how much they cared about civil rights and how fervently they believed in equality, before saying they would, nonetheless, vote for Parker. Charles Waterman, who voted for Parker in committee, claimed that, whenever anyone wrote to him accusing Parker of racism or arguing that he could not be a fair judge, he would write back asking for proof and never got anything.

Wagner notwithstanding, no senator opposing Parker's confirmation went on record to condemn his past statements about Black citizens in North Carolina. For instance, James Couzens (R-MI) had informed the NAACP that he was opposed to Parker because of his 1920 comments[46] but, when the time came, he chose not to take part in the floor debate, save for a quick clarification about what another senator had said previously.

Part of the reason for this was strategic. The NAACP understood that, if they tried to get more senators to make speeches similar in substance to Wagner's, it might have the effect of galvanizing support for Parker among Southern Democrats, some of whom were already on the fence about the nominee due to his prior party affiliation and because he had

[46] NAACP Papers, supra, Letter from Vandenberg to White, April 26, 1930. Letter from Couzens to White, April 26, 1930.

been nominated by Hoover—the first Republican to get significant electoral support from the South since Reconstruction. Seligman even advised White that the NAACP should take a softer approach with the debate underway for fear of alienating Southerners who would otherwise vote "no."[47]

Instead, the NAACP and other civil rights groups worked behind the scenes exerting pressure on senators directly. Michigan's Vandenberg had previously told the NAACP he was against Parker, but White believed he was wavering up until the end and tried hard to keep him in line. After White found out through his sources that McCulloch would vote for Parker, he told his associates in Ohio to inform him of the "consequences."[48]When Hamilton Kean, a senator who had previously expressed disapproval of Parker's 1920 remarks, started having second thoughts, both the NAACP and Parker worked on him directly to try and sway him over to their respective sides. Kean ultimately decided to vote for Parker, writing in a telegram to the NAACP that, while he was proud to represent 125,000 Black constituents and felt it was his duty to protect their rights, he accepted Parker's promise to be a fair judge to all.[49]

The NAACP got help from an unlikely source. Robert Gray Taylor of the Committee on Race Relations had previously thrown in his lot with Parker, rescinding his organization's initial opposition after reading the judge's letter to Senator Hatfield addressing the NAACP's charges against him. However, on April 29, he changed his mind and sent a telegram to every U.S. senator and released a copy to the press rescinding the recision. Claiming that Parker had written a letter to Overman that ignored the committee's original protest, Taylor argued that Parker had never denied nor disavowed his 1920 remarks, leading to the decision to fight his nomination once again.[50] Taylor later told Parker that, while he had the highest regard for him, personally, and understood why he felt he had to say what he did in 1920, the executive committee, nevertheless,

[47] NAACP Papers, supra, Memo from Seligmann to White, May 1, 1930.

[48] NAACP Papers, supra, Telegram from White to Harry Davis, May 1, 1930.

[49] NAACP Papers, supra, Telegram from Kean to NAACP, May 5, 1930.

[50] NAACP Papers, supra, Memorandum from Miss Randolph to Seligmann, April 29, 1930.

felt the protest was appropriate because Parker had demonstrated, in their eyes, that he still believed in those comments.[51]

Parker seized on the part of Taylor's statement about ignoring the committee's original protest, telling his supporters that Taylor was sore that he hadn't been mentioned alongside the NAACP in his letter and was now exacting revenge. He suggested to Northcott and Blair to advise senators to call attention to this because it would make him look ridiculous.[52]

Personal slight or not, Taylor immediately went to work alongside White and others to exert pressure on senators to vote against Parker, and kept the NAACP secretary informed on developments on the Hill. Taylor, for instance, told the association that all New England senators other than David Walsh would be voting for Parker[53] and assured him that Thomas Schall (R-MN) was still on board.[54]

They also got help from an unwitting source from inside the Hoover Administration that went a long way towards their goal of fracturing Southern support for Parker.

"A Major Political Stroke"

On April 30, Kenneth McKellar (D-TN) took the floor and made clear he was against Parker, calling his *Red Jacket* decision "puerile."[55] Like many of his colleagues, he spoke about *Hitchman*, yellow-dog contracts and whether Parker should have applied *Tri-City*—things plenty of other senators had already spoken about and things many additional senators were planning on addressing in the days ahead. It was nothing new.

Then he unveiled something new.

Towards the end of his speech, he responded to Fess' long address from the day before in which he had warned against politicizing the confirmation process. Arguing that the pro-Parker side had gotten the ball

51 Parker Papers, supra, Letter from Taylor to Parker, April 30, 1930.

52 Parker Papers, supra, Letter from Parker to Northcott and Blair, April 28, 1930.

53 NAACP Papers, supra, Telegram from Taylor to Mr. & Mrs. Pierpont Hazzard, May 5, 1930.

54 NAACP Papers, supra, Memorandum from Miss Randolph to White, May 7, 1930.

55 *Congressional Record*, Proceedings and Debates of the Second Session of the Seventy First Congress of the United States of America, Vol. LXXII—Part 8, April 29–May 16, 1930, 8038.

rolling when it came to playing politics, McKellar read into the record a letter from First Assistant Secretary of the Interior Joseph Dixon to Walter Newton, Hoover's secretary, making the case that Parker's appointment could pay future dividends for the administration and the GOP.

> North Carolina gave President Hoover 65,000 majority. In my judgment it carries more hope of future permanent alignment with the Republican Party than any other of the Southern States that broke from their political moorings last year.
> If the exigencies of the situation permit, I believe the naming of Judge Parker to the Supreme Court would be a major political stroke. North Carolina has had no outstanding recognition by the administration.
> The naming of Judge Parker at this time would appeal mightily to State pride. It would be the first distinctive major appointment made from the South. It would go a long way toward satisfying the unquestioned feeling that the administration has not yet recognized the political revolution of 1928.[56]

Montana's Walsh and Wheeler, two other Parker opponents, then interjected and engaged in a colloquy with McKellar that had the stated effect of clarifying certain points. First, it was established that the letter was written on March 13, five days after Sanford's death. Then, Walsh seemed to recall that Dixon had run for Senate in Montana against Wheeler, a fact the latter confirmed.[57]

Overman then demanded to know where the letter had come from, and McKellar answered that it had been in the Judiciary Committee's files. That stunned Overman, as he had never seen nor heard of it before. McKellar said that he got it from Norris—something the Judiciary Committee chairman confirmed, stating the file had been on his desk for some time and any senator could have come and taken a look at it. What was not addressed was why the letter hadn't been copied and sent to the other members of the committee—particularly the members of the subcommittee who had handled Parker's nomination. Overman was trying to get to that point, but backed off after McKellar got defensive

[56] Ibid., 8040.

[57] Ibid., 8040–8041.

and wondered if his colleague was trying to imply that he had stolen it or come into possession of it improperly.[58]

McKellar conceded that there was no indication that the Dixon letter had actually influenced the president, nor was there any reason to believe that there had been any political motivation behind Parker's nomination.[59] Nevertheless, the letter served its purpose by serving as a concrete reminder to Southern Democrats about the potential drawbacks of Parker's appointment to the court. Newspapers reported that, after McKellar unveiled his Dixon revelation, three Southern senators who had previously decided to support Parker to spite the NAACP had decided to switch their positions.[60]

Meanwhile, a little over a week after McKellar's speech, Hoover received a message from Willebrandt that Senators Black, Walter George and J. Thomas Heflin were using the Dixon letter as an excuse to vote against Parker. Willebrandt informed Hoover that Heflin, in particular, was under a lot of pressure to vote against Parker because he was facing reelection and one of the charges against him was that he was "not a good Democrat."[61] It's not clear whether these three senators were the ones the papers had been referring to—nevertheless, it spoke to the effect the letter had on certain Southern Democrats and made it clear that Parker had his work cut out for him.

The letter even had an effect with the newspapers in Parker's home state. For instance, the Democratic-aligned *News and Observer* criticized state political figures for supporting the judge and maintaining that it should not have required the unveiling of the Dixon letter to make clear the dangers of backing a Republican.[62] Others were more skeptical of the potential effects of the letter, with *The Charlotte News* wondering how the appointment of one man could change an entire state's politics[63] and *The News and Record* pointing out that political considerations always play a role in Supreme Court nominations.[64]

[58] Ibid., 8041–8042.

[59] Ibid., 8040–8041.

[60] "Defeat Judge Parker is Predicted," *Johnson City Staff News*, May 1, 1930.

[61] Hoover Papers, supra, Message from Willebrandt to Hoover, May 7, 1930.

[62] "A Master Political Stroke," *The News and Observer*, May 2, 1930.

[63] "Is Political Conviction Merely Casual?" *The Charlotte News*, May 2, 1930.

[64] "The Dixon Letter," *The News and Record*, May 2, 1930.

With Parker losing support, Hoover's attorney general, William Mitchell, tried to do damage control. On May 3, Mitchell sent a letter to Stephens of Mississippi assuring him that the president had never seen the Dixon letter until McKellar entered it into the record and it was republished in newspapers across the country. Mitchell also assured Stephens that the main reason for Parker's nomination was because of his judicial record, work ethic and reputation, and revealed that he had, personally, read every one of Parker's judicial opinions and found them to be first-rate and illustrative of his standing as one of the best circuit judges in the country. Mitchell brought up the fact that the Fourth Circuit hadn't been represented on the court for 60 years and revealed that he had looked at judges from the Third, Fifth and Ninth Circuits, as well, and that Parker's qualifications and accomplishments had been impressive. Mitchell also noted that there were already three Democrats on the bench and that Sanford had been a Southern Republican. Therefore, he argued that Hoover had simply maintained the previous balance on the bench.[65]

Wheeler and Caraway were incredulous at Mitchell's assurance that Hoover had not seen the Dixon letter. Black, meanwhile, wanted clarification on whether Mitchell meant that Parker was the best judge in the Fourth Circuit or the best judge out of the ones considered for the position. "I understood that because I understood no Democrat was considered," Black said.[66]

"There Will Be Judgeships Always Open"

Once senators were finished debating Mitchell's letter, Ashurst then took the floor and threw another curveball. The Arizona senator had become an implacable foe of Parker's confirmation, often engaging in personal attacks and heated rhetoric—like the "weaklings" comment he had made earlier and then doubled down on. On this occasion, he was so outraged and vociferous with his comments that *The Evening Sun* would report that his voice could be heard "a block away."[67]

[65] *Congressional Record*, Proceedings and Debates of the Second Session of the Seventy First Congress of the United States of America, Vol. LXXII—Part 8, April 29–May 16, 1930, 8341–8342.

[66] Ibid., 8342–8343.

[67] "Ashurst Asks Lobby Probe of Parker Support," *The Evening Sun*, May 5, 1930.

His comments touched off a mad scramble and utter pandemonium in the otherwise august and solemn chamber. Perhaps that's why there was such uncertainty about what he had actually said. *The Evening Sun* reported his words as: "Federal judgeships, ambassadorships, and other high appointments are being offered senators to win their support in this fight. A Senator would be a spineless reptile to sit silent in acquiescence to such efforts to place any man on the Supreme Bench."[68]

The New York Times stated that "men with Judge Parker's consent are being offered federal judgeships and other appointments to office if they will vote for this nominee," and noted that Ashurst had called for the Senate Lobbying Committee to investigate.[69]

The News and Observer used more vague terminology, saying "men are being offered federal judgeships and other appointments to office if they will vote for this nominee" while adding that Ashurst had said "spineless cactus" not "reptile." The paper also published some of the rumors to that effect flying around in D.C., claiming that Dill had been offered a spot on the bench and Deneen, who had been defeated for renomination by Ruth Hanna McCormick, was being considered for an ambassadorship.[70] Both senators denied the allegations, although that would not be the end of the matter—at least not for Dill.

Regardless of what his actual words were, Ashurst's accusations touched off a firestorm of finger-pointing and recriminations. After a stunned Stephens said he agreed the Lobbying Committee should investigate the matter, Caraway then complained of being virtually stalked by two, if not three, ex-governors of North Carolina who were all Parker allies and asked if the committee could look into that too. Some senators later claimed their offices had been entered unlawfully and ransacked. McKellar accused the Secret Service of being responsible, but Reed Smoot (of Smoot-Hawley fame) thought it might have just been building employees.[71]

68 Ibid.

69 "Judgeship Offer for Vote for Parker is Charged; No Politics, Says Mitchell," *The New York Times*, May 6, 1930.

70 "Ashurst's Sensational Allegation of Lobbying Features Parker Fight," *The News and Observer*, May 6, 1930.

71 *Congressional Record*, Proceedings and Debates of the Second Session of the Seventy First Congress of the United States of America, Vol. LXXII—Part 8, April 29–May 16, 1930, 8358.

In the meantime, Fess, who had become the main floor leader for the pro-Parker forces, expressed outrage that Ashurst could make such a charge and demanded to know whether he was saying that Hoover himself had made the offers. Ashurst responded that he never said the president was the one making the offers, just that the offers were being made. Fess refused to let the point go, claiming Ashurst was engaged in sophistry as only the president could make such appointments; therefore, he must be saying the president was making the offers. Ashurst shrugged off the point by saying, to laughter, that if Fess really believed that then he was like "a babe in the woods that I do not perceive how he could have advanced so far in American politics."[72]

Majority Leader Watson demanded to know if Ashurst was casting aspersions on him, which prompted the Arizona senator to proclaim that he was not accusing any senator of wrongdoing, nor did he have any knowledge of any senator actually saying yes to such a deal.[73]

Parker, meanwhile, angrily denounced the allegations that he had consented to such a scheme and immediately sent a telegram to Ashurst and Overman making that clear. "This statement is absolutely untrue and I resent it as an attack upon my character," he said.[74]

After being grilled as to whether or not he had evidence of Parker's knowledge or assent, Ashurst demurred. He eventually amended his comments to read: "I now say, call the lobby committee together and you will find that federal judgeships or other appointment to office are being offered for votes for this nominee."[75]

That wasn't the end of it, though. When grilled as to whether there was any truth to the reports of a possible *quid pro quo*, Ashurst stated that Dill had told him that the latter had been offered a judgeship if he voted for Parker. That prompted Dill to take the floor and issue a denial, claiming Ashurst had misinterpreted his words. In Dill's retelling, he had an informal conversation with someone from his state who suggested that

[72] *Congressional Record*, Proceedings and Debates of the Second Session of the Seventy First Congress of the United States of America, Vol. LXXII—Part 8, April 29–May 16, 1930, 8358–8359.

[73] Ibid., 8358–8359.

[74] Parker Papers, supra, Telegram from Parker to Ashurst, May 6, 1930.

[75] *Congressional Record*, Proceedings and Debates of the Second Session of the Seventy First Congress of the United States of America, Vol. LXXII—Part 8, April 29–May 16, 1930, 8343.

the senator would be able to name his price from the administration in exchange for a commitment to vote for Parker. Dill said he wasn't interested in anything since he was planning on retiring soon and looking forward to life as a private citizen.

"He said, 'Well, in that case there will be judgeships always open.' I laughed about it and said, 'Well, I would rather be a private citizen than a judge'," Dill recounted, adding that, he didn't take it as a serious offer and never expected it to become part of the debate.[76]

Norris then demanded to know the identity of the man who had spoken to Dill. The Washingtonian declined to identify him, saying he was a personal friend and a private citizen who was not part of the administration in any way. "He did not claim that the President had told him to talk as he did, but rather indicated he could do a lot for me at home," Dill stated.[77] "I do not think he has done anything politically for me in the past and I doubt if he would do anything in the future." In response to further inquiries, Dill stated that he did not believe the man had any strong desire to see Parker on the bench beyond the fact that the mystery man was a Republican who wanted what was best for the party.[78]

"The Senator would not think, then, that the suggestion made to him in that way by the Senator's trusted personal friend invests this whole matter with a degree of odium never heard of before in the American nation?" Glass asked.

"No; because I have often had men suggest to me that it would be to my political advantage if I would vote in a certain way, and I did not get excited and think my honor and integrity had been challenged, and I considered there was nothing sinister in this conversation," Dill responded.[79]

Perhaps sensing that their side was on the ropes and needed some time to ride out the bad headlines and convince senators not to jump ship, Watson and Overman tried to delay the final vote, ostensibly so the Judiciary Committee could investigate the matter. Ashurst objected, saying everything he had said on the record would be exactly what he said to the committee, so there was no need for a delay.

[76] Ibid., 8426–8427.

[77] Ibid., 8427.

[78] Ibid., 8427.

[79] Ibid., 8427.

Joseph Robinson then spoke up and said he also didn't see the point of putting off the vote. The powerful minority leader and 1928 vice presidential nominee had been absent for much of the debate due to his commitments at a naval disarmament conference in London. Upon his return to the chamber at the end of April, he had been seen as a wildcard due to his influence within the Democratic caucus.[80] While he claimed he would reserve judgment until after he reviewed the entire record, Robinson seemingly tipped his hand—and it was bad news for Parker. Like Ashurst and Norris, Robinson was eager to vote as quickly as possible rather than agree to the delay as proposed by Watson. Additionally, Robinson later had an exchange with another senator over how much time to allot for debate the following day before proceeding to the final vote. Robinson wanted to vote immediately after the opening gavel, whereas others wanted a little more time.[81]

Norris then spoke up, saying that, as chairman of the Judiciary Committee, he had no problem conducting the investigation but didn't see how that should affect Parker's nomination, since the judge was not accused of any wrongdoing. The Nebraskan had heard his fair share of rumors and gossip about horse-trading or *quid pro quos*.[82] In fact, he had a memo in his files containing information on a purported deal between Hoover and Senators Harrison and Glass. According to the memo, a New York man named William Deppe claimed Glass and Harrison had promised Hoover they would help get Parker's nomination over the line in exchange for the appointment of a Southern Democrat as judge on the U.S. Court of Claims. Deppe claimed the man Harrison and Glass wanted was Richard Whaley, a former U.S. representative for the 1st District of South Carolina. Norris tried to get proof of the deal and, after not getting any, dismissed the rumor and did not publicize it.[83] In the end, Harrison and Glass did vote for Parker and Whaley was nominated by Hoover later that month, although there was never any proof of a deal.

[80] "Urged Judge Parker As Political Move," *The New York Times*, May 1, 1930.

[81] *Congressional Record*, Proceedings and Debates of the Second Session of the Seventy First Congress of the United States of America, Vol. LXXII—Part 8, April 29–May 16, 1930, 8427, 8431–8432.

[82] Ibid., 8427–8428.

[83] George Norris Papers, supra, Memo to Norris, May 2, 1930.

Norris then nonchalantly pointed out that allegations of vote-buying or deal-making were inevitable in their line of work. Noting that this particular fight had drawn a lot of interest nationwide and had spurred lots of people and groups, on both sides, into action, Norris wasn't surprised that the offers were coming fast and furious.[84] "I know there has been very great pressure on some Senators who have told me so," Norris said.[85] "But that is always so, and it will always be so."

"Certain Radical Senators"

Sensing that there was not a lot of support for his motion to have the Judiciary Committee investigate, Watson withdrew it, stating that he was satisfied that there were no allegations of wrongdoing or unethical behavior by Parker or the president. The Senate then agreed to vote on the nomination on May 7 with each side getting 45 minutes to make their final case and no senator being allowed to speak longer than 15 minutes.

That day, once again before a packed gallery, senators squared off to make their final case for and against the nominee. Glass, Simmons and Fess spoke for Parker, with each senator arguing that the attacks against the judge were unfair and unwarranted. Glass noted that, politically, it would have been easy and probably better for him to vote against Parker, but he could not justify rejecting a respected, well-qualified judge who had done a great job for the Fourth Circuit. As for *Red Jacket*, Glass delivered the now well-worn argument that Parker had been doing his duty and had no choice but to rule the way he did. "I think Judge Parker is a friend to the laboring interests," Glass opined.[86] "The whole background of the man suggests that he would feel obliged to be the friend of the laboring interest."

Simmons expanded on Parker's background and biography and agreed with Glass that the judge's modest beginnings, lifetime of hard work, and accomplishments as a lawyer and judge made it clear that he was not hostile to labor. Simmons also expressed disbelief that the nomination of

84 *Congressional Record*, Proceedings and Debates of the Second Session of the Seventy First Congress of the United States of America, Vol. LXXII—Part 8, April 29–May 16, 1930, 8428.

85 Ibid., 8428.

86 Ibid., 8475–8476.

an otherwise qualified judge was in question because of "1 out of the 115 opinions he has written."[87]

The two of them addressed the 1920 statements, but only briefly. Glass waited until the end of his speech to start criticizing the NAACP and its pressure tactics, saying he did not understand how they came to be the arbiters of who deserved to be on the Supreme Court. His time then ran out and, when he was offered additional time to expand on this point, Glass declined.[88] Simmons also waited until his time was almost up, and the final line in his speech talked about how unfair it was that Parker was being protested because of one judicial opinion and "an additional protest on the part of a Negro association touching some statement now in dispute which they allege that he made in political discussion years before he went on the bench."[89]

Meanwhile Fess, as he had done throughout the entire debate, invoked names like Joseph Story and John Marshall and argued that the opposition to Parker was unprecedented. His colleagues had become so used to his academic lectures that Glass jokingly asked that Fess be allotted several additional hours so he could continue talking about the history of the Supreme Court.[90]

Summing up for the Parker opponents were Hiram Johnson, Henrik Shipstead and Borah. Johnson, a progressive who had run for vice president on the Progressive Party ticket with Theodore Roosevelt in 1912, not only criticized Parker for *Red Jacket* as well as the political motivations behind his nomination, but claimed Parker was not qualified for the job. Johnson dismissed Parker's background, calling him a failed, perennial candidate for office who then became a disciple of the discredited Daugherty before becoming a judge. "You could go into any village, any town, or any city in this country and among the profession you could find the replica of that kind of appointee," Johnson said.[91]

Johnson was hardly the first senator to be decidedly unimpressed with Parker's credentials. Earlier in the debate, Caraway, who had voted against Parker in the Judiciary Committee, had expressed his bewilderment that

[87] Ibid., 8479.

[88] Ibid., 8476.

[89] Ibid., 8479.

[90] Ibid., 8486.

[91] Ibid., 8476.

"this extraordinary lawyer, who possesses all the virtue and all the character attributed to him, was so unknown" and his wonderment over "how he ever concealed all these virtues."[92] Nevertheless, Johnson's words hit hard and, because they came on the same day as the final vote, they were carried in nearly every newspaper across the country.

Shipstead, a pro-labor senator representing the Farmer-Labor Party in Minnesota (the FLP merged with the Democrats in 1944), did one better than Fess and talked about common law and equity and how certain rights were so fundamental they could never be taken away. In that regard, Shipstead opposed Parker because he had been a party to enforcing an injunction that took away fundamental rights from laborers. The issue of injunctions was an important one to Shipstead—the senator had proposed a law two years earlier that would have limited the ability of courts to issue injunctions. The AFL had been heavily involved in drafting the bill and had taken some of the blame for its failure to pass. The bill ultimately formed the basis for the successful Norris-LaGuardia Act, which finally outlawed yellow-dog contracts and restricted the use of injunctions in labor disputes.[93]

Appropriately, it was Borah that ended up having the final word. His views and arguments were well known to everyone in the chamber at that point and, rather than rehash them, the Idahoan decided to respond to some of the speeches from the other side. First, Borah took issue with the assertion that passing judgment or setting certain criteria for confirmation undermined judicial independence. Responding to Fess, Borah even invoked some historical figures of his own, such as Oliver Ellsworth, who helped lead the opposition to John Rutledge and several senators, including Clay, Webster and Calhoun, who were opposed to Roger B. Taney—all because they found certain views the nominees held to be unsound and antithetical to their beliefs.[94]

[92] Ibid.

[93] William E. Forbath, "The Shaping of the American Labor Movement," *Harvard Law Review* 102, no. 6 (1989), 1228–1230. See also Parker Papers, supra, Letter from T.C. Townsend to Parker. Townsend theorized that Green's opposition to Parker was an attempt to regain some political power after the failure of the Shipstead Bill.

[94] *Congressional Record*, Proceedings and Debates of the Second Session of the Seventy First Congress of the United States of America, Vol. LXXII—Part 8, April 29–May 16, 1930, 8486. Roger B. Taney was the fifth chief justice of the Supreme Court, most famously known for delivering the majority opinion in the *Dred Scott v. Sandford* case (1857). When President Andrew Jackson nominated Taney to the Supreme Court in 1835

"We are insisting that here is a great problem involving human rights, a question of whether we should embody into the jurisprudence of the country a principle which we believe to be at enmity with the welfare of not only the great working classes but with the public good, and we say that we are not willing to place a man upon that bench who is committed to the doctrine," Borah intoned.[95] "We are on safe grounds, we are in company with great leaders and men whose fidelity is to the government no man dare challenges."

After announcing the various vote pairs,[96] the roll call began in earnest. Predictably, Borah, Norris, Johnson, Wheeler and the other "Sons of the Wild Jackass" voted "no" while Parker's avowed allies, including Fess, Overman, Hebert, Glass and Simmons, voted in favor. Vandenburg, whose vote was being watched by the NAACP, voted against Parker, as did Royal Copeland, Wagner's Democratic colleague from New York. Kean, as promised, voted in favor, as did McCulloch. Southern Democrats were split, with Black, William Julius Harris (D-GA), Park Trammell (D-FL), and both senators from Arkansas, Texas and Tennessee voting against while Blease and both senators from Virginia, Louisiana and Mississippi voted for. Quite a few Southerners ended up not voting or paired with others, including George, Heflin and Ellison Smith (D-SC). According to the *Congressional Record*, all three were paired: George and Heflin would have voted no while Smith would have voted yes. Kentucky's Robsion,

(initially for an associate justice role and later as chief justice), Taney faced significant opposition due to his strong support for Jackson's controversial policies, particularly his role in dismantling the Second Bank of the United States.

[95] Ibid., 8486.

[96] Vote pairing used to be a fairly common occurrence in the Senate—especially when absences were more frequent and parties had less ideological consistency. Essentially, a live pair is an agreement between two senators not to vote on a certain matter. The senators have to be on opposite sides of a pending vote so that neither side is negatively affected. There could be all sorts of reasons for wanting to be paired—reluctance to take a public stand on a certain issue, not wanting to come back to Washington to cast a vote, illness, campaigning, etc. Paired senators have to declare which side they are on and how they would have voted if present for the *Congressional Record*. According to Richard Watson, Jr.'s "The Defeat of Judge Parker: A Study in Pressure Groups and Politics," supra, anti-Parker senators who were absent from Washington were having trouble finding pairs, so some like La Follette Jr. had to rush back to D.C.

who was so concerned about losing the Black vote in his upcoming election, ended up being paired and would have voted "no."[97] He ended up losing his reelection anyway.

The result was in question until the very end, when the final tally had Parker losing 41–39. Had one senator switched his vote from "no" to "yes," Vice President Curtis would have been able to cast a tie-breaking vote. Instead, it marked the first time since 1894 that the Senate had rejected a Supreme Court nominee on an up-and-down vote.

After the result became official, the people who led the opposition to Parker took a victory lap. Green called the vote a "victory for justice, righteousness and human rights" and that the only people who would be upset about the result were those who love yellow-dog contracts and exploiting laborers. "There will be great rejoicing in the homes and in the communities of working people over the defeat of Judge Parker," Green said in a statement, while expressing gratitude to the "staunch defenders of human rights" who voted against Parker.[98] The AFL would later reflect that it had been some time since the American trade union movement was as motivated and energized as it was during the Parker fight.[99]

White also took a bow and reveled in what the *Christian Science Monitor* called "the first national demonstration of the Negro's power since Reconstruction days."[100] He also promised that the fight against "nullification of the Fourteenth and Fifteenth Amendments" was just beginning, and called the Parker vote "a crushing rebuke to President Hoover's lily-white policy." The NAACP head then called on Black voters to remember the senators who voted for Parker and hold them responsible at the ballot box, specifically criticizing New England's senators other than David Walsh.[101] In another statement, White noted that

97 *Congressional Record*, Proceedings and Debates of the Second Session of the Seventy First Congress of the United States of America, Vol. LXXII—Part 8, April 29–May 16, 1930, 8487.

98 "Nominee's Career Assailed," *The New York Times*, May 8, 1930.

99 American Federation of Labor, *Bulletin of the Metal Trades Department* 12, no. 6 (June 1930).

100 Richard Kluger, "The Story of John Johnson Parker: The First Demonstration of Negro Political Power Since Reconstruction," *The Journal of Blacks in Higher Education*, no. 46 (Winter 2004–2005), 125.

101 NAACP Papers, supra, "Parker Defeat Only a Beginning Says Negro Organization Head," May 8, 1930.

"Negroes felt stirred on the issue of the Parker nomination as on no issue in recent years" and vowed that they would mobilize again if needed to defend their fundamental rights.[102]

Borah also received many plaudits for his starring role. Labor leaders sent him letters and telegrams expressing their appreciation and gratitude for his actions, as did Harvard law professor and future Supreme Court Justice Felix Frankfurter, who told Borah that he had "rendered high service" to the country and the court.[103] Borah, for his part, said he felt he did the right thing and took satisfaction in the outcome, telling Green that "a real victory has been won for human rights" and that Parker's defeat served notice that people were tired of "the utter disregard of the rights of the individual when pitted against the rights of property."[104]

Among those who did not say anything was the man who had nominated him. Hoover never issued a statement following Parker's defeat[105]; instead, two days later, he simply sent the Senate the name of former Teapot Dome investigator Owen J. Roberts as his new nominee. However, there was a draft press release that has been preserved in his presidential papers bearing the date "May 8, 1930" that was written in response to the Senate vote. In it, the president issued a strong defense of Parker's credentials, qualifications and fitness, and a denunciation of the tactics used to take him down. The statement did not mention labor or the NAACP specifically, but expressed dismay over the utilization of propaganda that muddied the waters and turned Parker into a lightning rod for things that had largely been out of his control. "[N]ew influences have been introduced into the selection of men for the Court which must give concern," the statement said.[106] "In any event, these activities have confused the main issue and have placed many senators in the position of appearing to vote for or against some one of these issues with which Judge Parker had little to do."

Parker, for his part, was magnanimous in defeat. He made clear his disappointment at the Senate vote, but expressed his gratitude to his

[102] NAACP Papers, supra, "Negro Aid Body Welcomes Defeat of Judge Parker," May 7, 1930.

[103] Borah Papers, supra, Letter from Frankfurter to Borah, May 9, 1930.

[104] Borah Papers, supra, Letter from Borah to Green, May 8, 1930.

[105] Rappleye, supra, 148.

[106] Hoover Papers, supra, Final Draft of statement of Parker defeat, May 8, 1930.

friends and allies who had tried their best to help get his nomination over the line. He also kept his head down and immediately went back to work at the Fourth Circuit.[107] A few days after his rejection, Parker made a special trip to D.C. to visit Hoover and some of his Senate allies, to personally thank them for their support. He even did Hoover a favor by calling for Roberts' quick and prompt confirmation.[108] Parker also sent a note to Roberts wishing him well.[109] Unlike Parker, Roberts was confirmed by voice vote and joined the court in June, whereupon he became the one of the two swing votes on the Hughes court and ended up casting one of the most famous deciding votes in Supreme Court history.

In the days, weeks and months that followed, Parker received hundreds of letters and messages from friends, supporters, colleagues, and strangers expressing a litany of emotions ranging from sympathy, sadness, disappointment to anger over his rejection. Harlan Fiske Stone wrote a letter to Parker, expressing sympathy over his Senate defeat and calling it "an unhappy combination of circumstances."[110] Shepard also chalked it up to "a combination of sinister circumstances",[111] while Robert N. Page, his opponent in the 1910 House of Representatives race, condemned the vote and noted that one of the reasons why he quit Congress was because he thought many politicians there were a bunch of cowards who put party over country.[112] One of his main surrogates, Thomas W. Davis, wrote a letter condemning the Senate as being full of "little men" and "men of prejudice" who were "without courage and full of fear."[113]

In almost every circumstance, Parker took the high road and refused to cast blame or express bitterness over his humiliating defeat. Most of the time, he stuck with his public statement, expressing regret over the Senate vote and gratitude for his loyal friends and supporters. "I shall

[107] "Parker Thanks Loyal Friends for Aiding Him," *The Morning Union*, May 8, 1930.

[108] "Judge Parker Calls on Friends in Washington to Express His Thanks," *The News and Record*, May 13, 1930.

[109] Parker Papers, supra, Telegram from Parker to Roberts, May 9, 1930.

[110] Parker Papers, supra, Letter from Stone to Parker, June 4, 1930.

[111] Parker Papers, supra, Letter from Shepard to Parker, May 8, 1930.

[112] Parker Papers, supra, Letter from Page to Parker, May 8, 1930.

[113] Parker Papers, supra, Letter from Davis to Parker, May 10, 1930.

never allow myself to become discouraged or imbittered by my defeat," he said.[114]

There were a couple of instances, however, when the mask slipped. Parker sent a letter to Taylor returning a gift to the Committee on Race Relations head, stating: "I have no ill feeling towards you; but I do not feel that you have treated me justly."[115] He also wrote a letter to his former philosophy professor at UNC, Henry Horace Williams, calling his defeat a "radical attack on the Administration and the Supreme Court." Parker posited that labor and the NAACP, the latter of which he referred to as a "quasi-socialistic organization," were put up to the protest by "certain radical Senators" and that these groups utilized "false propaganda" to make their case. Parker said he would have been confirmed had it not been for some Southern senators who demonstrated a "desire to play small politics."[116]

Parker closed his letter to his former professor by noting that he had thought about retiring from the bench and returning to private practice, where he was certain his newfound notoriety would allow him to make a very good living. However, he had decided not to do that and, instead, wanted to continue excelling on the circuit court bench. "I have not yet reached the end of my efforts nor, I believe, the zenith of my capacity. While I cannot take my seat upon the Supreme Bench, I can at least demonstrate to the country that I am worthy of that position," Parker said in his letter.[117] "I am inclined to think that my position on the Circuit Bench affords greater opportunities both for worthwhile achievement and for worthwhile service."

[114] Parker Papers, supra, Letter from Parker to Wade Cooper, May 10, 1930.

[115] Parker Papers, supra, Letter from Parker to Taylor, June 4, 1930.

[116] Parker Papers, supra, Letter from Parker to Williams, May 26, 1930.

[117] Ibid.

CHAPTER 8

From the Ashes: Parker's Life After Rejection

If John J. Parker thought the Senate rejection would provide him with a sense of finality or closure, he was sorely mistaken.

The closeness of the vote, the sense that he had been a victim of politics and the desire among his supporters to right what they saw as a miscarriage of justice, all ensured that his name would come up whenever there was a subsequent vacancy on the Supreme Court. Indeed, it started immediately after the Senate vote, with several of his friends floating the possibility that Hoover might just resubmit Parker's name and dare the Senate to vote it down again or give him a recess appointment.

That's when they weren't telling him that if he couldn't beat them he should join them. Jonas and some other North Carolina Republicans tried to encourage Parker to run for Senate that fall for the seat then held by Simmons.[1] (Bailey ended up defeating Simmons in the primary and winning the general election by more than 20 points—in his memoir, Simmons attributed his vote for Parker as one reason why he lost.[2]) Parker shot that down, however, saying it would be a "great mistake" to run[3]

[1] "White House Still Silent on Parker Defeat in Senate," *The News Journal*, May 8, 1930.

[2] J. Fred Rippy (ed.), *F.M. Simmons: Statesman of the New South. Memoirs and Addresses* (Durham, NC: Duke University Press, 1936), 66.

[3] Parker Papers, supra, Letter from Parker to Charles Jonas, June 12, 1930.

V. Li, *Supreme Pressure*,
https://doi.org/10.1007/978-3-032-07864-3_8

while noting that he was not willing to give up his seat on the bench.[4] Perhaps he also felt conflicted over the possibility of taking on someone who had done so much to try and get him confirmed to the Supreme Court. Plus, it's not like North Carolina had suddenly become more hospitable terrain for Republicans over the last decade—Hoover's win in 1928 notwithstanding. Parker still faced the same headwinds and hurdles he had faced in 1910, 1916, and 1920.

Or maybe he knew that, if he ran, he'd have to face the race question once again. If he wanted any chance of winning, he'd have to embrace lily-whitism once again, and that would just confirm everything the NAACP and Wagner had said about him. Plus, he was on record despising race-baiting demagogues who used the scary prospect of Black voters to keep the actual ballot-casters in line and happy with the status quo. Running for public office would only force him to deal with these people again. And the stance he took during his confirmation hearing about how he had always been fair to the parties in front of him, to say nothing of his opinions backing civil rights groups that had challenged anti-miscegenation laws like the one at issue in *City of Richmond v. Deans*, would surely be used against him by Democrats.

He wouldn't have to worry about the NAACP—at least in North Carolina, where Black voters were still largely disenfranchised. That wasn't the case in states where Blacks could vote, and the NAACP made it clear that it would make good its threat to take on senators in those states who had voted to confirm Parker.

For instance, even before the Senate took its final vote, NAACP official Robert Bagnall had started campaigning in Kansas against Henry Allen, a strong Parker supporter who was up for reelection that November. White and the board then decided that another Parker ally, Roscoe McCulloch of Ohio, would be their other main target that year. That would hardly be the end of things, though—something made crystal clear when Du Bois printed in *The Crisis* a list of all of the senators who had voted for Parker, complete with helpful information like what states they were from and when they were up for reelection.[5]

[4] Parker Papers, supra, Letter from Parker to Charles Jonas, May 29, 1930.

[5] Goings, *The NAACP Comes of Age*, supra, 54.

There were people in the association who disagreed with the campaign to target pro-Parker senators. For instance, William Pickens, a field organizer, and Kelly Miller, a professor at Howard University, argued that Parker should not necessarily be the litmus test, and that a senator's overall record should be considered. After all, Heflin of Alabama, a renowned racist who had once shot a Black man on a Washington, D.C. streetcar for swearing at a white woman and who had once said that Blacks were decreed by God to be servants to the white man, had been paired against Parker, but that didn't mean he was now their friend or ally.[6]

Both McCulloch and Allen lost their reelection bids—and the NAACP's efforts against them got a lot of attention and established it as a power player in electoral politics. How effective they had actually been is up for debate. As Kenneth Goings pointed out in *The NAACP Comes of Age: The Defeat of Judge John J. Parker*, both defeated senators had been appointed to their seats to fill unexpired terms, so they weren't incumbents in the usual sense of the word. McCulloch had also been heavily targeted by labor, as the Ohio State Federation of Labor started coordinating with Green within a few days after Parker's defeat to find someone to run against the Senator that fall.[7] Finally, Republicans were hugely unpopular heading into the 1930 elections, thanks to the worsening Depression, and Democrats picked up eight Senate seats that year.

Nevertheless, it was clear that the NAACP had become a force to be reckoned with. George McGill, the Democrat who defeated Allen in Kansas, went so far as the join the NAACP and thank them for delivering the Black vote in a way "I could never have done myself."[8]

The following year, the NAACP opposed David Baird, Jr., a Republican from New Jersey who had voted for Parker. Baird had also been appointed to his seat but, unlike Allen and McCulloch, chose not to run for reelection in 1930. Instead, he ran for governor of New Jersey in 1931, and the NAACP decided to get involved. The association later claimed to have passed out over 100,000 copies of a flier entitled: "Why the NAACP Should Defeat Baird" and took credit for Baird not only

[6] Ibid., 56–57.

[7] William Green Papers on Microfilm, #5761 mf., Kheel Center for Labor-Management Documentation and Archives, Cornell University Library.

[8] Ibid., 62.

losing his race but running behind other Republicans on the ticket that year.[9]

In 1932, the NAACP went after Majority Leader James Watson, not just for his Parker vote but because they felt like he had abandoned them during the fight over the Dyer Anti-Lynching Bill in 1922. The decision to go after Watson had engendered some opposition within the NAACP and, at a conference of the Indiana branch, two officials were asked to resign because of their support for the senator.[10] Watson ultimately lost that November—one of many Republicans that found themselves out of a job as Franklin D. Roosevelt and the Democrats swept their way to power in a landslide.

After that, the Parker revenge tour sputtered out. In 1934, Fess, Kean, Hebert and Hatfield all lost, but that was attributable more to the overall unpopularity of the Republican Party, which got wiped out nationally as Democrats increased their Senate majority to 69. After that campaign, *The Crisis* published a piece entitled "The End of the Parker Fight," which took credit for defeating "all of the senators who voted for Parker and who could be reached by the colored voters." While the magazine and White conceded that there were a few who had escaped, such as Hastings of Delaware, the NAACP proudly declared that their organized opposition to the judge and his supporters had been "the most sensational and significant political movement by Negroes in the last generation."[11] The piece ended with an ominous warning for anyone who thought about ignoring the plight of Black citizens in this country: Ask former Senators Allen, Watson, Fess and the others how it worked out for them.[12]

"Greater Opportunities Both for Worthwhile Achievement and for Worthwhile Service"

Parker had made it clear that he still had a lot to accomplish as a federal judge. Over the next three decades, he did just that, amassing the kind of the record and reputation that critics like Johnson and Caraway had claimed he lacked at the time of his Supreme Court nomination.

[9] Ibid., 69.

[10] Ibid., 70–71.

[11] Ibid., 73.

[12] "Finish of the Parker Fight," *The Crisis*, December 1934, 364.

For instance, when North Carolina called on the foremost legal minds in the state to rewrite and amend its constitution in 1931, Parker was one of the main names on the list. His suggestions reflected his long-held desire to make government more efficient—for instance, he recommended that the governor be allowed to appoint all state executive officials other than lieutenant governor. He also proposed the governor be allowed to veto bills (in 1995, North Carolina finally granted its chief executive this power, becoming the last state in the country to do so). As for judicial reforms, Parker suggested the creation of a Department of Justice under the control of the state attorney general and the adoption of nonpartisan judicial elections. He also reiterated some of the things he had argued for previously, like allowing prosecutions by information instead of indictment for all but capital cases, and permitting jurors to hand down verdicts in civil and non-capital criminal cases by a three-fourths majority instead of by a unanimous vote.

Above all, he advocated for incremental changes rather than a full-scale overhaul of the state's constitution. "[A] complete change in the fundamental law would breed confusion, and a suggestion of a complete change would probably meet very detailed opposition," he wrote in a letter to Gardner, the governor who appointed him to the commission.[13]

The proposed constitution was set to be voted on in the November 1934 general election, but then the state Supreme Court issued an advisory opinion seven weeks before election day, ruling that the vote could not take place then.[14] Momentum for the effort then stalled and dissipated, although some of the 1934 proposed reforms did end up enshrined in North Carolina's next, successful effort to reform the constitution in 1971.

In the meantime, Parker moved on to other projects and initiatives while continuing to serve on the circuit court bench. In 1943, President Franklin D. Roosevelt formed the Advisory Board on Just Compensation to the War Shipping Administration and appointed Parker and two other respected circuit judges, Learned Hand of the Second Circuit and Joseph Chappell Hutcheson Jr. of the Fifth. The three were tasked with

13 Parker Papers, supra, Letter from Parker to Governor O. Max Gardner, November 21, 1931.

14 "Court Ruling Calls Off Election on Constitution," *The News and Observer*, September 20, 1934.

coming up with rules for determining how much the WSA would pay for requisitioning, buying or chartering vessels and boats for the war effort.[15]

When World War II finally came to an end, the White House had another important assignment for Parker. The International Military Tribunal had been established at Nuremberg, Germany with the immediate task of trying important Nazi political and military leaders for war crimes, and President Harry Truman had decided to send two leading Americans to take part: former Attorney General Francis Biddle would serve as a judge and Supreme Court Justice Robert Jackson would be a prosecutor. Truman also decided to appoint Parker as an alternate judge who, under the rules established by the IMT, would still take part in all the courtroom proceedings and judicial conferences and deliberations, but not vote on the court's decisions. Parker was hesitant about accepting Truman's offer—he would have to live in Germany and be away from his family and court for an extended period of time. He also had another reason for being reluctant, which we'll explore in the next section. However, he told contemporaries that he felt duty bound to accept a request from the president of the United States.

Later on, in 1953, he played a rare, public role in speaking out against the proposed Bricker Amendment, which would have amended the Constitution to restrict the president's ability to enter into treaties with other countries. "The President and the Senate have not betrayed us in the past," he said, testifying before the Senate Judiciary Committee in March 1953. "Why should we think they will betray us in the future?" Parker added there were other mechanisms in the Constitution to ensure the president did not enter into unpopular treaties that could violate the rights and liberties of American citizens. Surely "no such treaty could get the support of two-thirds of the Senate," he argued.[16]

[15] "Executive Order 9387—Establishing an Advisory Board on Just Compensation and Prescribing Its Functions," *The American Presidency Project,* October 15, 1943, www.presidency.ucsb.edu/documents/executive-order-9387-establishing-advisory-board-just-compensation-and-prescribing-its, accessed September 26, 2024.

[16] "Judge Parker Flays Treaty Power Curbs," *The Charlotte Observer*, March 25, 1953.

"Such an Appointment Would Wipe Out the Defeat That I Sustained Some Years Ago"

As mentioned earlier, the nature of his defeat in 1930 meant that Parker's name would, inevitably, pop up whenever there was a vacancy on the Supreme Court. Sometimes, it was more a matter of wishful thinking—either on his part or from his friends and supporters, who never stopped pushing for him to get what they felt he had long deserved.

There were a few instances over the next three decades where it was more than wishful thinking and there was a possibility that he might, belatedly, get the redemption both he and his friends and supporters desperately wanted.

In 1932, Hoover was defeated for reelection in a landslide at the hands of Franklin D. Roosevelt. While a Democrat in the White House would have seemed to preclude Parker's chances of securing a Supreme Court nomination, that wasn't necessarily the case. Back then, bipartisan gestures were not as rare as sightings of Haley's comet, and it was not out of the question for a president from one party to appoint Supreme Court justices from the other. Taft had named several Democrats to the Supreme Court, including promoting Edward Douglass White to the chief justiceship, while Hoover had crossed party lines to appoint Benjamin Cardozo in 1932.

Roosevelt, however, didn't have time for bipartisanship—at least not at that point in his presidency. Much of his expansive and ambitious New Deal, which had been designed to help an American public still in the throes of the Great Depression, had been stymied by the court and declared unconstitutional. The administration did notch a few wins early on, but the court, with Justice Owen Roberts often joining the conservative Four Horsemen, usually sided with businesses or entities challenging the federal government.

On May 27, 1935, things came to a head as the court dealt FDR a triple body blow that eventually became known as "Black Monday." A unanimous Court struck down parts of the National Industrial Recovery Act in *Schechter Poultry Corp. v. United States* as violating the non-delegation doctrine and exceeding Congress' power to regulate commerce power.[17] In *Humphrey's Executor v. United States*, the court, in another unanimous decision, struck down FDR's attempt to replace

[17] *A.L.A. Schechter Poultry Corp. v. United States*, 295 U.S. 495 (1935).

a member of the FTC with one of his own appointees.[18] Finally, in *Louisville Joint Stock Land Bank v. Radford*, a unanimous court struck down the Frazier-Lemke Farm Bankruptcy Bill, which had made it more difficult for banks to repossess farms.[19]

Those decisions were all unanimous, but others showed a more divided court. In January 1936, a 6–3 court, with Roberts writing for Hughes and the Horsemen, ruled that the Agricultural Adjustment Act was unconstitutional.[20] In May 1936, a 5–4, majority consisting of Roberts and the Horsemen, struck down the Bituminous Coal Conservation Act of 1935, a bill that would have deemed coal mining to be interstate commerce, thereby allowing the government to do things like set coal prices and production levels and regulate wages and hours.[21] The following month, in *Morehead v. New York ex rel. Tipaldo*, the same five justices overturned a New York minimum wage law, with Justice Pierce Butler calling it "repugnant to the due process clause of the Fourteenth Amendment" in his majority opinion.[22]

Roosevelt was furious. Following Black Monday, the president criticized the court for using a "horse and buggy definition of interstate commerce."[23] After some public blowback, Roosevelt kept quiet about the court until *Morehead*, when he complained that the majority had created a "no-man's-land" that was free from both state and federal regulation.[24]

Then, two things happened. First, Roosevelt was reelected in a massive landslide, winning both the popular and electoral vote by larger margins than 1932. He won 46 states and 523 out of 531 electoral votes, while his 60.8 percent of the popular vote was the largest since 1820, when

[18] *Humphrey's Executor v. United States*, 295 U.S. 602 (1935).

[19] *Louisville Joint Stock Land Bank v. Radford*, 295 U.S. 555 (1935).

[20] *United States v. Butler*, 297 U.S. 1 (1936).

[21] *Carter v. Carter Coal Company*, 298 U.S. 238 (1936).

[22] *Morehead v. New York ex rel. Tipaldo*, 298 U.S. 587 (1936).

[23] "On this day, Supreme Court invalidates key FDR program," *National Constitution Center*, https://constitutioncenter.org/blog/when-fdrs-blue-eagle-laid-a-supreme-court-egg, accessed October 2, 2024.

[24] William E. Leuchtenburg, "When Franklin Roosevelt Clashed With the Supreme Court—and Lost," *Smithsonian Magazine*, https://www.smithsonianmag.com/history/when-franklin-roosevelt-clashed-with-the-supreme-court-and-lost-78497994/, May 2005, accessed April 14, 2025.

James Monroe was reelected without any real opposition. Democrats also romped to gigantic majorities in both the House and Senate, taking 334 seats in the former and ending up with 69 seats in the latter.

The win seemingly gave Roosevelt a mandate to do whatever he wanted, and he had just the thing in mind. In February, weeks after his inauguration, Roosevelt proposed the Judicial Procedures Reform Bill of 1937, ostensibly to help with the backlog of cases in all federal courts. Popularly known as the "Court Packing Bill," Roosevelt proposed adding one new judge or justice for each one over the age of 70 or with ten years of service, not exceeding six new justices for the Supreme Court and two on any lower federal court.

Despite framing the bill as a means of helping courts be younger and more efficient, Roosevelt dropped that pretense almost immediately after proposing it. In a fireside chat the following month, he argued the American public badly needed help and the Supreme Court was standing in the way of attempts by Congress and the White House to meet their responsibility to the people who were still suffering from unemployment, hunger, homelessness, and other effects of the Great Depression. Likening the three branches of government to horses plowing a field, Roosevelt intoned: "Two of the horses are pulling in unison today; the third is not." He also added that the American people clearly wanted that third horse to fall in line and that they were tired of the court "acting not as a judicial body, but as a policy-making body."[25]

The bill split the Democrats and gave Republicans their first bit of political fortune since Hoover's salad days. Vice President John Nance Garner went on the Senate floor and expressed his disapproval by holding his nose and giving it a thumbs down. Arkansas Democrat Joseph Robinson, who was now Majority Leader of the Senate, personally opposed the bill but, ever the loyal soldier, decided to use every bit of his influence and power to try and get it passed for Roosevelt. Their fellow Democrat, Wheeler, decided to lead the fight against the bill and was aided behind the scenes by his fellow "Sons of the Wild Jackass" Borah and Norris, who were disturbed by the president's power grab. While they were hardly shrinking violets, Borah and Norris, nevertheless, decided to

[25] March 9, 1937: Fireside Chat 9: On "Court-Packing," *Miller Center*, https://millercenter.org/the-presidency/presidential-speeches/march-9-1937-fireside-chat-9-court-packing, accessed October 2, 2024.

keep a low profile, as did the rest of the GOP caucus, figuring that it was better to let the Democrats fight among themselves.

Eventually, the tide turned against Roosevelt and his allies and the Court Packing Bill died. First Chief Justice Hughes wrote a letter to Wheeler refuting Roosevelt's claim that the courts were backed up. Then, the court ruled for Roosevelt in several New Deal cases—most notably in *West Coast Hotel Co v. Parrish*, in which Roberts seemingly switched his stance and joined Brandeis, Stone, Cardozo and Hughes in upholding a state minimum wage law similar to the one that the court struck down in *Morehead*.[26]

Roberts' vote immediately led to speculation that he had flip-flopped under pressure due to the Court Packing Bill. However, that argument is undercut by the fact that the Justices voted on the case in December 1936, two months before Roosevelt announced his bill. Nevertheless, there was obvious long-running tension between the Court and White House, and Administration officials had floated the idea of expanding the membership of the High Court as early as 1933.[27] So while Roosevelt's bill would not have had any direct influence on the vote on *West Coast Hotel Co.*, the Justices surely felt some pressure and probably knew something was coming their way.

Perhaps more relevant is that the *West Coast Hotel* vote took place a month after FDR's reelection in 1936. Both Roberts and Hughes have said that they were stunned by the magnitude of FDR's landslide victory and Roberts later wrote that it was "difficult to see how the Court could have resisted the popular urge for uniform standards throughout the country – for what in effect was a unified economy."[28] Regardless of his motives, what is clear is that Roberts' vote, which was nicknamed "The Switch in Time that Saved the Nine," had the effect of easing a lot of the pressure put on them as a result of the Court Packing Bill and marked the end of the *Lochner* era as the court began upholding New Deal legislation far more frequently than in the past. It also made Parker

[26] *West Coast Hotel Co. v. Parrish*, 300 U.S. 379 (1937).

[27] William Edward Leuchtenburg, *The Supreme Court Reborn: The Constitutional Revolution in the Age of Roosevelt*, (New York: Oxford University Press, 1996).

[28] Owen Roberts, *The Court and the Constitution* (Cambridge, MA: Harvard University Press, 1951), 61. Sutherland seemingly made a veiled reference to Roberts in his dissent, arguing that "the meaning of the Constitution does not change with the ebb and flow of economic events."

allies wonder what might have been, since the judge had taken a fairly pro-government view of New Deal-related cases that reached his docket. Would the "switch in time" have even been necessary had Parker been confirmed back in 1930?

Roosevelt, however, pressed on and seemed determined to get his bill passed. But then, in the summer of 1937, the bill was dealt two death blows. First Van Devanter retired,[29] finally giving Roosevelt a chance to make his first Supreme Court appointment. Given how closely divided the court was, as well as the fact Van Devanter was an arch-conservative and leading member of the Four Horsemen, Roosevelt could now transform the court without adding a single extra seat.[30]

Then, in July, Robinson dropped dead of a massive heart attack. The majority leader had been likened to a traffic cop in the way he waved New Deal legislation through the Senate and onto Roosevelt's desk; if anyone could have passed the bill through sheer force of will, it would have been Robinson. His death seemingly killed the bill's chances, and the Senate effectively defeated it after that month, sending it back to the Judiciary Committee. A severely watered-down version of the bill passed in August, which focused more on revising procedures in the lower courts and added no new federal judges for the president to appoint.

Roosevelt then nominated Hugo Black, an ardent New Dealer who had supported the Court Packing Bill, to fill Van Devanter's seat and the Alabama senator was confirmed—albeit without the usual senatorial courtesy. Turns out, Black was unpopular with his colleagues and there were rumors he was a member of the Ku Klux Klan—rumors that turned

[29] According to *Time*, Borah and Wheeler worked with Van Devanter to announce his retirement at a strategically important moment in the Court Packing debate. Borah and Van Devanter lived in the same apartment complex and were cordial with one another. "National Affairs: Justice Retired," *Time*, May 31, 1937.

[30] Or not. Robinson had seemingly been promised the first available seat on the court as a reward for shepherding the Court Packing Bill through the Senate. Despite his fealty to Roosevelt, the president sensed Robinson was a closet reactionary and feared that once freed from his responsibilities as Democratic floor leader, he would become the newest Horseman. Roosevelt actually felt more pressure to get the bill passed after Van Devanter's retirement because he didn't want to give that seat to Robinson. Instead, he hoped to give Robinson one of the newly created seats, so he could blunt the influential Arkansan's impact on the court. Robinson's untimely death rendered all of that moot. Jeff Shesol, *Supreme Power: Franklin Roosevelt vs. The Supreme Court* (New York: W.W. Norton & Company, Inc., 2010).

out to be true. Nevertheless, he was confirmed 63–16 and became one of the longest-serving and most influential justices in Supreme Court history.

Father Time then took care of the rest, as more justices either retired or died, giving FDR ample opportunities to shape the court in his favor. Solicitor General Stanley Reed followed in 1938, replacing Sutherland. Longtime FDR allies Frankfurter and SEC Chairman William O. Douglas were appointed in 1939 to replace Cardozo and Brandeis, respectively, while Attorney General Frank Murphy got the nod in 1940 to replace Butler. In all, Roosevelt ended up naming more justices to the Supreme Court than any other president besides George Washington.

From his perch on the Fourth Circuit, Parker watched the events with great interest. Horrified by the Court Packing Bill, Parker was thrilled when it was watered-down and saw the president's retreat as the best thing for preserving judicial independence. He was also opposed to the other provisions in the original bill, including one that would allow lower level judges to float from one district to another based on need.[31] "The future of our institutions depends upon the independence of the judiciary; and I sincerely trust that nothing will happen to impair that independence," he wrote in a letter to Thomas Davis.[32]

However, he refrained from criticizing Roosevelt or the Court Packing Bill publicly. He made some oblique references to the dangers of unchecked power by any branch of the government[33] but saw eye-to-eye with the president when it came to taking an expansive view of federal power in order to promote the general welfare of the country. He also noted that "certain phases of production" had expanded and grown to the point that local governments could no longer exercise control over them because they had become inextricably linked with interstate commerce.[34] In essence, FDR's warnings of a commercial "no-man's-land" had been resolved by expanding federal power and taking a broad interpretation of the commerce clause—something Parker was clearly okay with.

Parker wasn't just simpatico with Roosevelt when it came to these constitutional matters. The judge began sending Roosevelt personal

[31] Parker Papers, supra, Letter from Parker to David Blair, April 29, 1937.

[32] Parker Papers, supra, Letter from Parker to Davis, April 29, 1937.

[33] "Speaker Says Democracy In Grave Danger," *The Bristol News Bulletin*, April 15, 1937.

[34] "Federal Government Needs More Power," *The Greenville News*, April 23, 1937.

letters and notes of praise, similar to what he had done with Hoover. "I feel the country is to be congratulated upon the virile leadership which you have furnished in this period of national danger," Parker wrote in a January 11, 1941 letter.[35] "Allow me to congratulate you on the speech last evening," Parker wrote to FDR on May 28, 1941.[36] "Men of all parties and all classes in this section of the country are already behind your foreign policy." Roosevelt even responded with a warm letter of his own, thanking Parker for his "nice letter" and "heartening" show of support.[37]

Perhaps coincidentally, at around that same time, there were whispers that Justice McReynolds, the last remaining Horseman, who had once said he would never let a president he had once referred to as a "crippled son of a bitch" replace him, was considering retirement. With tensions rising as a result of the war in Europe and the Pacific, Roosevelt was looking to make a bipartisan gesture as a means of promoting national unity. Therefore, Parker's name floated onto the list and, once again, his friends tried their best to make sure it moved to the top.

"I have only one interest in this matter and that is to see an injustice corrected and a distinguished friend and North Carolinian elevated to this high place. I will never rest content until this has been done," Gardner, who was now in private practice after leaving the governor's mansion, wrote to Parker in January 1941.[38]

Frank Graham, president of UNC, sent a telegram to Roosevelt recommending that he appoint "the outstanding judicial administrator in all the eleven circuits."[39] Meanwhile, Northcott sent a letter to Senator Joseph Guffey (D-PA) asking for his endorsement of Parker's potential nomination, writing "a great injustice was done him in his rejection for confirmation when he was formerly appointed" and that it came about because of "lack of knowledge of the man and proper appreciation of his great ability." Northcott also argued that Parker was "properly liberal" and once again played the geographic card, noting that McReynolds was the only justice from the South on the court.[40]

35 Parker Papers, supra, Letter from Parker to Roosevelt, January 11, 1941.

36 Parker Papers, supra, Letter from Parker to Roosevelt, May 28, 1941.

37 Parker Papers, supra, Letter from Roosevelt to Parker, June 3, 1941.

38 Parker Papers, supra, Letter from Gardner to Parker, January 3, 1941.

39 Parker Papers, supra, Telegram from Graham to Roosevelt, January 23, 1941.

40 Parker Papers, supra, Letter from Northcott to Guffey, January 27, 1941.

Meanwhile, newspapers clearly thought that Parker had a good chance to be nominated, once again, for the Supreme Court. *The Charlotte Observer* reported on January 24, 1941 that there was a growing belief Parker would get the nod, noting that it was customary in situations where the president's party already had a majority on the court to appoint a justice from the opposite party.[41] Influential columnist Drew Pearson reported that Roosevelt was considering nominating a Republican in the interests of national unity, and stated Parker was the top choice if he chose to go that route. Pearson noted that Parker had compiled a fairly liberal record as a circuit court judge and had proven to be a more reliable vote for the administration than Roberts.[42]

For his part, Parker clearly coveted the seat. "Nothing would please me more than to be appointed to the Supreme Court, not merely because of the honor of the position but also because such an appointment would wipe out the defeat that I sustained some years ago," he wrote in a May 1938 letter.[43] However, he dissuaded his friends from putting on the full-court press like they did in 1930, noting that it might do him more harm than good.[44] Instead, he thought a word from some influential folks to administration officials might be the better option.[45]

Despite his obvious desire for another shot at the Supreme Court, Parker did not seem confident about his chances. He knew Senator James F. Byrnes (D-SC) had a close relationship with Roosevelt and heard that he wanted McReynolds' seat. Parker figured it was possible that Roosevelt might not want to lose such a capable and trusted lieutenant to the court and, if anything, might give Byrnes a job in his administration, which he ended up doing the following year. Attorney General Robert Jackson also wanted a seat, but Parker heard he was holding out for the chief justiceship.

Sure enough, FDR ended up nominating Byrnes, who was easily confirmed by his fellow senators. A few months later, Hughes retired and

[41] "Judge John Parker Given Good Chance for Supreme Court," *The Charlotte Observer*, January 24, 1941.

[42] Drew Pearson, "The Daily Washington Merry Go Round," *The Anderson Herald*, January 28, 1941.

[43] Parker Papers, supra, Letter from Parker to Douglas McKay, May 9, 1938.

[44] Ibid.

[45] Parker Papers, supra, Letter from Parker to Northcott, January 24, 1941.

Roosevelt accomplished his feat of bipartisanship by elevating the Republican Stone to the chief justiceship. To take Stone's old seat, Roosevelt appointed Jackson, who accepted the offer even though he had wanted the center chair.

The following year, Byrnes, who was bored on the court, resigned to become the head of Roosevelt's Office of Economic Stabilization. However, his influence and power extended far beyond that job, and he became so important and indispensable to Roosevelt that he became known as "assistant president."[46] Once again, Parker's name was bandied about for the seat and, once again, several of his friends made entreaties on his behalf to the president.

And, once again, they came up short. Roosevelt nominated Wiley Rutledge, a circuit court judge from the U.S. Court of Appeals for the District of Columbia. Parker sent him a congratulatory message, to which Rutledge responded that he would have liked Parker to have gotten the nod (in possibly a moment of levity, Rutledge added a handwritten note that second choice was Norris).[47] Rutledge would serve from 1943 to 1949, when he suffered a stroke and died at the young age of 55.

Parker's next chance came in 1945, when Roberts resigned from the court. Truman was under pressure to appoint a Republican, since Roberts' departure left only one, Stone, on the court,[48] and it seemed poetic that Parker could be appointed to the very seat that had been denied him 15 years earlier. Pearson once again backed Parker and told the judge he was on the shortlist alongside Senators Warren Austin (R-VT) and Harold Burton (R-OH), and Judge Orie Phillips of the U.S. Court of Appeals for the Tenth Circuit. Pearson also revealed he had spoken with Walter White and came away with the impression that the NAACP would not seek a rematch should Parker be nominated again.[49] Ultimately, the NAACP made it clear it would be neutral on Parker were he to be nominated for Roberts' seat.[50]

46 "A Manager of Men," *The New York Times*, April 10, 1972.

47 Parker Papers, supra, Letter from Rutledge to Parker, January 13, 1943.

48 "Keep Supreme Court Bipartisan," *The Star Press*, July 11, 1945. "Voters in Favor of Bipartisan Lineup on Supreme Court," *The Daily Times*, August 29, 1945.

49 Parker Papers, supra, Letter from Pearson to Parker, July 19, 1945.

50 "NAACP Won't Back Parker," *The Baltimore Sun*, September 8, 1945.

Truman did make Parker an offer—only it was for the IMT job. Parker was concerned that Truman sending him to Nuremberg was designed to get him out of the way so he could appoint someone else. Nevertheless, he felt reassured by Truman telling him that "this appointment would have no bearing whatever upon the Supreme Court."[51]

Unfortunately for Parker, he seemed not to have considered the possibility that there would be no bearing because Truman had already made up his mind. Indeed, he ended up nominating Burton, a good friend from their days together in the Senate. The two had served together on the Senate Special Committee to Investigate the National Defense Program, also known as the Truman Committee, which looked into U.S. war preparation efforts and sought to identify and correct inefficiencies in the process. Parker admitted to being surprised at the selection, but thought Burton would be a satisfactory justice. "I expect that my failure to be appointed this time means that I shall never get on the Supreme Court, but I am not worrying about the matter," Parker wrote in a letter to Northcott.[52] "I am satisfied that I shall be happier on the Circuit Court of Appeals."

There was one last ray of hope for Parker. In 1952, Dwight D. Eisenhower ended 20 years of Democratic rule and won the White House. With a Republican back in the Oval Office, especially a moderate like Eisenhower, Parker's chances were seemingly enhanced. And when Chief Justice Frederick Vinson died in September 1953, Parker's friends reached out to Eisenhower, encouraging the general to right the wrong from 1930 and make Parker the 14th chief justice in American history. North Carolina bar associations endorsed him for the post and several well-known lawyers and political figures in the state circulated petitions in his favor.[53]

Never a well-respected judge or legal scholar, Vinson had presided over a fractious court, rife with bitter ideological differences and personal feuds. Perhaps with that in mind, Parker's supporters emphasized his credentials and status as one of the most respected judges in the country—to say nothing of his personal amiability. "He never loses his

[51] Parker Papers, supra, Letter from Parker to Senator Josiah Bailey, September 12, 1945.

[52] Parker Papers, supra, Letter from Parker to Northcott, September 20, 1945.

[53] "Parker To Speak in Capital," *Winston-Salem Journal*, September 16, 1953.

temper and is always successfully working out difficult and perplexing problems," U.S. District Judge Ashton Hilliard Williams of the Eastern District of South Carolina wrote to Eisenhower in a letter dated September 9, 1953, one day after Vinson's death.[54] "He is a master planner and diplomat. He is also one of the best judges in the United States. I think that his opinions rank among the best of any of our Federal Judges. No man on the Supreme Court can write a better opinion than Judge Parker can."

Once again, Parker was facing a gigantic obstacle—this time, in the form of the outgoing governor of California, Earl Warren. Eisenhower and Warren had vied for the 1952 GOP nomination for president and, after the general prevailed, the governor had been a good soldier and campaigned loyally for his party's standard bearer. According to Ed Cray, who wrote a biography of Warren published in 1997, Eisenhower had promised Warren the first available Supreme Court seat as a reward for his loyalty, and the outgoing governor had decided to hold the president to their deal.[55] Others have argued that there was no deal, but that Eisenhower always had Warren in mind for the chief justiceship, citing the governor's administrative and leadership skills.[56] Either way, it was widely reported that Warren had the inside track for the center chair[57] and, in October 1953, he was given a recess appointment to the court before being officially confirmed the following March.

After Warren's appointment, Parker's name continued to be mentioned whenever there was a Supreme Court vacancy but, at that point, it was more out of obligation than possibility. John Marshall Harlan II, a long-time corporate lawyer with the firm that became Dewey Ballantine (and then Dewey & LeBoeuf) before being appointed by Eisenhower to the U.S. Court of Appeals for the Second Circuit in 1954, got the nod following Jackson's death the previous year. After Justice Sherman Minton retired in 1956, Eisenhower stunned the political world by appointing Democrat William J. Brennan, Jr., a justice on the New Jersey Supreme

54 Parker Papers, supra, Letter from Williams to Eisenhower, September 9, 1953.

55 Ed Cray, *Chief Justice: A Biography of Earl Warren* (New York: Simon & Schuster, 1997), 248–252.

56 James F. Simon, *Eisenhower Vs. Warren: The Battle for Civil Rights and Liberties* (New York: Liveright, 2018).

57 "Warren Held Frontrunner for Supreme Court Post," *The Victoria Advocate*, September 7, 1953.

Court, in an attempt at bipartisanship. Brennan would become Warren's right-hand man and a highly influential justice who helped lead a liberal revolution on the court, to the extent that Eisenhower reportedly called Warren and Brennan the two biggest mistakes he made during his presidency.[58] The following year, the last Supreme Court vacancy in Parker's lifetime occurred when Reed retired. Eisenhower decided to go with Charles Evans Whittaker, a U.S. Court of Appeals judge for the Eighth Circuit, who never settled into life on the court and left after only five years after suffering a nervous breakdown.

Perhaps Eisenhower wanted his own candidates to consider and wasn't interested in refighting old battles. Or maybe he and others in his administration knew that, if they nominated Parker at that point, he would once again be controversial in a way he hadn't been since 1930. After all, Warren arrived right as a blockbuster school desegregation case was pending on its docket—a case Parker had been involved with as a circuit judge. While the NAACP may have decided not to fight him in 1945, his ruling in the case that eventually became part of *Brown v. Board of Education of Topeka, Kansas*, would have ensured a rematch of epic proportions while making the 1930 fight look like a picnic.

"Petty Tyranny Unworthy of the Spirit of This Republic"

When he wasn't thinking about finally landing his dream job, Parker had plenty of other things to keep him busy. He was in demand as a speaker, traveling throughout the country giving speeches about law, government and society. He served on the United Nations' International Law Commission. He was a member and influential voice of the Judicial Conference of the United States. He was active in the American Bar Association, winning the ABA Medal in 1943 and serving as chairman of the Special Committee on Improving the Administration of Justice – a longtime passion of his. He helped establish state committees (dubbed "Parker Committees") focused on implementing its findings.

He also weathered a serious personal tragedy, as his son and namesake, John J. Parker, Jr., was paralyzed following a car accident in 1938.

[58] Ed Lazarus, "Justices Often Surprise the Presidents Who Pick Them," *Time*, May 26, 2009, https://content.time.com/time/specials/packages/article/0,28804,1900851_1900850_1900845,00.html, accessed October 17, 2024.

The younger Parker never really recovered and, after several years of poor health, died in 1941. "[O]f course his condition is a source of grief to all of us," Parker wrote in a 1939 letter to one of his friends.[59] He also noted that his wife, Maria, had taken their son's accident especially hard and had fallen into a deep depression. Shortly after his son's passing, Parker wrote to one of his son's doctors, thanking him for doing everything he could. "Unfortunately, his injury was such that we could not hope for very much improvement, but that was not the fault of any of the doctors," Parker wrote.[60] "On the contrary, I feel that he would have passed away many months ago but for the fine treatment that he has had."

He also still had his full-time job as a circuit court judge. In the years after his Senate rejection, Judge John J. Parker of the Fourth Circuit had plenty of opportunities to rule on important, interesting cases. Two cases, however, stand out and are illustrative of how he did, and did not, change after his failed Supreme Court nomination.

In 1942, Parker wrote the opinion in the case of *Barnette v. West Virginia State Board of Ed.*, but the roots of the case go back a few years. In 1937, a family of Jehovah's Witnesses had challenged a Pennsylvania state law that made standing and saluting the flag while reciting the Pledge mandatory under threat of expulsion, arguing that it was against their religion to do so. The case, captioned *Minersville School District v. Gobitis,* went to the Supreme Court, which ruled in 1940 that public schools could force students to salute the flag and recite the Pledge of Allegiance.[61] In an 8–1 decision, with only Stone dissenting, the court upheld the Pennsylvania law and ruled that the First and Fourteenth Amendments did not apply.

Writing for the majority, Frankfurter held that the law was constitutional and did not violate freedom of religion since it was passed for secular reasons and was enforced evenhandedly. He also made clear that state legislatures and school officials had the right to promote national unity and courts should be deferential. He also asserted that people upset with the decisions of a democratically elected legislature could simply use their votes or political activism to try and get the change they believed in—an odd position for someone who helped found the American Civil

[59] Parker Papers, supra, Letter from Parker to James P. Dees, November 23, 1939.

[60] Parker Papers, supra, Letter from Parker to Dr. W.M. Coppridge, June 13, 1941.

[61] *Minersville School District v. Gobitis*, 310 U.S. 586 (1940).

Liberties Union, whose primary purpose was to protect civil liberties for people who might not be able to stand up to the government.

However, Frankfurter also believed in assimilation and the forging of a common national identity. "The ultimate foundation of a free society is the binding tie of cohesive sentiment," Frankfurter wrote in his opinion,[62] adding: "We live by symbols" and that the flag is a symbol of "our national unity."

The opinion led to an uptick in violence against Jehovah's Witnesses throughout the country, as now they were branded as disloyal. Frankfurter's former organization, the ACLU, tracked the incidents and reported attacks in 1940 against nearly 1,500 Jehovah's Witnesses in 335 separate incidents across 44 states. The Justice Department investigated and later found that, "almost without exception," the flag salute was the catalyst.[63]

In the aftermath of the case, some members of the *Gobitis* majority immediately began having second thoughts. In 1941, Justice Murphy told his clerk that he regretted his vote to join the majority and asked him to keep an eye out for any case that could correct that decision.[64] The following year, the court ruled against another Jehovah's Witness—this time in the case of *Jones v. Opelika*, a challenge on freedom of speech and religious grounds to a local ordinance prohibiting the sale of books without a license. Murphy dissented alongside his frequent ideological allies on the court, Black and Douglas. What was noteworthy was that the three formally renounced *Gobitis*, stating they believed the case had been wrongly decided and should be overturned. Alongside Stone, who was now chief justice, there were now four solid votes to overturn *Gobitis*. As the 1942–1943 term started, they would just need one more vote—maybe it would come from Robert Jackson, who had taken Stone's old seat. Or maybe one of the other justices would be convinced by Murphy, Douglas and Black and renounce his prior vote. Or maybe another seat would open up on the court and go to someone who thought *Gobitis*

[62] Ibid.

[63] Vincent Blasi and Seana Shiffrin, "The Story of West Virginia State Board of Education v. Barnette: The Pledge of Allegiance and the Freedom of Thought," in *Constitutional Law Stories*, ed. Michael C. Dorf (New York: Foundation Press, 2004), 457–463.

[64] John Pickering, "Remembering U.S. Supreme Court Justice Frank Murphy," *Law Quadrangle News* 14 (Winter 2005), 43.

was bad law. Either way, *Gobitis* may not have been dead just yet, but the buzzards were certainly getting into place.

The stars quickly aligned for another challenge to compulsory flag salute laws when the Barnetts, a family of Jehovah's Witnesses, filed suit in U.S. District Court for the Southern District of West Virginia in 1942. Incorrectly listed as "Barnette" on the court paperwork, the family claimed a West Virginia Board of Education rule requiring school children to stand and salute the flag every day while reciting the Pledge violated the First and Fourteenth Amendments.

Essentially, the facts and legal arguments were nearly identical to *Gobitis*. Since that case was still good law, any lower court judge would have been well within their rights to simply refer to *Gobitis* and rule against the Barnetts. Not even *Red Jacket* was this straightforward—and, when the case ended up before Parker and his colleagues on the Fourth Circuit, it seemed preordained that they would defer to Frankfurter's opinion.

Except that's exactly the opposite of what happened. Writing for a unanimous three-judge panel, Parker noted that "[o]rdinarily we would feel constrained to follow an unreversed decision of the Supreme Court of the United States, whether we agreed with it or not," but in this case, since four of the seven justices on the court who had decided *Gobitis* had expressed disagreement with it, "we do not feel that it is incumbent upon us to accept it as binding authority."[65]

Parker's opinion was grounded in religious liberty and not free speech. Indeed, he even wrote that there was "nothing improper in requiring a flag salute in schools." Instead, Parker held that the government could not force people to act against their religious beliefs, other than in cases where not doing so would be harmful to the general welfare of the community, such as evading taxes, engaging in polygamy or other things like that. "To justify the overriding of religious scruples, however, there must be a clear justification therefor in the necessities of national or community life," Parker wrote. And in a bit of sarcasm, Parker opined that, surely, the republic would stand even if schoolkids refused to do so every morning in homeroom.

Parker made clear that his opinion was not meant as an endorsement of Jehovah's Witnesses or their beliefs. Instead, he pointed out that all

[65] *Barnette v. West Virginia State Board of Ed.*, 47 F. Supp. 251 (S.D.W. Va. 1942).

religions have beliefs and practices that some people consider "utterly foolish and lacking in reason." Therefore, it was not the job of the courts to decide which ones were valid and protected under the law and which ones were not.[66] In fact, the month after Parker handed down his opinion, U.S. District Judge William Baker of the Northern District of West Virginia sent him a letter along with a newspaper clip of Baker berating two Jehovah's Witnesses defendants and questioning their beliefs before sentencing them to the maximum punishment for violating federal Selective Service laws. According to the article, Baker quoted Scripture at length and essentially called them traitors for not being willing to defend their country during wartime. "You have certainly made a very forcible statement with respect to the position of Jehovah's Witnesses, and I have no doubt that it will have a salutary influence," Parker wrote to Baker in a November 19, 1942 letter.[67]

Whatever his personal feelings, Parker nevertheless felt that the Jehovah's Witnesses deserved the same amount of protection that any other religious group would get under the Constitution. To make that clear, he ended his opinion with a soaring piece of rhetoric that may very well have gone down in legal lore had the Supreme Court not outdone him the following year. "The salute to the flag is an expression of the homage of the soul," Parker wrote. "To force it upon one who has conscientious scruples against giving it, is petty tyranny unworthy of the spirit of this Republic and forbidden, we think, by the fundamental law. This court will not countenance such tyranny but will use the power at its command to see that rights guaranteed by the fundamental law are respected."

Unlike *Red Jacket*, there did not seem to be much discussion or debate among the judges, which was surprising considering they were about to disobey a binding Supreme Court precedent. U.S. District Judge Harry Watkins of the Northern and Southern Districts of West Virginia, who was one of the three judges on the case, sent a letter to Parker on October 5, 1942 saying he had "no suggestions or criticisms" of his *Barnette* opinion.[68] The following day, the third judge on the case, U.S. District Judge Ben Moore of the Southern District of West Virginia, sent a letter

[66] Ibid.

[67] Parker Papers, supra, Letter from Parker to Baker, November 19, 1942.

[68] Parker Papers, supra, Letter from Watkins to Parker, October 5, 1942.

to Parker saying he had no changes to suggest and called the opinion "a very able one."[69]

Maybe their attitude stemmed from a feeling that they knew what was going to happen next. When the Supreme Court got the case the following year, not only did Stone, Black, Douglas and Murphy vote to overturn *Gobitis*, but they were joined by Jackson and Rutledge. In a sweeping opinion that went further than Parker, the majority not only held that the school board's rules violated freedom of religion, but of speech too. In one of the most famous and oft-quoted passages in American jurisprudence, Jackson wrote: "If there is any fixed star in our constitutional constellation, it is that no official, high or petty, can prescribe what shall be orthodox in politics, nationalism, religion or other matters of opinion or force citizens to confess by word or act their faith therein. If there are circumstances which permit an exception, they do not now occur to us."[70]

Despite his ultimate vindication, it is still odd that Parker chose to break with established Supreme Court precedent. As William Burris pointed out in *Duty and the Law: Judge John J. Parker and the Constitution*, *Barnette* was the first and only time in his career where Parker chose not to follow a Supreme Court case that was still good law.[71] After all, Parker could have done what Borah or Green thought he should have done in *Red Jacket* and followed precedent while expressing disapproval of it. Clearly, he had faith in his prognostication skills because his sense that the court was going to overrule *Gobitis* was right on the money.

Or maybe Parker was trying to burnish his Supreme Court credentials at a time when it looked likely that Roosevelt would appoint a Republican in a gesture of bipartisanship. Perhaps he had learned from the *Red Jacket* affair and realized that *Barnette* was an easy way for him to prove he wasn't just some mindless drone and was willing to stand up for something he believed was correct.

Or maybe the West Virginia regulation shocked him to his core and offended his belief in religious freedom. According to David Manwaring's 1962 book *Render Unto Caesar: The Flag-Salute Controversy*, Parker seemed unsympathetic towards the state board of education from the

[69] Parker Papers, supra, Letter from Moore to Parker, October 6, 1942.

[70] *West Virginia State Board of Education v. Barnette*, 319 U.S. 624 (1943).

[71] Burris, supra, 196.

start. At one point, prior to the commencement of oral arguments, the judge tried to get state authorities to simply excuse the Jehovah's Witnesses from having to take part in the flag salute and Pledge, and even recessed for the day so that they could take his words under advisement. They refused and, during oral arguments the next day, Parker seemed annoyed and hostile towards the state's lawyer, who had made clear that he personally disapproved of the rule he was tasked with defending.[72]

Therefore, it was more or less a foregone conclusion that the Barnetts would win, and Parker made sure of that. In his opinion, Parker drove a stake through the heart of the doctrine that he and many other judges had long clung to: the notion that lower court judges were bound by Supreme Court decisions. With a wave of the proverbial hand, Parker simply turned aside the board's reliance on *Gobitis* as controlling precedent, stating that dismissing on these grounds "will not easily dispose of this case."[73] "[It is] unfortunate that a case of its kind should be in the court at a time when national unity is paramount," Parker wrote in his majority opinion.[74] Clearly, national unity wasn't so important to Parker that it required enforced behavior.

"Does Not Require Integration"

Perhaps that attitude about not forcing national unity was on his mind several years later when he ruled in another major case.

When Thurgood Marshall and his NAACP colleagues walked into the federal district courtroom in South Carolina in 1951 to argue the school desegregation case of *Briggs v. Elliott* before a three-judge panel, they knew they had one vote in the bag.

Judge Julius Waties Waring had long been a staunch supporter of civil rights and desegregation and had convinced Marshall into turning a narrow case that had been about inequality in segregated schools into a broad one questioning whether segregation in public schools was constitutional.[75]

[72] David Manwaring, *Render Unto Caesar; The Flag-Salute Controversy* (Chicago: University of Chicago Press, 1962), 212–213.

[73] Ibid.

[74] Ibid., 212–213.

[75] Lamb, Chris, "Thurgood Marshall's Unusual Meeting With a Judge Helped End Segregation," *The Washington Post*, May 17, 2022.

They also knew they had one vote against them. Judge George Bell Timmerman Sr. was known as a "Bible quoting fundamentalist and an outspoken advocate of white supremacy."[76] Marshall and his team weren't counting on him to have a sudden conversion.

The wildcard, and probable swing vote, was John J. Parker. If Parker held a grudge against the NAACP, he hadn't shown it in the two decades or so since the civil rights organization had helped torpedo his Supreme Court nomination. Even Walter White conceded that Parker had been a fair-minded judge since their clash and had compared him favorably to the legendary Justice John Marshall Harlan, the sole dissenter in *Plessy*. Meanwhile, Marshall had won several civil rights appeals before Parker, with the judge writing for the court in *Alston v. School Board of the City of Norfolk* (1940) requiring the city to equalize salaries for Black and white teachers, and *Rice v. Elmore* (1947) striking down all-white primaries in South Carolina.[77]

In general, Parker had developed a reputation as a fairly liberal judge to the extent that former South Carolina Governor Strom Thurmond, an avowed segregationist who had bolted the Democrats for a third-party presidential bid in 1948, was concerned that he and Waring could deliver an opinion in favor of the NAACP. South Carolina's brain trust, led by then Governor James F. Byrnes and attorney Robert McCormick Figg, Jr., were also worried and came up with a strategy of throwing money at the admittedly inferior Black schools and conceding the legal argument that they were unequal, hoping that it would force the judges to issue a narrow ruling while avoiding the main constitutional issue as to whether or not segregated public schools were legal.[78]

Byrnes, Figg and Thurmond need not have worried. A closer look at Parker's prior rulings in favor of the NAACP revealed that those cases were fairly narrow in scope and had been primarily focused on equality—not whether an essential feature of Jim Crow was constitutional or not. To get to where Marshall and the NAACP lawyers wanted to go in *Briggs*, Parker would have to rule that *Plessy v. Ferguson*, the 1896 decision

[76] Richard Kluger, *Simple Justice: The History of* Brown v. Board of Education *and Black America's Struggle For Equality* (Alfred A. Knopf: New York, 2004), 302.

[77] Kluger, supra, at 302–303. *Alston v. School Board of City of Norfolk*, 112 F.2d 992 (4th Cir. 1940) and *Rice v. Elmore*, 165 F.2d 387 (4th Cir. 1947).

[78] Ibid., 344–345.

legalizing "separate but equal," was unconstitutional and should be overturned. While he had been willing to defy precedent in *Barnette*, Parker's analysis had been built, in large part, on the fact that the Supreme Court seemed likely to overturn *Gobitis*. For *Briggs* and other school desegregation cases, it was anyone's guess how the Supreme Court would rule—and even if there were a majority there willing to overrule *Plessy*, that didn't mean Parker was going to do so on his end. In fact, Marshall was not counting on Parker's support and was expecting to lose 2–1, which was fine since the goal was to get before the Supreme Court anyway.[79]

Parker seemed to telegraph his position during the trial phase, remarking that "it is not the function of the court to determine what is the best educational policy. It is the function of the court to see that all men are given their rights."[80] Parker also made clear that the court would not "wet nurse" the South Carolina educational system.[81] He seemed skeptical or dismissive of the NAACP's social science evidence that segregation had resulted in feelings of self-inferiority among Black Americans, at one point even cutting off an NAACP witness testifying about the effects of segregation on Blacks' sense of citizenship. Towards the end of the hearing, he asked Figg what kind of decree the court should enter in light of his admission that the schools were not equal. "Assuming segregation is not abolished by the decree, it would be proper for this court to direct an equalization of education facilities," Parker said.[82] "And we wouldn't tell you how to do it."

Indeed, when the three-judge panel handed down its decision, Parker stayed true to form and found the schools were unequal and violated the separate but equal principle, but upheld the legality of segregation in general. According to Waring, when the judges spoke about their positions, Parker operated from the assumption that *Plessy* could not be overruled.[83] His opinion reflected that assumption, as he started off by waxing poetic about a country with such diverse beliefs, customs, and traditions, and extolling the virtues of the American constitutional system

[79] Ibid., 303.

[80] Kluger, *Simple Justice*, supra, 358.

[81] "Dixie Holds its Breath as Judges Ponder S.C. School Bias Suit," *Pittsburgh Courier*, June 9, 1951.

[82] Ibid., 364–365.

[83] Ibid., 365.

where the federal government "protects the fundamental rights of the individual" but "leaves to the several states the solution of local problems." Education was one such problem that was best handled at the local level, and Parker made clear that it was "equally well settled that there is no denial of the equal protection of the laws in segregating children in the schools for purposes of education, if the children of the different races are given equal facilities and opportunities."[84]

In a nod to his *Barnette* analysis, Parker implied that it was unlikely the Supreme Court would overturn or reconsider *Plessy*. In the previous year, the court had handed down a decision in the case of *Sweatt v. Painter* (Marshall was one of the lead attorneys for the plaintiff) that the University of Texas Law School had to be integrated because the state's lone Black law school had been so unequal and inferior that it violated the principle of "separate but equal." However, the court had expressly declined to re-examine or reconsider *Plessy*,[85] despite requests from Marshall and several amicus counsel that they do so.

"[T]he principal argument made on appeal is that the authority of *Plessy v. Ferguson* has been so weakened by subsequent decisions that we should no longer consider it as binding," Parker wrote.[86] "We do not think, however, that we are at liberty thus to disregard a decision of the Supreme Court which that court has not seen fit to overrule and which it expressly refrained from re-examining, although urged to do so, in the very recent case of *Sweatt v. Painter*."

As with his *Barnette* opinion, Parker even found the time to get a little sarcastic, pointing out that "seventeen states and the Congress of the United States have for more than three-quarters of a century required segregation of the races in the public schools" and that the Supreme Court, including liberals like Brandeis, Oliver Wendell Holmes and Stone, had voted to uphold it time and time again. "[I]t is a late day to say that such segregation is violative of fundamental constitutional rights. It is hardly reasonable to suppose that legislative bodies over so wide a territory, including the Congress of the United States, and great judges of high courts have knowingly defied the Constitution for so long a period

[84] *Briggs v. Elliott*, 98 F. Supp. 529 (E.D.S.C. 1951).

[85] *Sweatt v. Painter*, 339 U.S. 629 (1950).

[86] Kluger, supra, 276.

or that they have acted in ignorance of the meaning of its provisions," Parker wrote.[87]

Parker soon learned the limits of his prognostication skills. *Briggs* and several other cases were consolidated into *Brown v. Board of Education of Topeka*, with the Supreme Court hearing oral arguments in December 1952 when Vinson was still chief justice. With a sharply divided court that was either narrowly in favor of striking down public school segregation or keeping it in place, depending on which justice you asked,[88] Frankfurter got the case put over for re-argument the following term in the hopes that some clear consensus would emerge by then.

That consensus came in the form of Warren. Showing the type of leadership and coalition-building skills he was known for, Warren convinced his brethren that state-sponsored segregation in public schools was wrong and that a show of force in the form of a unanimous opinion was necessary in order to head off any possible resistance. Over the course of several months, Warren steadily lobbied and cajoled reluctant justices, particularly Reed, who reportedly wept from the bench when the opinion was handed down. In the end, Warren got his way, as a unanimous court ruled that "in the field of public education, the doctrine of 'separate but equal' has no place" and "separate educational facilities are inherently unequal."[89]

Of course, that wasn't the end of it. The parties came back before the Supreme Court the following term to argue over how to implement the *Brown* decree. In a case that became known as "*Brown* II," the Court decided that, rather than order immediate desegregation in public schools throughout the country and risk civil unrest and resistance, it would let local authorities come up with plans to implement the *Brown* decision "with all deliberate speed."[90] The court also tasked lower federal courts with monitoring state and local officials to make sure they were complying

[87] *Briggs*, supra.

[88] Kluger, *Simple Justice*, supra, 592–618 and Bernard Schwartz, *Decision: How the Supreme Court Decides Cases* (New York: Oxford University Press, 1996), 96. Justice Burton thought the vote was 6–3 in favor of overruling *Plessy* with himself, Black, Douglas, Minton and a wavering Frankfurter and Jackson in the majority. Frankfurter had it at 5–4 with the same lineup minus Jackson. On the other hand, Douglas had it as 5–4 to affirm *Plessy*, with himself, Black, Minton and Burton in dissent.

[89] *Brown v. Board of Education of Topeka*, 347 U.S. 483 (1954).

[90] *Brown v. Board of Education of Topeka*, 349 U.S. 294 (1955) ("Brown II").

in good faith and sent back the original cases to the jurisdictions in which they were filed.

That meant Parker would have a say over how *Brown* would be implemented in his circuit. In 1955, the case of *Briggs v. Elliott* went back before Parker and the Fourth Circuit. As with the original case, Parker and Timmerman sat on the bench, but Waring, the staunch supporter of civil rights and desegregation, had retired and had been replaced by circuit judge Armistead Mason Dobie.

The three judges issued a *per curiam* opinion that was widely acknowledged to have been written by Parker.[91] In it, Parker accepted *Brown* I and II and conceded that his original *Briggs* opinion had been overruled. "Whatever may have been the views of this court as to the law when the case was originally before us, it is our duty now to accept the law as declared by the Supreme Court," he wrote in the opinion.

In an earlier draft of his opinion, Parker then immediately added this passage: "The Court is the keystone of the arch of our constitutional structure; and, unless its decisions on constitution matters are accepted by the courts and the people of the country as declaring the law of the land, our constitution system cannot endure." Parker went further, adding that "the overruling decisions of the Supreme Court must be accepted as the correct statement of the law, otherwise our governmental system will not work and anarchy will result."[92]

However, Parker removed that part from his final draft and, instead, it went immediately from the sentence "Whatever may have been the views of this court as to the law when the case was originally before us ..." into an analysis of what *Brown* did and did not declare. It's unknown why he chose to remove the words he had written defending the Supreme Court. For a judge who had long believed in the economy of words and not writing long, florid passages that didn't actually have any actual legal bearing on the outcome of the case, it's possible that he simply made an editorial decision by deleting that passage. But, by doing so, his tone became one of grudging acceptance that could be read as somewhat cynical considering he immediately went into what he believed *Brown's* limits were.

[91] Morris A. Soper, Fred B. Helms and Orie L. Phillips, "A Tribute to Judge John J. Parker – The Gladsome Light of Jurisprudence," *North Carolina Law Review* 37, no. 1 (1958).

[92] Parker Papers, supra, draft opinion of *Briggs v. Elliott*, 1955.

For instance, he pointed out that the court did not give federal courts the right to "take over or regulate the public schools of the states." Furthermore, the court did not rule that "states must mix persons of different races in the schools" or that students had to attend certain schools against their will. Instead, Parker maintained that all the court did was outlaw state-sponsored segregation of public schools. "The Constitution, in other words, does not require integration. It merely forbids discrimination. It does not forbid such segregation as occurs as the result of voluntary action. It merely forbids the use of governmental power to enforce segregation," he wrote.[93] In other words, de facto segregation in public schools was okay, but *de jure* segregation was not. And if a school happened to be segregated on its own and not because of governmental regulation, then it could remain so, as long as it did not deny students of other races entry.

Was Parker's legal analysis correct, and did he make the only logical ruling given the twin opinions in *Brown* that he was handed? Or did he violate the spirit of the *Brown* cases, which clearly held that segregated schools were wrong and found that separating schoolkids "solely because of their race generates a feeling of inferiority as to their status in the community that may affect their hearts and minds in a way unlikely ever to be undone"?[94]

Regardless of whatever his motives may or may not have been, Parker's opinion would have far-reaching implications and essentially presaged the next phase in the ongoing war involving school segregation. As Richard Kluger pointed out in his book, *Simple Justice: The History of* Brown v. Board of Education *and Black America's Struggle For Equality*, and the NAACP lawyers focused on getting segregation outlawed and did not really think about how it would be dismantled. In an exchange with Timmerman during the 1952 re-argument of *Briggs* before the court, Marshall was asked how the state should achieve integration when there were too many Black students and not enough room in white schools to accommodate them. Marshall proposed mixing up the schools so that there would be white and Black kids in all schools, while flatly stating that not all students would go to the white schools.[95] Marshall

93 *Briggs v. Elliott*, 132 F. Supp. 776 (E.D.S.C. 1955).

94 *Brown v. Board*, supra.

95 Kluger, supra, 535.

and others underestimated just how angry and frightened that would make white families and strengthen their resolve to fight to maintain some semblance of the status quo. Indeed, states and localities that were desperate to preserve some level of racial segregation had long ago drawn up contingency plans to try and blunt the impact of *Brown*, such as privatizing schools, closing down public schools, utilizing vouchers and grants, and implementing a "school choice" scheme that would have the effect of having white students choose to go to all-white schools and Black students choose to go to all-Black schools. Some states began to turn to busing as a means to desegregate and integrate schools, a controversial issue that became a convenient lightning rod for people, not just in the South but all over the country.

The so-called Parker Doctrine "set the standard for evasiveness throughout the south," Kluger argued.[96] J. Harvie Wilkinson, III, concurred, stating that Parker was the figure who "most influenced school desegregation" in the years after *Brown*. "The distinction between 'Thou Shalt Integrate' and 'Thou Shalt Not Segregate' is all important. If *Brown* was read to require integration, Southern school boards would be under an immediate duty to submit plans for substantial racial mixing. If, as Parker contended, *Brown* merely prohibited segregation, then the question becomes what evidence courts will accept that school boards are no longer doing so."[97]

According to Wilkinson and Alexander Bickel, formerly all-white schools would simply admit a few token minorities and use that to satisfy their duty not to segregate.[98] "Anything other than outright defiance stood a fair chance of judicial approval," Wilkinson observed.[99] Therefore, during the first decade following the *Brown* decision, only a small handful of Black students were allowed to enroll at white schools and less

[96] Kluger, *Simple Justice: The History of* Brown v. Board of Education *and Black America's Struggle For Equality* (New York: Vintage Books, 1975), 751. In the revised edition issued in 2004, Kluger wrote a new final chapter that traced the history and progress (or lack thereof) of civil rights in the 50 years since *Brown*. The new chapter was less focused on the immediate aftermath of *Brown II* and therefore omitted reference to the "Parker Doctrine." Other historians, however, have utilized the term.

[97] J. Harvie Wilkinson, "The Supreme Court and Southern School Desegregation, 1955–1970: A History and Analysis." *Virginia Law Review* 64, no. 4 (1978): 507–508.

[98] Alexander Bickel, "The Decade of School Desegregation: Progress and Prospects," *Columbia Law Review* 64, no. 2 (1964), 205.

[99] Wilkinson, supra, 508.

than one out of 50 Black school children had class with white students in 11 states in the country.[100] As of 2024, nearly 70 years after *Brown*, schools continue to be highly segregated, with studies showing that racial segregation in the country's 100 largest school districts has grown by 64 percent since 1988.[101]

On the other hand, some scholars have argued that Parker's opinion was not necessarily unjustified. In *From Jim Crow to Civil Rights: The Supreme Court and the Struggle for Racial Equality*, Michael Klarman pointed out that Burton, himself, had advanced that same argument during deliberations for *Brown* II.[102] Others have argued that Parker's opinion was the only possible middle ground in an explosive situation where one side desperately wanted equality and civil rights and the other desperately wanted to hold onto their way of life. Having understood just how fragile the country was, Parker's incremental approach reflected his belief that forcing rapid change on the South would only lead to unrest and conflict. "No man in America has done more to steer the South and the country along lines of moderation than Judge Parker did by his clear analysis of the decision in *Brown v. Board of Education*," Fred Helms, former president of the North Carolina Bar Association, wrote in a tribute to Parker following his death in 1958, while arguing that *Brown* precipitated "a grave crisis – the most serious since the Civil War."[103]

Nevertheless, the Parker Doctrine, more or less, became the law given how often lower court judges cited it in the years following *Brown*. "I know how earnestly you have endeavored to moderate emotions in this area of race relations, and you have taken occasion to say in our court's opinions that which would help to lessen resistance to the Supreme Court's decisions," Simon Sobeloff, Parker's colleague on the Fourth Circuit, said to Parker.[104] "It was both true and useful to point out, as you have done in the past, that the law does not require wholesale

[100] Kluger, *Simple Justice*, supra, 755.

[101] Fabiola Cineas, "Why School Segregation is Getting Worse," *Vox*, May 15, 2024, www.vox.com/24156492/school-segregation-increasing-brown-board-of-education, accessed: October 17, 2024.

[102] Michael Klarman, *From Jim Crow to Civil Rights: The Supreme Court and the Struggle for Racial Equality* (New York: Oxford University Press, 2004), 358.

[103] "A Tribute to Judge John J. Parker – The Gladsome Light of Jurisprudence," supra, at 10.

[104] Parker Papers, supra, Letter from Sobeloff to Parker, June 25, 1957.

reshuffling of pupils to compel mixing; but I am wondering if it serves the desired purpose to keep repeating this assertion. I fear that such repetition is less likely to allay fears than to encourage inaction."

Unbowed, Parker and his colleagues on the Fourth Circuit reaffirmed his so-called Doctrine in several desegregation cases he heard before his 1958 death, including *School Bd. of City of Charlottesville v. Allen*,[105] in which a unanimous court found that Virginia officials had been trying to enforce racial segregation by rejecting applications from Black students to white schools, and *School Bd., City, Newport News, Va. v. Atkins*,[106] which upheld injunctions that prohibited racial discrimination in public schools in Norfolk and Newport News, Virginia.

It would not be until the late 1960s that the Parker Doctrine finally met its end. First, Judge John Minor Wisdom of the Fifth Circuit Court of Appeals broke with Parker and argued that states did, in fact, have a duty to promote integration. In three opinions written between 1965 and 1966, Wisdom held that states had wielded segregation as a weapon to relegate Blacks to a state of second-class citizenship and quasi-servitude, and now it was their duty to undo it. "[T]he only adequate redress for a previously overt system-wide policy of segregation directed against Negroes as a collective entity is a system-wide policy of integration," he wrote in *United States v. Jefferson County Bd. of Education*.[107]

Then, in 1968, a decade after Parker's death, the Supreme Court heard *Green v. County School Board of New Kent County*. Originally brought by the NAACP challenging a "freedom of choice" plan in Virginia that they alleged was designed to maintain some form of de facto racial segregation in public schools, the *Green* case showed just how ingrained the Parker Doctrine (or "Parker Dictum" as the NAACP referred to it—a term that the famously taciturn judge surely despised) had become in post-*Brown* school desegregation cases, especially in the South. During oral arguments, NAACP lawyer Samuel Tucker explicitly asked the court to reject the "Parker Dictum" and adopt Wisdom's reasoning while opposing counsel Frederick T. Gray of Virginia defended it and noted that it may have been dicta to start with "but it didn't remain dicta very

[105] *School Bd. of City of Charlottesville v. Allen*, 240 F.2d 59 (4th Cir. 1956).

[106] *School Bd., City, Newport News, Va. v. Atkins*, 246 F.2d 325 (4th Cir. 1957).

[107] *United States v. Jefferson County Bd. of Educ.*, 372 F.2d 836 (5th Cir. 1966).

long" because it had been "adopted by one court after another across this land."[108]

The Court finally put its foot down and decided to put an end to "all deliberate speed" and the Parker Doctrine. Writing for a unanimous court, Brennan struck down the "freedom of choice" plan, making clear that school boards had an "affirmative duty" to end segregation "root and branch," and emphasizing that "the time for mere 'deliberate speed' has run out."[109] "When this opinion is handed down, the traffic light will have changed from *Brown* to *Green*. Amen!" Warren wrote in a private note to Brennan.[110]

Ironically, Parker's failure to attain a Supreme Court seat may have actually allowed him to play a much larger and impactful role in the desegregation battle. It's difficult to engage in counterfactuals and hypotheticals because, on the one hand, if he had been confirmed in 1930, he would have occupied the seat that ultimately went to Burton, making Parker a potential swing vote in favor of maintaining segregated schools. However, it's also possible Burton and Minton might have still ended up on the court anyway. The two of them, plus Douglas and Black, assuming Roosevelt still puts them on the court in a world where Parker was confirmed in 1930, would have remained a formidable bloc when it came to *Brown*, and with Warren's appointment, they would have won no matter what. Assuming Frankfurter and Jackson would have still signed onto Warren's opinion, the only question would have been whether Parker would have bowed to the inevitable and put aside his own personal beliefs for the sake of unity or if he would have stuck to his guns and penned a lone dissent (or one for himself and Reed) that would have had little to no impact legally but might have given aid and comfort to resisters throughout the country.

Instead, from his perch on the Fourth Circuit, he ended up crafting an opinion that would be used and followed by other judges and officials in the South determined to delay or get around *Brown*. Parker would die in 1958 after suffering a heart attack in Washington, D.C., as he was

[108] "Green v. County School Board of New Kent County." *Oyez*. Accessed April 23, 2025. https://www.oyez.org/cases/1967/695.

[109] *Green v. County Sch. Bd. of New Kent County*, 391 U.S. 430 (1968).

[110] "Brown v. Board: Timeline of School Integration in the U.S.," *Learning For Justice*, Spring 2004 www.learningforjustice.org/magazine/spring-2004/brown-v-board-timeline-of-school-integration-in-the-us, accessed October 25, 2024.

preparing to attend the Judicial Conference. As a result, he did not live to see the passage of the 1964 Civil Rights Act and the 1965 Voting Rights Act, to say nothing of the various Supreme Court decisions and federal laws that ended *de jure* racial segregation throughout the country.

He also did not live to see how de facto racial segregation, especially at the public school level, remains in effect throughout the country to this day. The Parker Doctrine (or Dictum) may have been put to rest, but the ideological underpinnings behind it, to say nothing of its general attitude of unwillingness to embrace the *Brown* decision, are still alive and continue to affect race relations. In that sense, Warren and Brennan were wrong that the light had gone from *Brown* to *Green*. If anything, the light hasn't even reached *Brown* yet.

While his personal feelings towards racial segregation are not known, it is easy to infer that, based on his speeches during his political career and his judicial decisions post-*Brown* that he, at the very least, believed in the legality and correctness of the status quo and that Black Americans were better off staying out of the political process and not agitating for social change.

In the end, he saw his fealty to what he believed *Brown* said and what the law required at the expense of helping millions of less fortunate Americans who toiled under the badge of inferiority as him doing his duty as a judge. Perhaps it was appropriate, given how he had lost out on his dream job because, in his view, he had performed his judicial duties in *Red Jacket* and stuck to his guns by repeating and upholding his political ideals.

In doing so he either failed or refused to acknowledge something his critics charged him with during his ill-fated confirmation battle. It didn't matter to millions of Americans that Parker behaved the way a judge should have or was doing what he thought was for the greater good. It only mattered that, in doing so, he wasn't on their side.

CHAPTER 9

Epilogue

Nearly 40 years after Parker's defeat, another stately, distinguished looking judge from the Fourth Circuit was nominated to the Supreme Court. Like Parker, his nomination was highly controversial, drawing the organized resistance of both labor and civil rights groups. Like Parker, he was a Southerner and had been nominated by a newly-elected Republican president who had carried a number of states in the Solid South and was hoping to solidify those gains for the future. Like Parker, he faced hostility from certain quarters of the Senate, who were spoiling for a fight thanks to a prior, equally contentious and controversial, Supreme Court nomination.

Unlike Parker, Judge Clement F. Haynsworth of South Carolina showed up to testify before the Senate Judiciary Committee, allowing him to face his detractors and defend his record. His appearance had never been in doubt—starting with John Marshall Harlan II's nomination in 1955, it had become expected, almost mandatory, for nominees to show up and testify before the committee. Long gone were the days when judges like Parker demurred because they thought it was unseemly to publicly vie for a seat on the court. Whatever ethical qualms they may have still had about commenting on issues they could one day face on their dockets or defending their past actions had long been tossed aside in the name of pragmatism and political expediency. In other words, they saw how sitting back and trying to remain above the fray had worked out

V. Li, *Supreme Pressure*,
https://doi.org/10.1007/978-3-032-07864-3_9

for Parker and some of the nominees that came after him and realized that, if they wanted to win, they had to play the game.

That's because, in the years since the Parker nomination, the game had grown to accommodate many more players. According to *Making the Supreme Court* by Cameron and Kastellec, interest group involvement in High Court nominations dipped slightly after Parker, but then sharply increased starting with Haynsworth. Most nominations after that saw the same or higher level of interest group involvement than Parker before reaching its peak with Robert Bork.[1] The involved groups run the gamut from left-wing organizations to Christian conservatives—it all depends on the nominee and the President making the appointment.

That raises the stakes for all nominees since, after all, anyone can always find any reason to oppose a nominee, no matter how qualified they might be. Harlan II, for instance, had felt it necessary to show up because anti-civil rights senators such as Judiciary Committee Chairman James Eastland (D-MS) were still furious about *Brown* and were worried this Harlan would be like his grandfather, the original *Plessy* dissenter. There were also accusations that Harlan believed in one world government because of his involvement with the Atlantic Union, an organization that called for closer ties to NATO—a hot-button issue thanks to the ongoing controversy over the Bricker Amendment.[2] Harlan faced the committee and did well enough that he was eventually confirmed by a lopsided margin.

Not all nominees did as well as Harlan before the committee. When Earl Warren retired in 1968, Lyndon Johnson tried to elevate his friend and confidant, Justice Abe Fortas, to the chief justice chair (in a move to try and appeal to Southern Democrats, Johnson nominated his friend and fellow Texan, U.S. Circuit Judge Homer Thornberry of the Fifth Circuit, to replace Fortas). Conservatives from both parties, angry over the liberal jurisprudence of the Warren court, took their frustrations out on Fortas, forcing him to play defense for much of his hearing. Also putting him on his heels was his ongoing relationship with Johnson, as senators were concerned about what kind of advice Fortas was giving and what matters he was advising the president on. Republicans, meanwhile, questioned the

[1] Cameron and Kastellec, supra.

[2] Lewis I. Maddocks, "The Two Justices Harlan on Civil Rights and Liberties: A Study in Judicial Contrasts," *Kentucky Law Journal* 68, no. 2 (1979), article 3, 323.

timing of the move, noting that Warren's retirement and Fortas' elevation seemed designed to prevent Richard Nixon, the favorite to win the presidency in 1968, from being able to make the appointment Fortas didn't do himself any favors by appearing evasive, defensive and, at times, downright dishonest during his testimony.[3]

All of those factors coalesced into a perfect storm that eventually drowned Fortas' nomination. Southerners, led by Strom Thurmond, filibustered, and Johnson, knowing the nomination was doomed, nevertheless called in as many favors and pulled as many arms as he could in order to get a bare majority to invoke cloture—far short of the two-thirds margin necessary to cut off debate but a face-saving move that would allow Fortas to say he probably would have been confirmed had it gone to an up-and-down vote. Fortas withdrew his name and Nixon eventually appointed Warren Burger of the D.C. Circuit to be the new chief justice.

Fortas then was forced to resign following an ethics scandal. In May 1969, *Life* published a story in May 1969 under the headline: "Fortas of the Supreme Court: A Question of Ethics,"[4] reporting that Fortas had accepted $20,000 from Wall Street financier Louis Wolfson in 1966 at a time when the latter was under investigation by the SEC. Fortas returned the money later that year—after Wolfson had been indicted for fraud. That accusation was bad enough, with *Life* describing Wolfson, Fortas,

[3] Laura Kalman, *Abe Fortas* (New Haven, CT: Yale University Press, 1990), 336–337. For instance, Fortas denied recommending candidates for judgeships to the president when he clearly did. He also said he played a limited role in advising the president on Vietnam when, in fact, he had been one of Johnson's closest advisors. His lack of candor extended to his view on the court, stating he did not believe the court should spearhead social, political, or economic change—a laughable statement considering he was one of the biggest judicial activists on the court.

[4] Kalman, supra, 359–376. See also: Victor Li, *Nixon in New York* (Lanham, MD: Rowman & Littlefield, 2018), 218–221. Fortas believed *Life* had a vendetta against him because of a strong dissent he had penned in the case of *Time, Inc. v. Hill*, a First Amendment case handed down in 1967 involving *Life's* parent company, *Time*, that had been harshly critical of the magazine. Fortas' dissent had been set to be the majority opinion, until Hugo Black got the case reargued the following term, whereupon positions had shifted. The lawyer who argued on behalf of the Hills and against *Time/Life* before the Supreme Court was none other than Richard Nixon, who was then a partner at the Wall Street law firm of Nixon, Mudge, Rose, Guthrie, and Alexander and was preparing to run for President in 1968.

and Johnson all tangled up together in a vast web of influence peddling and corruption.[5]

Turns out, that was actually child's play compared to what the Nixon Administration had on Fortas and Wolfson. Attorney General John Mitchell had a copy of a contract between Fortas and Wolfson guaranteeing the justice $20,000 a year for life (and $20,000 a year for life to his wife should he predecease her) and took his evidence to Warren, who hadn't stepped down from the court yet. With a criminal probe and impeachment proceedings looking likely, Fortas resigned.

Nixon now had another vacancy to fill, and in stepped Haynsworth. The native South Carolinian was widely respected and highly regarded, having served on the Fourth Circuit since 1957, when he was appointed by Eisenhower. The ABA, which began evaluating Supreme Court nominees' qualifications in 1955, found him highly qualified.[6] Haynsworth had overlapped with Parker for a little less than a year, yet the two had become especially close during their time on the bench together, forming a relationship that was somewhere between mentor/protégé and surrogate father/son. Haynsworth would later reflect that it seemed like he had filled the void in Parker's life that had resulted from John Jr.'s untimely death in 1941.[7]

Haynsworth would, indeed, follow in Parker's footsteps in several ways. Like Parker, his judicial rulings tended to be narrow and fact-driven while deferential to precedent.[8] He also became chief judge of the Fourth Circuit in 1964, holding the job until 1981, when he took senior status. And, unfortunately for him, his Supreme Court nomination in 1969 ended up being derailed by many of the same factors and groups that had taken down his mentor in 1930.

Trouble started when AFL-CIO President George Meany tried to get Nixon to reconsider. When the president refused, Meany came out against

[5] William Lambert, "Fortas of the Supreme Court: A Question of Ethics," *Life*, May 5, 1969.

[6] "Evaluation Process and Ratings of Supreme Court Nominees by the American Bar Association," *Congressional Research Service*, March 22, 2022, https://crsreports.congress.gov/product/pdf/IN/IN11896, accessed: October 18, 2024.

[7] Bruce H. Kalk, "The Making of Mr. Justice Haynsworth? The Rise, Fall and Revival of Judge Clement F. Haynsworth." *The South Carolina Historical Magazine* 117, no. 1 (2016): 4–29.

[8] Ibid.

the nomination, citing a 1963 decision involving a South Carolina textile mill that shut down after an affiliate of the AFL-CIO was chosen to represent the mill's workers. The National Labor Relations Board had ruled against the mill, saying its closure violated federal law. Haynsworth, however, voted with the majority to overturn the decision.

What made this vote more than just one judge voting his conscience according to his interpretation of the law was that Haynsworth owned a significant amount of stock in, and served as a director for, a vending machine supplier that operated in several of the mills in question. Meany argued Haynsworth should have recused himself due to the conflict of interest. While Haynsworth had been unaware of the relationship between the vending company and factory, and he had been cleared of any wrongdoing in 1964, the allegations had legs thanks to the Fortas affair.[9] In fact, Meany's press strategy during the Haynsworth fight was pretty much just repeating accusations levied against Fortas and painting Haynsworth with the same brush.

The NAACP was also alarmed, and mobilized its forces to oppose a Supreme Court nomination for the first time since Parker. The main thrust of the association's opposition was Haynsworth's views on implementing *Brown*—notably his adherence to the Parker Doctrine. The NAACP sent a brief to senators, as well as to Nixon, highlighting some of his votes over the years, particularly *Green v. County School Board of New Kent County*,[10] in which Haynsworth upheld a "freedom-of-choice" plan that was unanimously struck down by the Supreme Court in 1968.[11]

As Stephen Wasby and Joel Grossman point out in "Haynsworth and Parker: History Does Live Again," Haynsworth's jurisprudence in relation to *Brown* was fairly consistent with other judges in the South during that time, and was not overly permissive of the kind of dilatory tactics that were common then. "His record is devoid of any evidence of outright

[9] Michael Bobelian, *Battle for the Marble Palace: Abe Fortas, Earl Warren, Lyndon Johnson, Richard Nixon and the Forging of the Modern Supreme Court* (Tucson, AZ: Schaffner Press, 2019), 361–362.

[10] *Green v. County School Board of New Kent Cty*, 382 F.2d 338 (4th Cir. 1967).

[11] *Green v. County Sch. Bd. of New Kent County*, 391 U.S. 430 (1968). NAACP Papers, supra, The Civil Rights Record of Clement F. Haynsworth, Jr., undated.

disobedience to the *Brown* decision, but it is also devoid of evidence of real acceptance of the principle or spirit of that decision," they found.[12]

Nevertheless, Haynsworth's seeming ambivalence was tantamount to outright opposition to *Brown* in the eyes of the NAACP and was more than enough for them to justify going after him. "It is all-out opposition, because, on his record, Judge Haynsworth is for marking time on Negro civil rights, not for going forward," NAACP Executive Director Roy Wilkins said in a letter sent to NAACP branch presidents.[13] "His vote on the high court could help undo what has been done since 1953."

Both organized labor and the NAACP were considerably weaker than they had been in 1930. Nevertheless, they were able to raise enough questions about Haynsworth that senators began running from him. There was also an undercurrent of discontent and even anger from some senators, especially those on the left, given what had happened to Fortas. Led by young, ambitious Senator Birch Bayh (D-IN), who had helped enact two constitutional amendments and had become famous for bravely rescuing Senator Ted Kennedy (D-MA) after their plane crashed in 1964, a group of liberals and moderates diligently made the case against Haynsworth and slowly but surely picked up support from others in the Senate. Meanwhile, Southern Democrats, particularly the powerful and influential Georgian Richard Russell, were solidly in support of Haynsworth but were wary of being too open, fearing that doing so would paint the nominee as a white supremacist and galvanize opposition to him.[14]

The Nixon White House was caught off guard by the level of opposition. Nevertheless, Administration officials soon recovered and organized a counteroffensive, calling in several outside interest groups to go to bat for Haynsworth, including bar associations, business executives, and even the American Medical Association. Senator William Saxbe (R-OH) remarked the intense pressure campaign was "as strong as anything we've ever seen" while Minority Leader Hugh Scott (R-PA) warned the White House that they were doing more harm than good. Indeed, Senator John

[12] Stephen Wasby and Joel B. Grossman, "Haynsworth and Parker: History Does Live Again," *South Carolina Law Review* 23, vol. 3 (1971), article 1, 357–358.

[13] NAACP Papers, supra, Letter from Roy Wilkins to NAACP Branch Presidents, August 19, 1969.

[14] Kalk, supra, 15–23.

Williams (R-DE) and others would end up voting against Haynsworth due to resentment over some of the Administration's strong-arm tactics.[15]

Sure enough, Haynsworth was defeated 55–45, with 17 Republicans joining 38 Democrats in voting no. "Haynsworth would have been confirmed in a minute ten years ago," one White House aide lamented.[16] "But his appointment came at a time when Christ himself would have drawn at least one 'no' vote on principle alone."

Haynsworth, like Parker, returned to his job on the Fourth Circuit and carved out a respectable career while engendering widespread sympathy for being a victim of politics and circumstances. Then-Senate Majority Leader Mike Mansfield (D-MT) would later state that he regretted his vote against Haynsworth, as did two of his influential colleagues, George McGovern (D-SD), the 1972 Democratic nominee for President, and Thomas Eagleton (D-MO), briefly McGovern's running mate. Even some of Haynsworth's would-be colleagues lamented what happened and what could have been, with Chief Justice Warren Burger calling him "one of the outstanding judges in the country" and Hugo Black and William O. Douglas both saying he would have been a fine Justice.[17] The Senate ultimately chose to honor Haynsworth in a different way—in 1982, they voted to rename the federal courthouse and post office building in Greenville, South Carolina, in his honor.

To fill the still-vacant seat, an angered Nixon decided to nominate another Southern judge—only one from "further down south and further to the right."[18] G. Harrold Carswell, a Fifth Circuit Court of Appeals judge, certainly fit those criteria. A former politician, Carswell had unsuccessfully run for the Georgia legislature in 1948 before moving to Florida and working as an attorney for a few years. Carswell then got the attention of the Eisenhower Administration, as he was named U.S. attorney for the Northern District of Florida from 1953 to 1958 before being appointed to the United States District Court for the Northern District of Florida. He was then promoted to the Fifth Circuit by Nixon in 1969.

[15] Bobelian, supra, 308. Kalk, supra, 23.

[16] Bobelian, supra, 306.

[17] Kalk, supra, 27–28. Also, Bob Woodward, and Scott Armstrong, *The Brethren* (New York: Simon and Schuster, 1979), 57.

[18] Bobelian, supra, 309.

Whereas the bespectacled and professorial-looking Haynsworth had seemed like the very image of a genteel Southern gentleman, Carswell very much looked like the firebrand he had once been. Much like how something Parker had said during his political career came back to haunt him, Carswell also had a ghost in his closet in the form of a campaign speech in his past—only this one made Parker's 1920 remarks look like the Gettysburg Address. "I am Southern by ancestry, birth, training, inclination, belief and practice. And I believe that segregation of the races is proper and the only practical and correct way of life in our states," Carswell said during an August 2, 1948, speech.[19] "I yield to no man, as a fellow candidate or as a fellow citizen, in the firm, vigorous belief in the principles of white supremacy, and I shall always be so governed."

Upon revelation of that speech, Carswell publicly renounced those views and called them "abhorrent."[20] That wasn't enough for the NAACP, which had taken the lead on Carswell after playing a more subordinate role to labor on Haynsworth. There were plenty of other instances in Carswell's career and life that raised red flags for the civil rights group. For instance, in 1955, he helped establish a private segregated golf club on public property in violation of a Supreme Court desegregation order—an allegation he denied by saying he was unaware of what was happening. Eleven years later, he sold real estate with a racial covenant forbidding occupation by Blacks.[21] Additionally, the NAACP opposed Carswell because of his desegregation decisions post-*Brown*, which they believed furthered the cause of Southern resistance and delay thanks to the Parker Doctrine.

Two days after Nixon nominated Carswell, the NAACP released a statement expressing its opposition to the judge due to his "pro-segregation record."[22] They also previewed another area of attack by questioning Carswell's credentials and qualifications, arguing that his career not only lacked distinction, but that he was a poor judge whose cases were often overturned by a higher court.

[19] "Carswell Disavows '48 Speech Backing White Supremacy," *The New York Times*, January 22, 1970, www.nytimes.com/1970/01/22/archives/carswell-disavows-48-speech-backing-white-supremacy-judge-disavows.html, accessed October 18, 2024.

[20] Ibid.

[21] Bobelian, supra, 311.

[22] NAACP Papers, supra, "NAACP Opposes Nomination of Judge Harrold Carswell," January 21, 1970.

This tactic ended up working quite well for the NAACP—especially once other groups and individuals who were not affiliated with the association concurred. The ABA gave him a "qualified" rating but others immediately disagreed, including Harvard Law Dean Derek Bok, who claimed Carswell had a low "level of competence" and Yale Law Dean Louis Pollak, who testified before the Judiciary Committee that Carswell had "more slender credentials than any nominee for the Supreme Court put forth this century."[23] Meanwhile, the Law Students Concerned for the Court, a group based out of Columbia Law School, found that Carswell was reversed by a higher court 58.8 percent of the time—almost triple the national average for a federal judge.[24]

"The total lack of distinction in his career is such that one must assume that President Nixon found him qualified for the Supreme Court chiefly because the civil rights community found him unacceptable," the NAACP said in its press release.[25]

Even Carswell's allies didn't think too highly of him. "They think Carswell's a boob, a dummy," Nixon's congressional liaison told the president.[26] "And what counter is there to that? He is." Senator Roman Hruska (R-NE), one of Carswell's biggest supporters, inadvertently gave the judge his epitaph, saying during a speech: "Even if he were mediocre, there are a lot of mediocre judges and people and lawyers, and they are entitled to a little representation, aren't they? We can't have all Brandeises and Frankfurters and Cardozos."[27]

The judge did have one thing going in his favor, though. Coming off a long, hard-fought battle over Haynsworth (to say nothing of the Fortas fight), the consensus was that the Senate wasn't going to get into another one over Carswell. Even Bayh, who had taken up the leadership role in opposing Carswell, privately doubted that he'd get more than 25 votes against the judge when the nomination was first announced.[28] But

[23] Bobelian, supra, 311–312.

[24] Bobelain, supra, 312.

[25] NAACP Papers, supra, "NAACP Opposes Nomination of Judge Harrold Carswell," January 21, 1970.

[26] Ibid., 312.

[27] Bob Woodward and Scott Armstrong, *The Brethren* (New York: Simon and Schuster, 1979), 74–75.

[28] "Birch Bayh: A Biography," https://libraries.indiana.edu/birch bayh-biography, accessed January 11, 2025.

as with Haynsworth, Bayh, who had suggested the tactic of scrutinizing Carswell's opinions, chipped away at the judge's support and on April 8, 1970, the Senate rejected him by a 51–45 vote.[29]

As with Haynsworth, a significant number of Nixon's own party defected—in this case, 13 Republicans voted "no." A furious Nixon made political hay out of the situation, tying himself even tighter to the South by lamenting that no Southern judge would receive a fair shot from the Senate. After privately threatening a group of senators that if they voted down Carswell, his next choice would be "someone from Mississippi," Nixon declined to nominate another Southerner, saying that doing so would subject them to unfair character assassination.[30] Instead, he chose Minnesota-based Harry Blackmun for the seat, and the Eighth Circuit judge was unanimously confirmed 94–0.

Nixon got his Southerner on his next try. In 1971, Lewis Powell, a Virginia lawyer and former president of the ABA, was confirmed 89–1 to replace Hugo Black on the court. During his 15 years as an associate justice, Powell emerged as the main swing vote on a closely divided court. While he tended to vote more with the conservatives, he also provided the decisive vote for liberals enough times that lawyers began tailoring their arguments specifically to try and win him over.[31] Perhaps the best indication of his influence was *Regents of the University of California v. Bakke*,[32] in which he voted with four justices to outlaw strict racial quotas, but then voted with the other four in recognizing that schools had a

[29] Unlike Haynsworth, Carswell's post-rejection life would be tumultuous and controversial. In 1970, Carswell resigned his judgeship to run for the U.S. Senate in Florida, specifically saying he wanted to "confront the liberals who shot me down." He lost badly in the GOP primary to Rep. Bill Cramer—notably, Nixon stayed out of the race and did not endorse his onetime High Court nominee. After the loss, Carswell went into private practice in Florida. He made headlines again in 1976, when he was arrested for making sexual advances on an undercover cop in a public men's room in Tallahassee and was later convicted of battery. Three years later, he was attacked by a man he purportedly met in a skating rink and invited back to his hotel room. In 1992, he died of lung cancer. See: "G. Harrold Carswell; Rejected for U.S. High Court," *The Los Angeles. Times*, August 1, 1992; "Carswell Attacked, Beaten in Downtown Atlanta Hotel," *The Sarasota Herald-Tribune*, September 12, 1979; Billy B. Hathorn, "Cramer v. Kirk: The Florida Republican Schism of 1970," Florida Historical Quarterly: Vol. 68: No. 4, Article 3. (1989).

[30] Bobelian, supra, 315.

[31] "Justice Powell Shaping Law as Swing Man on High Court," *The New York Times*, April 26, 1987.

[32] *Regents of the University of California v. Bakke*, 438 U.S. 265 (1978).

compelling interest in encouraging diversity. That compromise position was, essentially, the law of the land until 2023, when the Supreme Court struck down using race as a consideration in college admissions.[33]

Therefore, when Powell announced his retirement in 1987, the stakes could not have been higher, and whoever his replacement ended up being had the potential to control the direction of the court for the next generation.

Liberal groups understood the gravity of the situation—especially with a conservative like Ronald Reagan in the White House. And they were ready. Within 45 minutes of Reagan's nomination of conservative D.C. Circuit Judge Robert Bork, Ted Kennedy spoke on the Senate floor, denouncing the judge's views and ideology. Indeed, Bork was heading back to the West Wing after his public unveiling when he and the Reagan Administration official with him turned on C-SPAN and caught Kennedy's speech.[34]

Using a memorable turn of phrase that would forever define the judge, Kennedy portrayed "Robert Bork's America" as a place where "women would be forced into back-alley abortions," Blacks would have to sit in "segregated lunch counters," police could break into anyone's house they wanted, and children "could not be taught about evolution" and other topics that could be easily censored by the government. Kennedy also underscored the importance of this nomination, warning that Reagan was trying to tip the balance of the court into one that was in line with his own "reactionary vision of the Constitution." Kennedy then concluded by saying that "no Justice would be better than this injustice."[35]

Bork was outraged and claimed that Kennedy's speech did not contain a single truth in it. Reagan and his staff were caught off guard, not anticipating the speed and effectiveness of Kennedy's attack. Nor were they prepared for all of the civil rights and civil liberties groups (including the NAACP) that immediately amplified Kennedy's message. "We will go all out in seeing that Bork is not appointed to the Supreme Court," NAACP Executive Director Benjamin Hooks said.[36] One group, the People for

[33] *Students for Fair Admissions v. Harvard*, 600 U.S. 181 (2023).

[34] Ethan Bronner, *Battle for Justice: How the Bork Nomination Shook America* (New York: Union Square Press, 1989), 84–85.

[35] Bronner, supra, 84–85.

[36] "NAACP Plans 'All Out' Fight Against Bork," *United Press International*, July 5, 1987.

the American Way, even produced TV ads featuring Academy Award winning actor Gregory Peck denouncing Bork and his extreme views.[37]

It took months before Bork and Reagan Administration officials finally addressed Kennedy's accusations but, by then, it was too late. Bork had been painted as a dangerous extremist, and moderate Republicans were under pressure to vote against him. Not helping was his past (after his two superiors at the Justice Department resigned rather than fire Watergate special prosecutor Archibald Cox under orders from Nixon, then-Solicitor General Bork complied in an event later known as the "Saturday Night Massacre"), as well his long paper trail of controversial statements, speeches, and opinions, which demonstrated his fidelity to the then novel legal doctrine that the Constitution should be interpreted based on the original views of its framers. Also not helping was Bork's testimony before the Judiciary Committee, during which time he came across as combative and defensive. He was also inconsistent, at times backing away from some outspoken things he had said in the past.[38] Even his video rental history became fair game for the hearings, as Bork's argument that there was no right to privacy in the Constitution led to a newspaper investigation into his movie preferences (unlike what happened with Clarence Thomas, there was nothing sordid in his rental history—unless you count as salacious a love for Alfred Hitchcock thrillers and Cary Grant films).[39]

Bork was rejected by a 58–42 margin, with six Republicans joining all but two Democrats in voting "no." Ninth Circuit Judge Anthony Kennedy (no relation to Ted Kennedy) eventually got the seat[40] and, indeed, cast some pretty consequential deciding votes and wrote several monumentally important opinions in his 30-year career on the court.

[37] Ibid., 140–141.

[38] "The Bork Hearings; Bork Backs Away from His Stances on Rights Issues," *The New York Times*, September 17, 1987.

[39] Stephen Landesman, "By their videocassette rental records you shall know them," *The Ithaca Journal*, September 28, 1987.

[40] Reagan nominated D.C. Circuit Judge Douglas Ginsburg after Bork's rejection, but Ginsburg withdrew his name under pressure after it was reported that he had used marijuana as a professor at Harvard in the 1970s. Reagan then nominated Anthony Kennedy, who was easily confirmed. Ginsburg continued with his career on the D.C. Circuit and became Chief Judge in 2001. He took senior status in 2011.

There were some factors that were out of Bork's control that led to his nomination's demise. Had he been nominated the previous year, either for the chief justiceship that went to Justice William Rehnquist or for Rehnquist's now vacant seat that went to Antonin Scalia, Bork may very well have been confirmed. Republicans still controlled the Senate in 1986, and Democrats had trained their fire on Rehnquist, who had been controversial since he was first appointed as an associate justice by Nixon in 1972. Scalia, a conservative and originalist in Bork's image, was young, charismatic, and charming. While he emerged as an outspoken and polarizing force in later years, he was fairly unknown at the time—lacking a significant paper trail of controversial quotes, writings, and opinions. He also had history going for him, as the first Italian-American Supreme Court nominee in American history. Therefore, he essentially got a free pass from the Senate, getting confirmed 98–0, compared to 65–33 for the new chief.

Additionally, Rehnquist was replacing Chief Justice Warren Burger, a conservative. With Scalia taking Rehnquist's old seat, the balance of the court was not going to change—unlike the case with Powell's retirement. As Ethan Bronner wrote in his 1989 book *Battle for Justice: How the Bork Nomination Shook America*, Bork represented an existential threat to a large segment of the country. "Bork's attacks on a few cherished civil rights decisions, his oft-repeated contention that numerous high court rulings had to be overturned, and his belief that egalitarian trends were dangerous rendered him a threat to future—and perhaps some existing—civil rights advances," Bronner wrote.[41]

Bork was also hurt by his own nature. Whereas some nominees can be circumspect or evasive about views, Bork's long paper trail made that impossible. Combine that with his combative and confrontational style—especially when he was testifying before the Senate Judiciary Committee—and it's surprising that he even made it to the Senate in the first place. There's a reason why judicial nominees now are trained to say as little as possible about their views while trying to be charming and humble. For instance, the main thing that people remember about John Roberts' confirmation hearing after he was nominated to replace Rehnquist as chief justice in 2005 was not what he may or may not have said about abortion or privacy, but his genial nature and charm. That and his

[41] Bronner, supra, 317.

famous analogy of how justices are there to call balls and strikes and not play in the game.

The Bork nomination has been widely credited with creating the modern-day confirmation process, where ideology and partisan politics matter as much, if not more, than qualifications, and outside groups will always be involved, either as a trusted partner or formidable adversary. Subsequent Supreme Court nominees have been compared and contrasted to Bork, with any near defeat bringing back memories of 1987 and any overwhelming victory a testament to presidential administrations not wanting to relive that battle.

For instance, George H.W. Bush's first nominee, David H. Souter, was largely chosen because of his confirmability (he won 90–9). That was not the case with his second nominee, Clarence Thomas, an originalist in the mold of Bork and Scalia, who faced steep opposition even before Professor Anita Hill came forward with sexual harassment allegations. "We're going to 'Bork' him. We're going to kill him politically," feminist Florynce Kennedy said during a National Organization for Women conference in July 1991.[42] After the most explosive confirmation hearings since Bork, maybe of all time, Thomas eventually squeaked by and was confirmed by the Senate.

Most Supreme Court nominations since then have all had some degree of contentiousness, as partisanship has become more pronounced and obstruction more regular. They haven't all been as nasty or angry as Brett Kavanaugh's hearings in 2018, which were probably the nastiest since Thomas, and also featured allegations of sexual harassment and assault. But the days of unanimous or near-unanimous votes seem like bygone relics of a quaint past; much more common are near party line votes and committee hearings that resemble tennis matches, with senators sitting on one side lobbing attacks and senators sitting on the other defending them. Even the ones that didn't make it to the committee—like Harriet Miers in 2005 and Merrick Garland in 2016—resulted in angry recriminations and accusations of "Borking."

As stated before, maybe it should have been "Parkering." After all, the Parker fight wasn't the first time powerful senators derailed a nomination—Oliver Ellsworth, David Hill, Simon Cameron and others were

[42] Jane Coaston, "'Borking,' explained: why a failed Supreme Court nomination in 1987 matters," *Vox*, September 27, 2018, www.vox.com/2018/9/26/17896126/bork-kavanaugh-supreme-court-conservatives-republicans, accessed October 21, 2024.

certainly proof of that. While it was the first time outside interest groups organized successfully against a Supreme Court nominee, it wasn't the first time they entered the battlefield—Stanley Matthews, Charles Evans Hughes, and Louis Brandeis could attest to that. And it certainly wasn't the first time that politics, partisanship, and electoral considerations were considered at the expense of competence, qualifications, experience, or ability—otherwise John Tyler's choices would have been easily confirmed with or without Henry Clay's support.

But it was the first time that all of those factors combined to take down a Supreme Court nominee. The Parker nomination ended up being a perfect storm of political, ideological, and historical forces that turned what should have been an easy confirmation into a maelstrom that continues to rage to this day. It also became a proxy fight of sorts as many different factions fought each other in a culmination of decades of conflict over various aspects of American law and society. Progressives fought conservatives. Republicans quarreled with Democrats. Civil rights activists took on Jim Crow and the status quo. Labor battled big business. Southerners and Northerners clashed once again. However, those were but skirmishes—the main thrust of the war focused on the future of the Supreme Court and how it should interpret the Constitution. Should it be business as usual—in more ways than one? Or was it time for a change?

With so many macro forces at play, Parker ended up being a small part of a much larger fight between ideologies, policies, politics, and egos.

In other words, he was an incident.

Bibliography

Books

Dave Barry, *Dave Barry Slept Here: A Sort of History of the United States* (New York: Fawcett Columbine, 1989).

Richard Barry, *Mr. Rutledge of South Carolina* (New York: Duell, Sloan & Pearce, 1942).

Alexander Bickel, "The Decade of School Desegregation: Progress and Prospects," *Columbia Law Review* 64, no. 2 (1964).

Vincent Blasi and Seana Shiffrin, "The Story of *West Virginia State Board of Education v. Barnette*: The Pledge of Allegiance and the Freedom of Thought," in *Constitutional Law Stories*, ed. Michael C. Dorf (New York: Foundation Press, 2004).

Michael Bobelian, *Battle for the Marble Palace: Abe Fortas, Earl Warren, Lyndon Johnson, Richard Nixon and the Forging of the Modern Supreme Court* (Tucson, AZ: Schaffner Press, 2019).

Ethan Bronner, *Battle for Justice: How the Bork Nomination Shook America* (New York: Union Square Press, 1989).

William C. Burris, *Duty and the Law: Judge John J. Parker and the Constitution.* Bessemer (Bessemer, Alabama: Colonial Press, 1987).

Charles M. Cameron and Jonathan P. Kastellec, *Making the Supreme Court: The Politics of Appointments, 1930–2020* (New York: Oxford University Press, 2023).

Rob Christensen, *The Paradox of Tar Heel Politics* (Chapel Hill, NC: University of North Carolina Press, 2008).

Ed Cray, *Chief Justice: A Biography of Earl Warren* (New York: Simon & Schuster, 1997.

V. Li, *Supreme Pressure*, https://doi.org/10.1007/978-3-032-07864-3

Helen G. Edmonds, *The Negro and Fusion Politics in North Carolina, 1894–1901* (Chapel Hill, NC: Univ of North Carolina Press, 2003).
James W. Ely, Jr., *The Chief Justiceship of Melville W. Fuller, 1888–1910* (Columbia, SC: University of South Carolina Press, 1995).
Martin Fausold, *The Presidency of Herbert Hoover* (Lawrence, KS: University Press of Kansas, 1985).
Eric Foner, *The Second Founding: How the Civil War and Reconstruction Remade the Constitution* (New York: W.W. Norton, 2019).
Kenneth Goings, *The NAACP Comes of Age: The Defeat of John J. Parker* (Bloomington: Indiana University Press, 1990).
Joseph P. Harris, *The Advice and Consent of the Senate: A Study of the Confirmation of Appointments by the United States Senate* (New York: Greenwood Press, Publishers, 1968).
Douglas Irwin, "The Hawley-Smoot Tariff and the Great Depression, 1928–1932," in *Clashing Over Commerce: A History of U.S. Trade Policy*, ed. Douglas Irwin (Chicago: University of Chicago Press, 2017).
J. Myron Jacobson and Ron M. Mersky, *The Rejected: Sketches of the 26 Men Nominated for the Supreme Court but Not Confirmed by the Senate* (Milpitas, CA: Toucan Valley Publications, 1993).
Laura Kalman, *Abe Fortas* (New Haven, CT: Yale University Press, 1990).
Willard L. King, *Melville Weston Fuller– Chief Justice of The United States 1888–1910* (United Kingdom: Read Books Limited, 2013).
Michael Klarman, *From Jim Crow to Civil Rights: The Supreme Court and the Struggle for Racial Equality* (New York: Oxford University Press, 2004).
Richard Kluger, *Simple Justice: The History of* Brown v. Board of Education *and Black America's Struggle for Equality* (New York: Vintage Books, 1975).
Richard Kluger, *Simple Justice: The History of* Brown v. Board of Education *and Black America's Struggle For Equality* (Alfred A. Knopf: New York, 2004).
William Edward Leuchtenburg, *The Supreme Court Reborn: The Constitutional Revolution in the Age of Roosevelt* (New York: Oxford University Press, 1996).
Victor Li, *Nixon in New York* (Lanham, MD: Rowman & Littlefield, 2018).
David Manwaring, *Render Unto Caesar; The Flag-Salute Controversy* (Chicago: University of Chicago Press, 1962).
Marian McKenna, *Borah* (Ann Arbor, MI: University of Michigan Press, 1961).
John Charles McNeil, *Lyrics from Cotton Land* (Charlotte: The Stone & Barringer Company, 1907) (site: https://ia800209.us.archive.org/27/items/lyricsfromcotton00mcne/lyricsfromcotton00mcne.pdf).
George Norris, *Fighting Liberal: The Autobiography of George Norris* (New York: The MacMillan Company, 1945).
Lewis J. Paper, *Brandeis: An Intimate Biography of One of America's Truly Great Supreme Court Justices* (Secaucus, NJ: Citadel Press, 1983).

Charles Rappleye, *Herbert Hoover In The White House: The Ordeal Of The Presidency* (New York: Simon & Schuster, 2016).

J. Fred Rippy (ed.), *F.M. Simmons: Statesman of the New South. Memoirs and Addresses* (Durham, NC: Duke University Press, 1936).

Owen Roberts, *The Court and the Constitution* (Cambridge, MA: Harvard University Press, 1951).

Lon Savage, *Thunder in the Mountains: The West Virginia Mine War, 1920–21* (Pittsburgh: University of Pittsburgh Press, 1990).

Bernard Schwartz, *Decision: How the Supreme Court Decides Cases* (New York: Oxford University Press, 1996).

Jeff Shesol, *Supreme Power: Franklin Roosevelt vs. The Supreme Court* (New York: W.W. Norton & Company, Inc., 2010).

Robert Shogan, *The Battle for Blair Mountain: The Story of America's Largest Labor Uprising* (New York: Perseus Books Group, 2004).

James F. Simon, *Eisenhower Vs. Warren: The Battle for Civil Rights and Liberties* (New York: Liveright, 2018).

James Simon, *FDR and Chief Justice Hughes: The President, the Supreme Court, and the Epic Battle Over the New Deal* (New York: Simon & Schuster, 2012).

Paul Simon, *Advice & Consent: Clarence Thomas, Robert Bork and the Intriguing History of the Supreme Court's Nomination Battles* (Washington, D.C.: National Press Books, 1992).

Patricia Sullivan, *Lift Every Voice: The NAACP and the Making of the Civil Rights Movement* (New York: The New Press, 2009).

Alden L. Todd, *Justice on Trial: The Case of Louis D. Brandeis* (New York: McGraw-Hill, 1964).

Melvin Urofsky, *Louis D. Brandeis A Life* (New York: Random House, 2009).

Walter White, *A Man Called White: The Autobiography of Walter White* (Athens, GA, and London: Brown Thrasher Books: 1948).

J. Harvie Wilkinson, "The Supreme Court and Southern School Desegregation, 1955–1970: A History and Analysis." *Virginia Law Review* 64, no. 4 (1978).

Bob Woodward and Scott Armstrong, *The Brethren* (New York: Simon and Schuster, 1979).

David Zucchino, *Wilmington's Lie: The Murderous Coup of 1898 and the Rise of White Supremacy* (New York: Atlantic Monthly Press, 2020).

Articles

Henry Abraham, and Edward Goldberg, "A Note on the Appointment of Justices of the Supreme Court of the United States," *ABA Journal* 46, no. 2 (1960).

Billy Ball, "North Carolina's Wilmington Massacre and Trump's Insurrection Really Aren't So Different," *Cardinal & Pine*, November 10, 2021.

"Brown v. Board: Timeline of School Integration in the U.S.," *Learning For Justice*, Spring 2004 www.learningforjustice.org/magazine/spring-2004/brown-v-board-timeline-of-school-integration-in-the-us

"Cannon, Joseph G." In *Congress A to Z*, 6th ed. edited by McCutcheon, Chuck, 78, American Government A to Z Series. Washington, DC: CQ Press, 2014.

James Chapin, "Analysis: The end of the Southern strategy, part 2," *United Press International*, www.upi.com/Archives/2001/02/22/Analysis-The-end-of-the-Southern-strategy-part-2/7841982818000/.

Fabiola Cineas, "Why School Segregation is Getting Worse," *Vox*, May 15, 2024, www.vox.com/24156492/school-segregation-increasing-brown-board-of-education.

Jane Coaston, "'Borking,' explained: why a failed Supreme Court nomination in 1987 matters," *Vox*, September 27, 2018, www.vox.com/2018/9/26/17896126/bork-kavanaugh-supreme-court-conservatives-republicans.

David Dalin, "The Appointment of Louis D. Brandeis: First Jewish Justice on the Supreme Court," archived at https://web.archive.org/web/20190412031118/http://bir.brandeis.edu/bitstream/handle/10192/31435/LDB100Dalin.pdf?isAllowed=y&sequence=1.

Sheldon Gilbert, "A look at the closest Court confirmation ever," *National Constitution Center*, October 6, 2018.

"Green v. County School Board of New Kent County." *Oyez*. Accessed April 23, 2025. https://www.oyez.org/cases/1967/695.

Bruce H. Kalk, "The Making of Mr. Justice Haynsworth? The Rise, Fall and Revival of Judge Clement F. Haynsworth." *The South Carolina Historical Magazine* 117, no. 1 (2016).

Abby Lee Hood, "What Made the Battle of Blair Mountain the Largest Labor Uprising in American History," *Smithsonian Magazine*, August 25, 2021.

William Lambert, "Fortas of the Supreme Court: A Question of Ethics," *Life*, May 5, 1969.

Jennifer Latson, "The Surprising Story of Walter White and the NAACP," *Time*, July 1, 2015.

Ed Lazarus, "Justices Often Surprise the Presidents Who Pick Them," *Time*, May 26, 2009, https://content.time.com/time/specials/packages/article/0,28804,1900851_1900850_1900845,00.html.

Victor Li, "The 14th: A Civil War-era amendment has become a mini Constitution for modern times," *ABA Journal*, May 1, 2017.

"National Affairs: Justice Retired," *Time*, May 31, 1937.

John J. Parker, "Liberty and Law: The Role of Law in a Free Society," *American Bar Association Journal* 36, no. 7 (1950).

John J. Parker, "Social Progress and the Law," *ABA Journal*, Vol. 16, No. 11 (November 1930).

John Pickering, "Remembering U.S. Supreme Court Justice Frank Murphy," *Law Quadrangle News* 14 (Winter 2005).

William E. Leuchtenburg, "When Franklin Roosevelt Clashed With the Supreme Court—and Lost," *Smithsonian Magazine*, https://www.smithsonianmag.com/history/when-franklin-roosevelt-clashed-with-the-supreme-court-and-lost-78497994/, May 2005.

Walter White, "I Investigate Lynchings," *National Humanities Center, The Making of African-American Identity*, Vol. III, 1917–1968, https://nationalhumanitiescenter.org/pds/maai3/segregation/text2/text2read.htm.

Walter White, "The Negro and the Supreme Court," *Harper's Monthly Magazine*, January 1931.

Archival Collections

American Federation of Labor Papers. Retrieved from ProQuest History Vault database.

William Borah Papers, Library of Congress.

William Green Papers on Microfilm, Kheel Center for Labor-Management Documentation and Archives, Cornell University Library.

Herbert Hoover Papers, Herbert Hoover Presidential Library.

George Norris Papers, Library of Congress.

Papers of the National Association for the Advancement of Colored People, Factiva.

Lee S. Overman Papers, #570, Southern Historical Collection, Wilson Special Collections Library, University of North Carolina at Chapel Hill.

John Johnston Parker Papers, #03464, Southern Historical Collection, Wilson Special Collections Library, University of North Carolina at Chapel Hill.

Websites

"A Most Controversial Nominee: Louis Brandeis," *Fascinating Politics*, https://fascinatingpolitics.com/2022/03/27/a-most-controversial-nominee-louis-brandeis/.

"A Pocket Manual of North Carolina," 1911, *Carolana*, www.carolana.com/NC/NC_Manuals/NC_Manual_1911.pdf.

"A Pocket Manual of North Carolina," 1917, *Carolana,* https://www.carolana.com/NC/NC_Manuals/NC_Manual_1917.pdf.

"A Pocket Manual of North Carolina," 1921, *Carolana*, www.carolana.com/NC/NC_Manuals/NC_Manual_1921.pdf.

"A Storied Law Firm With a Strong History," *Hughes Hubbard & Reed*, www.hugheshubbard.com/culture/firm-history.

"A Timeline of Louis D. Brandeis' Confirmation, Part 1," *Brandeis and Harlan Watch*, https://brandeiswatch.wordpress.com/2020/08/04/a-timeline-of-louis-d-brandeiss-confirmation-part-1/, accessed June 5, 2024.

"Announcement in the Wilmington Messenger on November 9, 1898," *Wikipedia*, https://en.wikipedia.org/wiki/Wilmington_massacre#/media/File:Attention_White_Men.jpg.

"Birch Bayh: A Biography," https://libraries.indiana.edu/birch-bayh-biography.

"The Brandeis confirmation a century letter," *Oxford University Press Blog*, https://blog.oup.com/2016/06/the-brandeis-confirmation-a-century-later/.

"Cameron Morrison (1869–1953)," *North Carolina History Project*, https://northcarolinahistory.org/encyclopedia/cameron-morrison-1869-953/.

"Come quick, Pa—it's a Republican candidate!" *NC Miscellany*, October 17, 2015, https://blogs.lib.unc.edu/ncm/2015/10/17/come-quick-pa-its-a-republican-candidate/.

"The Democratic Handbook. 1898. Prepared by the State Democratic Executive Committee of North Carolina: Electronic Edition." *Documenting the American South*, https://docsouth.unc.edu/nc/dem1898/dem1898.html.

"Early UNC-State rivalry featured the first Shelby High football star and a man who went on to far greater fame," *Carolinas Sports Hub*, https://carolinassportshub.com/early-unc-state-rivalry-featured-the-first-shelby-high-football-star-and-a-man-who-went-on-to-far-greater-fame/.

"Election and Recall of Federal Judges: Abstract of Speech," Statements and Speeches of Robert Owen, *Federal Reserve Bank St Louis*, https://fraser.stlouisfed.org/title/statements-speeches-robert-l-owen-5328/election-recall-federal-judges-535691.

"Evaluation Process and Ratings of Supreme Court Nominees by the American Bar Association," *Congressional Research Service*, March 22, 2022, https://crsreports.congress.gov/product/pdf/IN/IN11896.

"Executive Order 9387—Establishing an Advisory Board on Just Compensation and Prescribing Its Functions," *The American Presidency Project,* October 15, 1943, www.presidency.ucsb.edu/documents/executive-order-9387-establishing-advisory-board-just-compensation-and-prescribing-its.

"Governor Cameron Morrison," *State Archives of North Carolina*, https://archives.ncdcr.gov/morrison-cameron/open.

"The History of John J. Parker," *VIP Mag*, www.vipmagsc.com/the-history-of-judge-john-j-parker/.

"Historical Background of Governor Cameron Morrison," *Charlotte Mecklenburg Library*, https://www.cmlibrary.org/blog/historical-background-governor-cameron-morrison#_ftn14.

"John Rutledge," *Oyez*, https://www.oyez.org/justices/john_rutledge.

"March 9, 1937: Fireside Chat 9: On "Court-Packing," *Miller Center*, https://millercenter.org/the-presidency/presidential-speeches/march-9-1937-fireside-chat-9-court-packing.

"On this day, Supreme Court invalidates key FDR program," *National Constitution Center*, https://constitutioncenter.org/blog/when-fdrs-blue-eagle-laid-a-supreme-court-egg.

"Robert Moton and the Colored Advisory Commission," *PBS*, www.pbs.org/wgbh/americanexperience/features/flood-moton-cac/.

Roll Call Vote To Pass H.R. 8206, *Voteview*, https://voteview.com/rollcall/RS0680199.

Roll Call Vote To Pass H.R. 9103, *Voteview*, https://voteview.com/rollcall/RS0670317.

"Secretary of Commerce, Undersecretary of Everything Else," *U.S. Department of Commerce*, https://library.doc.gov/digital-exhibits/hoover-digital-exhibit.

"The Senate Approves Louis D. Brandeis," *Visit The Capitol*, www.visitthecapitol.gov/artifact/senate-resolution-advise-and-consent-appointment-louis-d-brandeis-be-associate-justice.

"Senate Progressives vs. the Federal Courts," *U.S. Senate*, https://www.senate.gov/artandhistory/senate-stories/senate-progressives-vs-the-federal-courts.htm.

"Senator Carter Glass 1858–1946: The Good and the Bad," *Notes from Under Grounds*, https://smallnotes.library.virginia.edu/2021/09/01/senator-carter-glass-1858-1946-the-good-and-the-bad/.

"Shapiro on Dalin, 'Jewish Justices of the Supreme Court: From Brandeis to Kagan'," *H-Judaic*, https://networks.h-net.org/node/28655/reviews/1488181/shapiro-dalin-jewish-justices-supreme-court-brandeis-kagan.

"The Shelby Dynasty," NCPedia, https://dev.ncpedia.org/shelby-dynasty.

"To Advise and Consent to the Nomination of Charles Evans Hughes to be Chief Justice of the United States," *Govtrack.us*, www.govtrack.us/congress/votes/71-2/s175.

"To confirm the nomination of Louis D. Brandeis, to be an associate justice of the Supreme Court of the U.S.," *Govtrack.us*, https://www.govtrack.us/congress/votes/64-1/s147.

"To Pass H.R. 2667," *Govtrack.us*, www.govtrack.us/congress/votes/71-2/s295.

"Unsuccessful Nominations and Recess Appointments," *Federal Judicial Center*, www.fjc.gov/history/judges/unsuccessful-nominations-and-recess-appointments.

Court Opinions

A.L.A. Schechter Poultry Corp. v. United States, 295 U.S. 495 (1935).

American Steel Foundries v. Tri-City Central Trades Council, 257 U.S. 184, 42 S. Ct. 72, 66 L. Ed. 189.
Anchor Coal Co. v. United States, 25 F.2d 462 (S.D.W. Va. 1928).
Atlantic Coast Line R. Co. v. Standard Oil, 275 U.S. 257 (1927).
Atlantic Coast Line R. v. Standard Oil C., N.J, 12 F.2d 541 (4th Cir. 1926).
Barnette v. West Virginia State Board of Ed., 47 F. Supp. 251 (S.D.W. Va. 1942).
Berea College v. Kentucky, 211 U.S. 45 (1908).
Belvin v. United States, 12 F.2d 548 (4th Cir. 1926).
Bittner v. West Virginia-Pittsburgh Coal Co., 15 F.2d 652 (4th Cir. 1926).
Briggs v. Elliott, 98 F. Supp. 529 (E.D.S.C. 1951).
Briggs v. Elliott, 132 F. Supp. 776 (E.D.S.C. 1955).
Brown v. Board of Education of Topeka, 347 U.S. 483 (1954).
Brown v. Board of Education of Topeka, 349 U.S. 294 (1955) ("Brown II").
Buchanan v. Warley, 245 U.S. 60 (1917).
Carter v. Carter Coal Company, 298 U.S. 238 (1936).
Carolina & NW Ry. Co. v. Town of Lincolnton, 33 F.2d 719 (4th Cir. 1929).
Chandler v. Pennsylvania Railroad Co., 11 F.2d 39 (4th Cir. 1926).
City of Richmond v. Deans, 37 F.2d 712 (4th Cir. 1930).
The Civil Rights Cases, 109 U.S. 3 (1883).
Coppage v. Kansas, 236 U.S. 1 (1915).
Coronado Co. v. U.M. Workers, 268 U.S. 295, 45 S. Ct. 551 (1925).
Corrigan v. Buckley, 271 U.S. 323 (1926).
Duplex Printing Press Co. v. Deering, 254 U.S. 443 (1921).
Farmers & Merchants Bank v. Federal Res. Bank, 262 U.S. 649 (1923).
Great American Ins. Co. v. Johnson, 25 F.2d 847 (4th Cir. 1928).
Green v. County School Board of New Kent Cty, 382 F.2d 338 (4th Cir. 1967).
Green v. County Sch. Bd. of New Kent County, 391 U.S. 430 (1968).
Guinn v. United States, 238 U.S. 347 (1915).
Hitchman Coal & Coke Co. v. Mitchell, 245 U.S. 229 (1917).
Humphrey's Executor v. United States, 295 U.S. 602 (1935).
International Organization, United Mine Workers of America, et al. v. Red Jacket Coal and Coke Company, 18 F.2d 839 (4th Cir. 1927).
Lochner v. New York, 198 U.S. 45 (1905)
Louisville Joint Stock Land Bank v. Radford, 295 U.S. 555 (1935).
Minersville School District v. Gobitis, 310 U.S. 586 (1940).
Moore v. Dempsey, 261 U.S. 86 (1923).
Morehead v. New York ex rel. Tipaldo, 298 U.S. 587 (1936).
Nixon v. Herndon, 273 U.S. 536 (1927).
Plessy v. Ferguson, 163 U.S. 537 (1896).
Regents of the University of California v. Bakke, 438 U.S. 265 (1978).
School Bd. of City of Charlottesville v. Allen, 240 F.2d 59 (4th Cir. 1956).
School Bd., City, Newport News, Va. v. Atkins, 246 F.2d 325 (4th Cir. 1957).

The Slaughterhouse Cases, 83 U.S. 36 (1873).
South Dakota v. North Carolina, 192 U.S. 286 (1904).
Students for Fair Admissions v. Harvard, 600 U.S. 181 (2023).
Sweatt v. Painter, 339 U.S. 629 (1950).
Talbot v. Janson, 3 U.S. 133 (1795).
United Mine Workers v. Coronado Co., 259 U.S. 344, 42 S. Ct. 570 (1922).
United Railways & Electric Co. of Baltimore v. West, 280 U.S. 234 (1930).
United States v. Butler, 297 U.S. 1 (1936).
United States v. Cruikshank, 92 U.S. 542 (1876).
United States v. Jefferson County Bd. of Educ., 372 F.2d 836 (5th Cir. 1966).
United States v. Peters, 3 U.S. 121 (1795).
Wendell v. United States, 34 F.2d 92 (4th Cir. 1929).
West Coast Hotel Co. v. Parrish, 300 U.S. 379 (1937).
West Virginia State Board of Education v. Barnette, 319 U.S. 624 (1943).
Williams v. Mississippi, 170 U.S. 213 (1898).
Yick Wo v. Hopkins, 118 U.S. 356 (1886).

Government Publications

"Confirmation of Hon. John J. Parker to be an Associate Justice of the Supreme Court of the United States," United States Government Printing Office, 1930.
Congressional Record
Founders Online, National Archives
Hearing Before the Subcommittee of the Committee on the Judiciary, United States Senate, April 5, 1930.
Public Papers of the Presidents of the United States: Herbert Hoover. January 1 to December 31, 1930 (Washington, D.C.: United States Government Printing Office, 1976).
Senate.gov

Journal Articles

Douglas Carl Abrams, "A Progressive–Conservative Duel: The 1920 Democratic Gubernatorial Primaries in North Carolina," *The North Carolina Historical Review* 55, no. 4 (1978).
Scott H. Ainsworth and John Anthony Maltese, "National Grange Influence on the Supreme Court Confirmation of Stanley Matthews," *Social Science History* 20, no. 1 (1996).
Louis Brandeis, "The Living Law," *Illinois Law Review* 10, no. 7 (1916).

Jeremy Buchman, "Judicial Lobbying and the Politics of Judicial Structure: An Examination of the Judiciary Act of 1925," *The Justice System Journal* 24, no. 1, Court Administration (2003).

Daniel Curran, "Polk, Politics, and Patronage: The Rejection of George W. Woodward's Nomination to the Supreme Court," *The Pennsylvania Magazine of History and Biography* 121 (1997).

Robert Durden, "Governor Daniel L. Russell Explains His 'South Dakota Bond' Scheme," *The North Carolina Historical Review* 38, no. 4 (1961).

Daniel Farbman, "Redemption Localism," 100 N.C. L. Rev. 1527 (2022).

Peter Graham Fish, "A 'Freshman' Takes Charge: Judge John J. Parker of the United States Court of Appeals, 1925–1930," *Journal of Southern Legal History* 10 (2002).

Peter Graham Fish, "Judge Parker and the Public Service State," *Duke Law Magazine* 37–44 (1985).

Peter Graham Fish, "Red Jacket Revisited: The Case that Unraveled John J. Parker's Supreme Court Appointment," *Law and History Review* 5, no. 1 (1987).

William E. Forbath, "The Shaping of the American Labor Movement," *Harvard Law Review* 102, no. 6 (1989).

G.F. Garcia, "Black Disaffection from the Republican Party During the Presidency of Herbert Hoover, 1928–1932", *The Annals of Iowa* 45, no. 6 (1980).

Oona Hathaway, "Review: The Politics of the Confirmation Process," *The Yale Law Journal* 106, no. 1 (1996).

Darlene Clark Hine, "The NAACP and the Supreme Court: Walter F. White and the Defeat of John J. Parker, 1930," *Negro History Bulletin* 40, no. 5 (1977).

James L. Hunt, "The Making of a Populist: Marion Butler, 1863–1895, Part II," *The North Carolina Historical Review* 62, no. 2 (1985).

Richard Kluger, "The Story of John Johnson Parker: The First Demonstration of Negro Political Power Since Reconstruction," *The Journal of Blacks in Higher Education*, no. 46 (Winter 2004–2005).

William Alexander Mabry, "Negro Suffrage and Fusion Rule in North Carolina," *The North Carolina Historical Review* 12, no. 2 (1935).

Lewis I. Maddocks, "The Two Justices Harlan on Civil Rights and Liberties: A Study in Judicial Contrasts," *Kentucky Law Journal* 68, no. 2 (1979).

George S. McCowan, "Chief Justice John Rutledge and the Jay Treaty," *The South Carolina Historical Magazine* 62, no. 1 (1961).

Chris Messer, "The Tulsa Race Riot of 1921: Toward an Integrative Theory of Collective Violence," *Journal of Social History*, no. 4 (2011).

Richard M. Mizelle, Jr. "Black Levee Camp Workers, The NAACP, and the Mississippi Flood Control Project, 1927–1933," *The Journal of African American History* 98, no. 4 (2013).

Morris A. Soper, Fred B. Helms and Orie L. Phillips, "A Tribute to Judge John J. Parker—The Gladsome Light of Jurisprudence," *North Carolina Law Review* 37, no. 1 (1958).

Clyde Spillenger, "Elusive Advocate: Reconsidering Brandeis as People's Lawyer," *The Yale Law Journal* 105 (1996).

Joseph F. Steelman, "The Trials of a Republican State Chairman: John Motley Morehead and North Carolina Politics, 1910–1912," *The North Carolina Historical Review* 43, no. 1 (January 1966).

Allen W. Trelease, "The Fusion Legislatures of 1895 and 1897: A Roll-Call Analysis of the North Carolina House of Representatives," *The North Carolina Historical Review* 57, no. 3 (1980).

Richard Watson, Jr. "The Defeat of Judge Parker: A Study in Pressure Groups and Politics," *The Mississippi Valley Historical Review* 50, no. 2 (1963).

Stephen Wasby and Joel B. Grossman, "Haynsworth and Parker: History Does Live Again," *South Carolina Law Review* 23, vol. 3 (1971).

Dissertations

Alan Bromberg, "Pure Democracy and White Supremacy: The Redeemer Period in North Carolina, 1876–1894," University of Virginia Ph.D. dissertation, 1977.

Newspapers

The Afro-American.
The Anderson Herald.
The Arizona Republic
The Asheville Citizen-Times.
The Asheville Times.
The Baltimore Sun.
The Bristol News Bulletin.
The Buffalo News.
The Caucasian.
The Charlotte News.
The Columbia Record.
The Concord Times.
The Crisis.
The Daily Record (Wilmington, N.C.).
The Daily Tar Heel.
The Daily Times.
The Davie Record.
The Des Moines Register.

The Dispatch (Lexington, N.C.).
The Evening Star.
The Evening Sun.
The Greensboro Daily Record.
The Greensboro Telegram.
The Greenville News.
The Ithaca Journal.
Johnson City Staff News.
The Lincoln Nebraska State Journal.
The Los Angeles Times.
The Messenger and Intelligencer (Wadesboro, N.C.)
The Minnesota Post.
The Monroe Journal.
The Morning Union.
The New Pittsburgh Courier
The New York Times.
The News and Advance (Lynchburg, VA).
The News and Observer (Raleigh).
The News and Record (Greensboro).
The News Journal.
The Oklahoma Weekly Leader.
The Oxford Public Ledger.
The Pittsburgh Courier.
The Reading Times.
The Reidsville Review.
The St. Louis Dispatch.
The St. Luke Herald.
The Sarasota Herald-Tribune.
The Semi-Weekly Messenger.
The Springfield Daily Republican.
The Star Press.
The State Journal (Raleigh).
The Streator Daily Times-Press.
The Washington Daily News.
The Washington Post.
The Western North Carolina Times.
The Wilmington Dispatch
The Winston-Salem Journal.
The Victoria Advocate.
The Virginia-Pilot.
United Press International.

Index

V. Li, *Supreme Pressure*, https://doi.org/10.1007/978-3-032-07864-3

T

FSC
www.fsc.org
MIX
Papier | Fördert
gute Waldnutzung
FSC® C083411

Kolibri 360 GmbH
Ferdinand-Jühlke-Straße 7
99095 Erfurt, Deutschland
produktsicherheit@kolibri360.de